The Ultimate Country & Victorian Home Plan Collection is our best-selling Country & Victorian style homes in a variety of sizes. These plans cover a broad range of architectural styles as well as a wide variety of lifestyles and budgets. Each design page features floor plans, a front view of the house, interior square footage of the home, number of bedrooms, baths, garage size and foundation types. All floor plans show room and exterior dimensions.

Technical Specifications -

At the time the construction drawings were prepared, every effort was made to ensure that these plans and specifications meet nationally recognized building codes (BOCA, Southern Building Code Congress and others). Because national building codes change or vary from area to area some drawing modifications and/or the assistance of a professional designer or architect may be necessary to comply with your local codes or to accommodate specific building site conditions. We advise you to consult with your local building official for information regarding codes governing your area.

Blueprint Ordering -

Fast and Easy - Your ordering is made simple by following the instructions on page 480. See page 479 for more information on which types of blueprint packages are available and how many plan sets to order.

Your Home, Your Way - The blueprints you receive are a master plan for building your new home. They start you on your way to what may well be the most rewarding experience of your life.

The Ultimate Country & Victorian Home Plan Collection is published by HDA, Inc. (Home Design Alternatives) 944 Anglum Rd., St. Louis, MO 63042. All rights reserved. Reproduction in whole or in part without written permission of the publisher is prohibited. Printed in the U.S.A © 2004. Artist drawings and photos shown in this publication may vary slightly from the actual working drawings. Some photos are shown in mirror reverse. Please refer to the floor plan for accurate layout.

CONTENTS

House shown on front cover is Plan #578-071D-0010 and is featured on page 351. Photographer; Gregg Krogstad for Architects Northwest, Inc., Woodinville, Washington

The Ultimate Country & Victorian HOME PLAN Collection

About The Cover Home . . .

*L*ooking inside this stunning Victorian dream home creates visions of the past with all the modern amenities of the present and future.

The inlaid wood design on the floor of the entry rotunda (photo, above) is reminiscent of the kind of detail found in turn-of-the-century homes. When looking down from the second floor, it truly is a stunning reminder of American craftsmanship at its finest.

The substantial stone fireplace in the two-story family room (photo, below) creates a rustic, casual feel to this space. Directly adjacent to the breakfast nook and kitchen, this room has a friendly, inviting feel for intimate family gathering.

Charming and cozy, the formal living room (photo, above) invites guests in with its Traditional fireplace and ceiling details.

This state-of-the-art media room (photo, below) is filled with 21st century technology while maintaining a cozy atmosphere. The handsome corner fireplace and rich wood beamed ceiling keep the surroundings warm and inviting for all those film enthusiasts who enjoy the room.

Graced with French doors leading to the covered porch, the formal dining room (photo, below) is designed to impress guests and visitors alike.

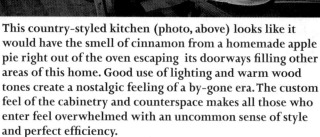

This country-styled kitchen (photo, above) looks like it would have the smell of cinnamon from a homemade apple pie right out of the oven escaping its doorways filling other areas of this home. Good use of lighting and warm wood tones create a nostalgic feeling of a by-gone era. The custom feel of the cabinetry and counterspace makes all those who enter feel overwhelmed with an uncommon sense of style and perfect efficiency.

A pleasant breeze will delight all those who step onto the outdoor covered porch (photo, below). Large enough for entertaining, this stylish, yet casual space is the perfect escape during all seasons. With warmth from the beautiful stone fireplace in the winter and fall, or a subtle breeze to stir the air from ceiling fans above in the spring and summer, this place is sure to become a family favorite year-round.

Enter the double-doors of the second floor loft (photo, above) and find an unbelievable treasure. The second floor turret creates the ultimate private retreat. The turret ceiling in this home has been adorned with a heavenly custom mural making it even more of a fantasy escape. Not just for relaxing, this space would make a sensational home office or nursery flooded in sunlight from windows all around.

For more information on this home, see page 351.
Photos courtesy of Architects Northwest, Woodinville, Washington
Photos shown may vary slightly from the actual working drawings. Please refer to the floor plan for accurate layout.

Stately Country Home For The "Spacious Age"

Features

- 2,727 total square feet of living area

- Wrap-around porch and large foyer create an impressive entrance

- A state-of-the-art vaulted kitchen has a walk-in pantry and is open to the breakfast room and adjoining screen-in-porch

- A walk-in wet bar, fireplace, bay window and deck access are features of the family room

- Vaulted master bedroom enjoys a luxurious bath with skylight and an enormous 13' deep walk-in closet

- 4 bedrooms, 2 1/2 baths, 2-car side entry garage

- Walk-out basement foundation

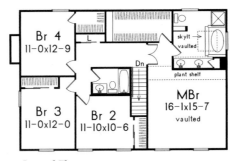

Second Floor
1,204 sq. ft.

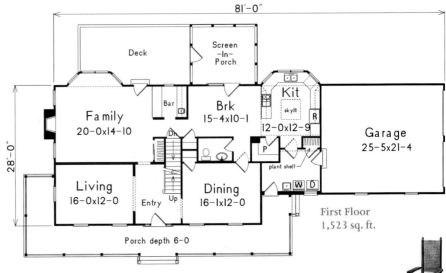

First Floor
1,523 sq. ft.

Quick & Easy Customizing

Make Changes To Your Home Plan In 4 Steps

Here's an affordable and efficient way to make changes to your plan.

1. Select the house plan that most closely meets your needs. Purchase of a reproducible master is necessary in order to make changes to a plan.

2. Call 1-800-373-2646 or e-mail customize@hdainc.com to place your order. Tell the sales representative you're interested in customizing a plan. A $50 nonrefundable consultation fee will be charged. You will then be instructed to complete a customization checklist indicating all the changes you wish to make to your plan. You may attach sketches if necessary. If you proceed with the custom changes the $50 will be credited to the total amount charged.

3. FAX the completed customization checklist to our design consultant. Within 24-48* business hours you will be provided with a written cost estimate to modify your plan. Our design consultant will contact you by phone if you wish to discuss any of your changes in greater detail.

4. Once you approve the estimate, a 75% retainer fee is collected and customization work gets underway. Preliminary drawings can usually be completed within 5-10* business days. Following approval of the preliminary drawings your design changes are completed within 5-10* business days. Your remaining 25% balance due is collected prior to shipment of your completed drawings. You will be shipped five sets of revised blueprints or a reproducible master, plus a customized materials list if required.

Before

After

Sample Modification Pricing Guide

The average prices specified below are provided as examples only. They refer to the most commonly requested changes, and are subject to change without notice. Prices for changes will vary or differ, from the prices below, depending on the number of modifications requested, the plan size, style, quality of original plan, format provided to us (originally drawn by hand or computer), and method of design used by the original designer. To obtain a detailed cost estimate or to get more information, please contact us.

Categories	Average Cost*
Adding or removing living space	Quote required
Adding or removing a garage	Starting at $400
Garage: Front entry to side load or vice versa	Starting at $300
Adding a screened porch	Starting at $280
Adding a bonus room in the attic	Starting at $450
Changing full basement to crawl space or vice versa	Starting at $495
Changing full basement to slab or vice versa	Starting at $495
Changing exterior building material	Starting at $200
Changing roof lines	Starting at $360
Adjusting ceiling height	Starting at $280
Adding, moving or removing an exterior opening	$65 per opening
Adding or removing a fireplace	Starting at $90
Modifying a non-bearing wall or room	$65 per room
Changing exterior walls from 2"x4" to 2"x6"	Starting at $200
Redesigning a bathroom or a kitchen	Starting at $120
Reverse plan right reading	Quote required
Adapting plans for local building code requirements	Quote required
Engineering and Architectural stamping and services	Quote required
Adjust plan for handicapped accessibility	Quote required
Interactive Illustrations (choices of exterior materials)	Quote required
Metric conversion of home plan	Starting at $400

*Prices and Terms are subject to change without notice.

Affordable Atrium Ranch

Features

- 2,334 total square feet of living area
- Roomy front porch gives home a country flavor
- Great room has a fireplace, TV alcove, pass-through snack bar to kitchen, atrium with bayed window wall and stair to family room
- Vaulted master bedroom features a double-door entry and walk-in closet
- 3 bedrooms, 2 baths, 2-car garage
- Walk-out basement foundation

Lower Level
557 sq. ft.

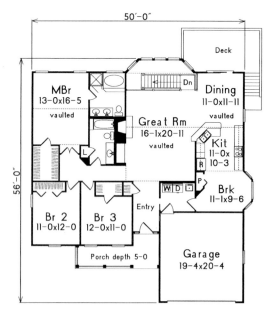

First Floor
1,777 sq. ft.

Rear View

To order call toll-free 1-800-DREAM HOME or visit www.houseplansandmore.com

Country Lodge With Screened Porch And Fireplace

Features

- 1,568 total square feet of living area
- Multiple entrances from three porches help to bring the outdoors in
- The lodge-like great room features a vaulted ceiling, stone fireplace, step-up entrance foyer and opens to a huge screened porch
- The kitchen has an island and peninsula, a convenient laundry room and adjoins a spacious dining area which leads to a screened porch and rear patio
- The master bedroom has two walk-in closets, a luxury bath and access to the screened porch and patio
- 2 bedrooms, 2 baths, 3-car side entry garage
- Crawl space foundation

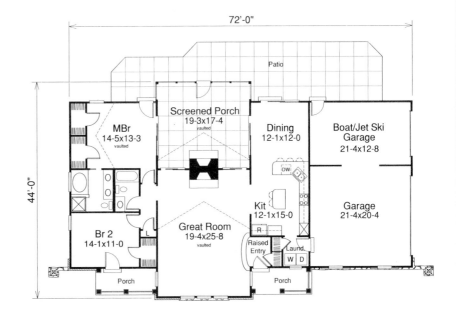

Functional Layout For Comfortable Living

Features

- 1,360 total square feet of living area
- Kitchen/dining room features island workspace and plenty of dining area
- Master bedroom has a large walk-in closet and private bath
- Laundry room is adjacent to the kitchen for easy access
- Convenient workshop in garage
- Large closets in secondary bedrooms maintain organization
- 3 bedrooms, 2 baths, 2-car side entry garage
- Basement foundation, drawings also include crawl space and slab foundations

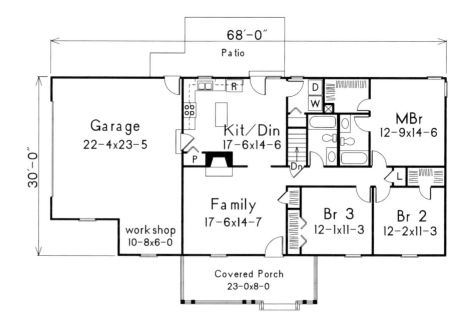

Paint-By-Number Wall Murals

Solar System
#75902

Photo colors may vary from kit colors

Create a unique room with ✑WALL ART™

You will be the envy of friends when you decorate with a Paint-By-Number Wall Mural.

Choose from over 100 custom designs for all ages and transform your room into a paradise.

You don't have to be an artist to paint a Wall Art mural. The whole family can participate in this fun and easy weekend project.

Your Wall Art kit includes everything but the wall!

Wall Art murals are available in a variety of sizes starting at the *low price of $49.97.*

ORDER TODAY!

It's As Easy As 1 - 2 - 3!

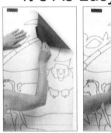  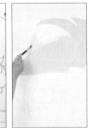

1. Tape   2. Trace   3. Paint

To order or request a catalog, call toll free

1-877-WALLMURAL (925-5687)

24 hours a day, 7 days a week,
or buy online at

www.wallartdesigns.com

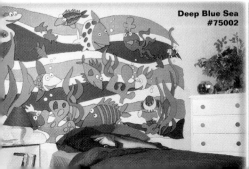

Deep Blue Sea
#75002

Route 66
#76305

Bug Collection
#75001

Impressive Victorian Blends Charm And Efficiency

Features

- 2,286 total square feet of living area
- Fine architectural detail makes this home a showplace with its large windows, intricate brickwork and fine woodwork and trim
- Stunning two-story entry with attractive wood railing and balustrades in foyer
- Convenient wrap-around kitchen enjoys a window view, planning center and pantry
- Oversized master bedroom includes a walk-in closet and master bath
- 4 bedrooms, 2 1/2 baths, 2-car garage
- Basement foundation, drawings also include crawl space and slab foundations

Second Floor
1,003 sq. ft.

Br 4
10-2x
10-8

Br 3
11-7x10-8

MBr
12-8x15-11
vaulted

Br 2
12-4x10-8

open to
below

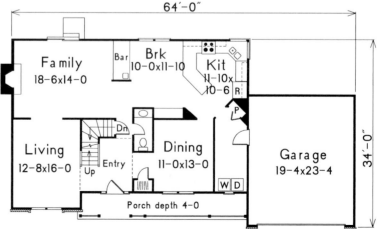

64'-0"

Family
18-6x14-0

Bar

Brk
10-0x11-10

Kit
11-10x
10-6

Living
12-8x16-0

Entry

Up

Dining
11-0x13-0

Garage
19-4x23-4

34'-0"

Porch depth 4-0

First Floor
1,283 sq. ft.

Zoned For Great Entertaining

Features

- 3,204 total square feet of living area

- The master bedroom highlights a sunny sitting area, tray ceiling, huge walk-in closet and a corner spa tub in the bath

- Decorative columns introduce the expansive great room which features a fireplace, built-in shelves and a serving counter shared with the kitchen

- A handy office just off the entry doubles as a guest room and has private access to a full bath

- A full bath near the rear door from the kitchen is convenient

- 4 bedrooms, 4 baths, 3-car side entry garage

- Basement or crawl space foundation, please specify when ordering

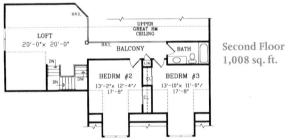

Second Floor
1,008 sq. ft.

LOFT
20'-0"x 20'-0"

BALCONY

BATH

UPPER
GREAT RM
CEILING

BEDRM #2
13'-2"x 12'-4"/
17'-8"

BEDRM #3
13'-10"x 11'-0"/
17'-8"

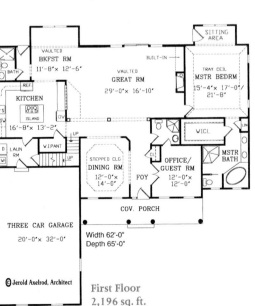

SITTING AREA

BKFST RM
11'-8"x 12'-6"

VAULTED

BUILT-IN

BATH

VAULTED
GREAT RM
29'-0"x 16'-10"

TRAY CEIL
MSTR BEDRM
15'-4"x 17'-0"/
21'-8"

REF.

KITCHEN
16'-8"x 13'-2"
ISLAND

W.I.PANT

LAUN RM

WICL

STEPPED CLG
DINING RM
12'-0"x
14'-0"

OFFICE/
GUEST RM
12'-0"x
12'-0"

FOY

MSTR
BATH

COV. PORCH

THREE CAR GARAGE
20'-0"x 32'-0"

Width 62'-0"
Depth 65'-0"

Jerold Axelrod, Architect

First Floor
2,196 sq. ft.

Tranquility Of An Atrium Cottage

Features

- 1,384 total square feet of living area
- Wrap-around country porch for peaceful evenings
- Great room enjoys a large bay window, stone fireplace and rear views through an atrium window
- Atrium opens to 611 square feet of optional living area below
- 2 bedrooms, 2 baths, 1-car side entry garage
- Walk-out basement foundation

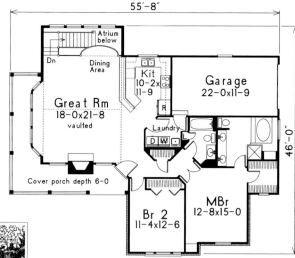

First Floor
1,384 sq. ft.

55'-8"

Atrium below

Dn

Dining Area

Kit
10-2x11-9

Garage
22-0x11-9

Great Rm
18-0x21-8
vaulted

Laundry

D W

R

46'-0"

Cover porch depth 6-0

Br 2
11-4x12-6

MBr
12-8x15-0

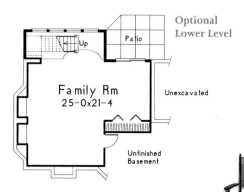

Optional
Lower Level

Up

Patio

Family Rm
25-0x21-4

Unexcavated

Unfinished Basement

Rear View

Bay Window Graces Luxury Master Bedroom

Features

- 1,668 total square feet of living area
- Large bay windows grace the breakfast area, master bedroom and dining room
- Extensive walk-in closets and storage spaces are located throughout the home
- Handy covered entry porch
- Large living room has a fireplace, built-in bookshelves and sloped ceiling
- 3 bedrooms, 2 baths, 2-car drive under garage
- Basement foundation

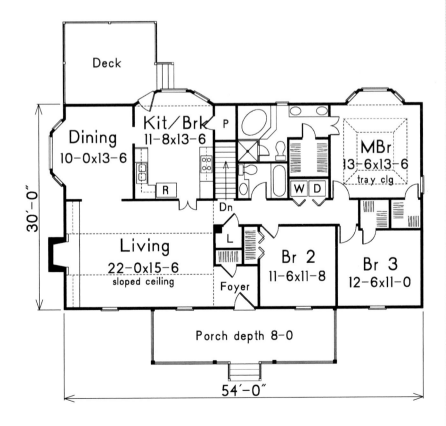

Amazing Carpentry Details Adorn This Home's Facade

Features

- 4,220 total square feet of living area
- A large covered porch surrounds and connects to the living room with fireplace
- Unbelievable octagon-shaped sitting room connects the master bedroom to its own private bath with whirlpool tub
- Bay windows brighten bedrooms #3 and #4
- Bonus room on the second floor is included in the square footage
- 4 bedrooms, 3 1/2 baths, 3-car garage
- Crawl space foundation

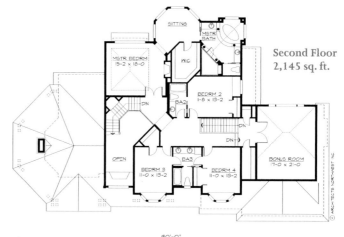

Second Floor
2,145 sq. ft.

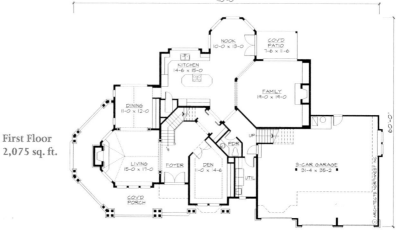

First Floor
2,075 sq. ft.

To order call toll-free 1-800-DREAM HOME or visit www.houseplansandmore.com

Cozy Covered Porches

Features

- 2,698 total square feet of living area
- Great room feels spacious with a vaulted ceiling and windows over-looking the covered porch
- Master bath has a glass shower and whirlpool tub
- Laundry area includes counterspace and a sink
- 4 bedrooms, 3 baths, 2-car side entry garage
- Crawl space or slab foundation, please specify when ordering

Second Floor
885 sq. ft.

First Floor
1,813 sq. ft.

Transom Windows Create Impressive Front Entry

Features

- 1,800 total square feet of living area
- Energy efficient home with 2" x 6" exterior walls
- Covered front and rear porches add outdoor living area
- 12' ceilings in the kitchen, breakfast area, dining and living rooms
- Private master bedroom features an expansive bath
- Side entry garage has two storage areas
- Pillared styling with brick and stucco exterior finish
- 3 bedrooms, 2 baths, 2-car side entry garage
- Crawl space foundation, drawings also include slab foundation

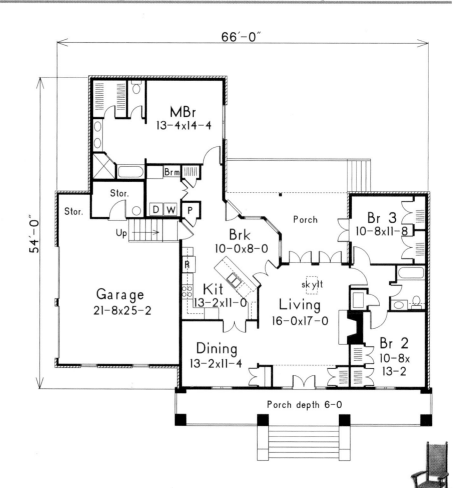

Charming House, Spacious And Functional

Features

- 2,505 total square feet of living area
- The garage features extra storage area and ample workspace
- Laundry room is accessible from the garage and the outdoors
- Deluxe raised tub and immense walk-in closet grace master bath
- 3 bedrooms, 2 1/2 baths, 2-car side entry garage
- Basement foundation, drawings also include crawl space foundation

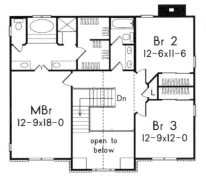

Second Floor
1,069 sq. ft.

Br 2
12-6x11-6

MBr
12-9x18-0

Dn

open to
below

Br 3
12-9x12-0

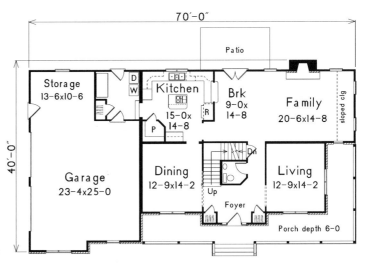

70'-0"

Patio

40'-0"

Storage
13-6x10-6

Kitchen
15-0x
14-8

Brk
9-0x
14-8

Family
20-6x14-8

sloped clg

D
W

P

R

Garage
23-4x25-0

Dining
12-9x14-2

Up

Dn

Living
12-9x14-2

Foyer

Porch depth 6-0

First Floor
1,436 sq. ft.

Terrific Rear Patio

Features

- 3,176 total square feet of living area
- Varied ceiling heights throughout
- Beautifully designed foyer has a prominent center staircase and a lovely adjacent gallery space
- A casual sitting room connects the secondary bedrooms
- 3 bedrooms, 3 1/2 baths, 2-car rear entry garage
- Basement, crawl space or slab foundation, please specify when ordering

Rear View

First Floor
2,310 sq. ft.

Second Floor
866 sq. ft.

To order call toll-free 1-800-DREAM HOME or visit www.houseplansandmore.com

Stately Entry

Features

- 4,652 total square feet of living area
- A grand foyer introduces a formal dining room and library with beamed ceiling and built-ins
- Covered porches at the rear of the home offer splendid views
- A magnificent master bedroom has a 10' ceiling, a private sitting area and a luxurious dressing room with walk-in closet
- Secondary bedrooms have window seats, large closets and private bath access
- 4 bedrooms, 3 1/2 baths, 3-car side entry garage
- Walk-out basement foundation

Second Floor
1,238 sq. ft.

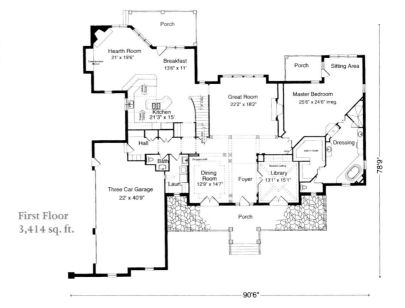

First Floor
3,414 sq. ft.

Atrium's Dramatic Ambiance, Compliments Of Windows

Features

- 1,721 total square feet of living area
- Vaulted dining and great rooms are immersed in light from the atrium window wall
- Breakfast room opens onto the covered porch
- Functionally designed kitchen
- 3 bedrooms, 2 baths, 3-car garage
- Walk-out basement foundation, drawings also include crawl space and slab foundations
- 1,604 square feet on the first floor and 117 square feet on the lower level

Rear View

To order call toll-free 1-800-DREAM HOME or visit www.houseplansandmore.com

Home Has Character Of Days Gone By

Features

- 2,445 total square feet of living area
- A dramatic, skylighted foyer preludes the formal, sunken living room, which includes a stunning corner fireplace
- A built-in desk and a pantry mark the smartly designed kitchen which opens to the breakfast room and beyond to the family room
- Sunken and filled with intrigue, the family room features a fireplace plus French doors that open to a backyard deck
- 4 bedrooms, 2 1/2 baths, 3-car garage
- Basement foundation

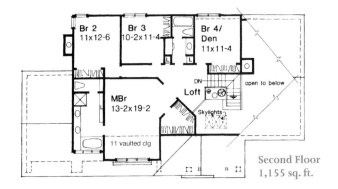

Second Floor
1,155 sq. ft.

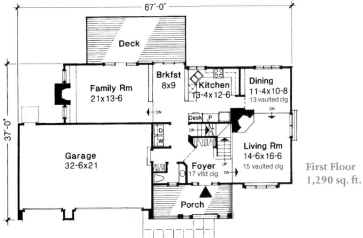

First Floor
1,290 sq. ft.

Charming Country Styling In This Ranch

Features

- 1,600 total square feet of living area
- Energy efficient home with 2" x 6" exterior walls
- Impressive sunken living room features a massive stone fireplace and 16' vaulted ceiling
- The dining room is conveniently located next to the kitchen and divided for privacy
- Special amenities include a sewing room, glass shelves in kitchen and the master bath and a large utility area
- Sunken master bedroom features a distinctive sitting room
- 3 bedrooms, 2 baths, 2-car side entry garage
- Slab foundation, drawings also include crawl space and basement foundations

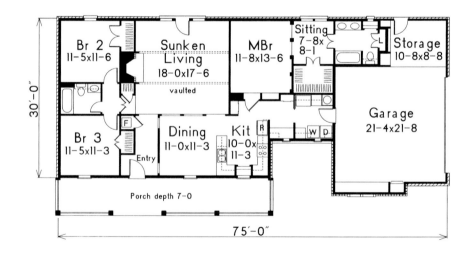

Private Breakfast Room Provides Casual Dining

Features

- 1,708 total square feet of living area
- Massive family room is enhanced with several windows, a fireplace and access to the porch
- Deluxe master bath is accented by a step-up corner tub flanked by double vanities
- Closets throughout maintain organized living
- Bedrooms are isolated from living areas
- 3 bedrooms, 2 baths, 2-car garage
- Basement foundation, drawings also include crawl space foundation

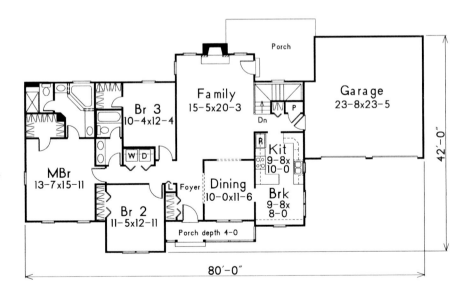

Pillared Front Porch Generates Charm And Warmth

Features

- 1,567 total square feet of living area
- Living room flows into the dining room shaped by an angled pass-through into the kitchen
- Cheerful, windowed dining area
- Future area available on the second floor has an additional 338 square feet of living area
- Master bedroom is separated from other bedrooms for privacy
- 3 bedrooms, 2 baths, 2-car side entry garage
- Partial basement/crawl space foundation, drawings also include slab foundation

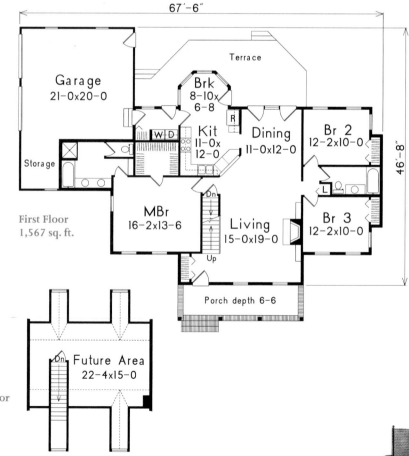

Garage 21-0x20-0

Terrace

Brk 8-10x 6-8

Kit 11-0x 12-0

Dining 11-0x12-0

Br 2 12-2x10-0

Storage

First Floor 1,567 sq. ft.

MBr 16-2x13-6

Living 15-0x19-0

Br 3 12-2x10-0

Dn

Up

Porch depth 6-6

67'-6"

46'-8"

Optional Second Floor

Future Area 22-4x15-0

Dn

Layout Creates Large Open Living Area

Features

- 1,285 total square feet of living area
- Accommodating home with ranch-style porch
- Large storage area on back of home
- Master bedroom includes dressing area, private bath and built-in bookcase
- Kitchen features pantry, breakfast bar and complete view to the dining room
- 3 bedrooms, 2 baths
- Crawl space foundation, drawings also include basement and slab foundations

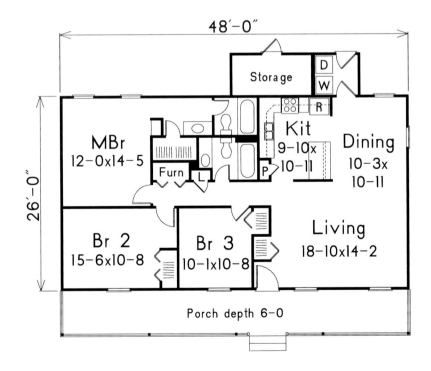

Classic Ranch Has Grand Appeal With Expansive Porch

Features

- 1,400 total square feet of living area
- Master bedroom is secluded for privacy
- Large utility room has additional cabinet space
- Covered porch provides an outdoor seating area
- Roof dormers add great curb appeal
- Living room and master bedroom feature vaulted ceilings
- Oversized two-car garage has storage space
- 3 bedrooms, 2 baths, 2-car garage
- Basement foundation, drawings also include crawl space foundation

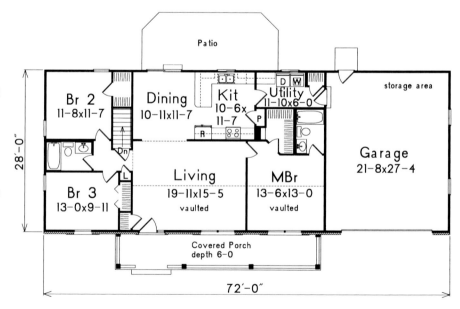

Patio

Br 2
11-8x11-7

Dining
10-11x11-7

Kit
10-6x
11-7

Utility
11-10x6-0

storage area

Dn

28'-0"

Br 3
13-0x9-11

Living
19-11x15-5
vaulted

MBr
13-6x13-0
vaulted

Garage
21-8x27-4

Covered Porch
depth 6-0

72'-0"

Country-Style Porch Adds Charm

Features

- 1,619 total square feet of living area
- Private second floor bedroom and bath
- Kitchen features a snack bar and adjacent dining area
- Master bedroom has a private bath
- Centrally located washer and dryer
- 3 bedrooms, 3 baths
- Basement foundation, drawings also include crawl space and slab foundations

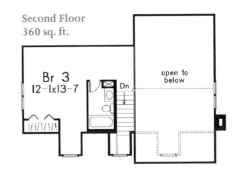

Second Floor
360 sq. ft.

Br 3
12-1x13-7

open to below

Dn

Deck

Br 2
12-7x12-3

Kit/Dining
22-9x
12-6

D
W

R

L

Dn

28'-2"

MBr
12-1x15-0

Living
15-5x15-4
vaulted

Up

Porch depth 7-6

52'-6"

First Floor
1,259 sq. ft.

Dormers Add Charm

Features

- 2,107 total square feet of living area
- Kitchen has pantry and adjacent dining area
- Master bedroom has a bath and a large walk-in closet
- Second floor bedrooms have attic storage
- Bonus room above the garage has an additional 324 square feet of living area
- 3 bedrooms, 2 1/2 baths, 2-car garage
- Walk-out basement, basement, crawl space or slab foundation, please specify when ordering

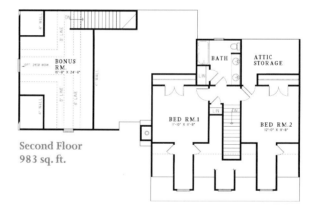

Second Floor
983 sq. ft.

First Floor
1,124 sq. ft.

Colossal Southern Colonial

Rear View

Features

- 4,187 total square feet of living area
- 10' ceilings on the first floor and 9' ceilings on the second floor
- Secluded bedroom on the first floor has its own private bath and could convert to a mother-in-law suite
- Second floor sitting area accesses outdoor balcony through lovely French doors
- Octagon-shaped breakfast room is a nice focal point
- Future gameroom over the garage has an additional 551 square feet of living area
- 4 bedrooms, 4 1/2 baths, 3-car side entry garage
- Slab foundation

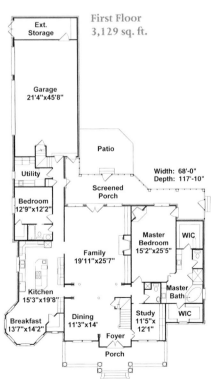

First Floor
3,129 sq. ft.

Ext. Storage

Garage
21'4"x45'8"

Patio

Utility

Width: 68'-0"
Depth: 117'-10"

Bedroom
12'9"x12'2"

Screened Porch

Family
19'11"x25'7"

Master Bedroom
15'2"x25'5"

WIC

Kitchen
15'3"x19'8"

Master Bath

WIC

Breakfast
13'7"x14'2"

Dining
11'3"x14'

Study
11'5"x12'1"

WIC

Foyer

Porch

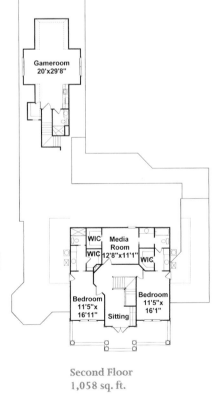

Gameroom
20'x29'8"

WIC
WIC

Media Room
12'8"x11'1"

WIC

Bedroom
11'5"x16'11"

Sitting

Bedroom
11'5"x16'1"

Second Floor
1,058 sq. ft.

Country Style With Wrap-Around Porch

Features

- 1,597 total square feet of living area

- Spacious family room includes a fireplace and coat closet

- Open kitchen and dining room provide a breakfast bar and access to the outdoors

- Convenient laundry area is located near the kitchen

- Secluded master bedroom enjoys a walk-in closet and private bath

- 4 bedrooms, 2 1/2 baths, 2-car detached garage

- Basement foundation

Br 4
12-0x12-4

Br 3
14-0x10-0

Dn

Second Floor
615 sq. ft.

Br 2
14-0x10-10

41'-0"

MBr
12-0x14-0

Dn Up

Dining
11-0x10-0

Kit
10-0x
10-0

Garage
21-4x25-4

21'-0"

Family
14-0x16-10

First Floor
982 sq. ft.

Porch Depth 7-0

Excellent Ranch For A Country Setting

Features

- 2,758 total square feet of living area
- Vaulted great room excels with fireplace, wet bar, plant shelves and skylights
- Fabulous master bedroom enjoys a fireplace, large bath, walk-in closet and vaulted ceiling
- Trendsetting kitchen and breakfast area adjoins the spacious screened porch
- Convenient office near kitchen is perfect for computer room, hobby enthusiast or fifth bedroom
- 4 bedrooms, 2 1/2 baths, 3-car side entry garage
- Basement foundation

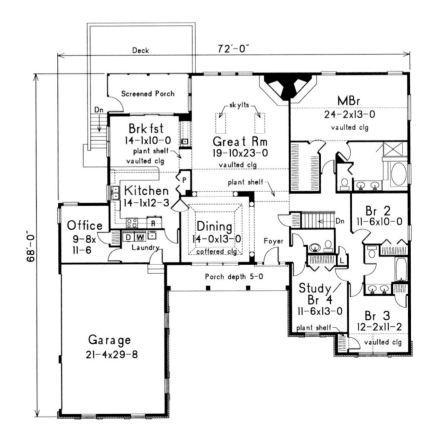

Deck

72'-0"

Screened Porch

Dn

Brkfst
14-1x10-0
plant shelf
vaulted clg

skylts

Great Rm
19-10x23-0
vaulted clg

MBr
24-2x13-0
vaulted clg

Kitchen
14-1x12-3

P

plant shelf

Office
9-8x
11-6

Dining
14-0x13-0
coffered clg

Foyer

Br 2
11-6x10-0

Dn

L

Laundry

68'-0"

Porch depth 5-0

Study/
Br 4
11-6x13-0

plant shelf

Br 3
12-2x11-0

vaulted clg

Garage
21-4x29-8

Charming Victorian Has Unexpected Pleasures

Features

- 2,935 total square feet of living area
- Gracious entry foyer with handsome stairway opens to separate living and dining rooms
- Kitchen has vaulted ceiling and skylight, island worktop, breakfast area with bay window and two separate pantries
- Large second floor master bedroom features a fireplace, raised tub, dressing area with vaulted ceiling and skylight
- 4 bedrooms, 2 1/2 baths, 2-car side entry garage
- Basement foundation

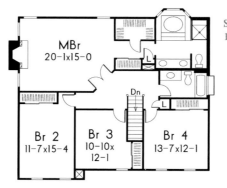

Second Floor
1,320 sq. ft.

MBr
20-1x15-0

Dn

Br 2
11-7x15-4

Br 3
10-10x
12-1

Br 4
13-7x12-1

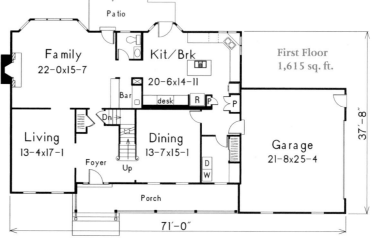

Patio

Family
22-0x15-7

Kit/Brk
20-6x14-11

First Floor
1,615 sq. ft.

Bar

desk R P P

Dn

Living
13-4x17-1

Dining
13-7x15-1

Garage
21-8x25-4

37'-8"

Foyer

Up

D W

Porch

71'-0"

Classic Columned Home

Features

- 2,969 total square feet of living area
- Formal entry has an open stairwell to the second floor and balcony overlook with upper porch access
- 9' ceilings on the first floor
- Large great room has fireplace, access to patio/deck and view to rear
- Kitchen features a center island, walk-in pantry and bayed breakfast room
- 3 bedrooms, 2 1/2 baths, 2-car side entry garage
- Slab or crawl space foundation, please specify when ordering

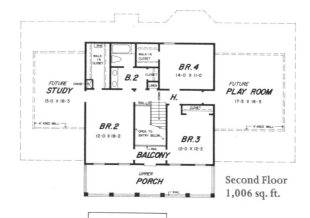

Second Floor
1,006 sq. ft.

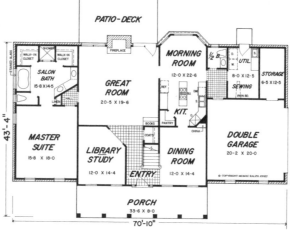

First Floor
1,963 sq. ft.

A Substantial Home With Luxurious Touches

Features

- 2,820 total square feet of living area
- Convenient wet bar is located between the kitchen and family room
- Kitchen, breakfast room and large family room flow together for informal entertaining
- Luxurious master bedroom suite enjoys a fireplace and generous closet
- Oversized foyer leads to private living and dining rooms
- 4 bedrooms, 2 1/2 baths, 2-car garage
- Basement foundation, drawings also include slab and crawl space foundations

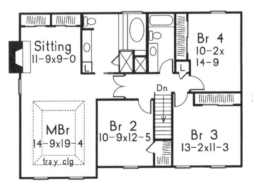

Sitting
11-9x9-0

Br 4
10-2x
14-9

MBr
14-9x19-4
tray. clg.

Br 2
10-9x12-5

Dn

Br 3
13-2x11-3

Second Floor
1,312 sq. ft.

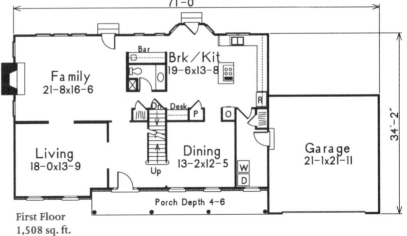

71'-0"

Bar

Brk/Kit
19-6x13-8

Family
21-8x16-6

Desk
Dn
P

R

O

Living
18-0x13-9

Up

Dining
13-2x12-5

W
D

Garage
21-1x21-11

34'-2"

Porch Depth 4-6

First Floor
1,508 sq. ft.

Charming Wrap-Around Porch

Features

- 1,879 total square feet of living area
- Open floor plan on both floors makes home appear larger
- Loft area overlooks great room or can become an optional fourth bedroom
- Large storage in rear of home has access from exterior
- 3 bedrooms, 2 baths
- Crawl space foundation

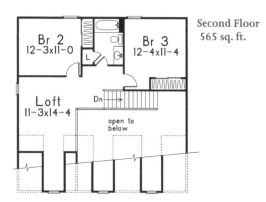

Second Floor
565 sq. ft.

Br 2
12-3x11-0

Br 3
12-4x11-4

Loft
11-3x14-4

Dn

open to below

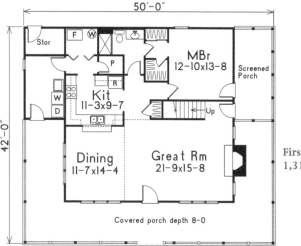

50'-0"

42'-0"

Stor

F W

MBr
12-10x13-8

Screened Porch

P

R

Kit
11-3x9-7

W

D

Up

Dining
11-7x14-4

Great Rm
21-9x15-8

First Floor
1,314 sq. ft.

Covered porch depth 8-0

Unique Three-Way Fireplace

Features

- 2,126 total square feet of living area
- Elegant bay windows in the master bedroom welcome the sun
- Double vanities in the master bath are separated by a large whirlpool tub
- Secondary bedrooms each include a walk-in closet
- Nook has access to the outdoors onto the rear porch
- 3 bedrooms, 2 baths, 2-car side entry garage
- Slab foundation

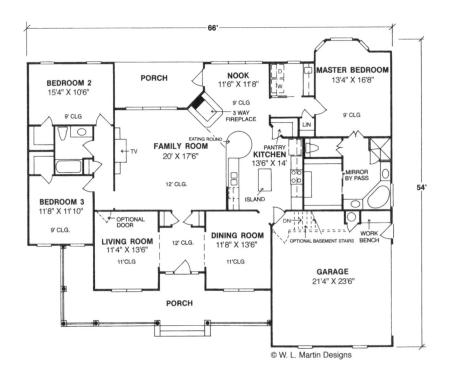

© W. L. Martin Designs

A Charming Home Loaded With Extras

Features

- 1,997 total square feet of living area
- Screened porch leads to a rear terrace with access to the breakfast room
- Living and dining rooms combine adding spaciousness to the floor plan
- Other welcome amenities include boxed windows in the breakfast and dining rooms, a fireplace in the living room and a pass-through snack bar in the kitchen
- 3 bedrooms, 2 1/2 baths
- Basement foundation

Rear View

First Floor
1,111 sq. ft.

Second Floor
886 sq. ft.

Extraordinary Charm

Features

- 2,787 total square feet of living area
- 9' ceilings on the first and second floors
- Enormous shop area in garage is ideal for hobbies, a workshop or extra storage
- Interesting gallery is the focal point of the entry
- Optional second floor has an additional 636 square feet of living area
- 4 bedrooms, 2 1/2 baths, 3-car side entry garage
- Crawl space, basement or slab foundation, please specify when ordering

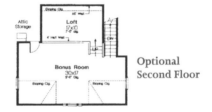

Optional
Second Floor

First Floor
2,787 sq. ft.

Plan #578-069D-0016

Dormers And Porch Are Nice Touches

Features

- 1,925 total square feet of living area
- Angled snack bar in kitchen provides extra dining space overlooking into the great room and dining area
- Wonderful master bath includes a sunny whirlpool tub, corner oversized shower and a makeup counter
- Dining area has sliding glass doors leading to the outdoors
- 3 bedrooms, 2 1/2 baths, 2-car garage
- Slab or crawl space foundation, please specify when ordering

Second Floor
596 sq. ft.

BEDROOM # 3
14' x 10'

BATH # 2
5' x 12'

BEDROOM # 2
14' x 14'

STOR

DOWN

CLOSET

First Floor
1,329 sq. ft.

Massive Double Columned Front Porch

Features

- 2,452 total square feet of living area
- Second floor balcony overlooks vaulted entry and two-story living room
- Living room features two-story glass rear wall
- Kitchen and breakfast area are open to family room with built-ins and a fireplace
- Master bedroom and breakfast room have access to rear deck
- 4 bedrooms, 2 1/2 baths, 2-car garage
- Basement foundation

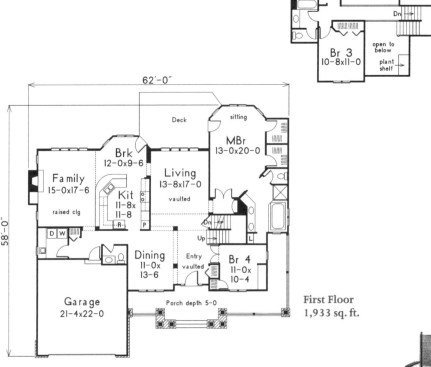

Second Floor
519 sq. ft.

Br 2
11-8x13-8

open to below

Dn

Br 3
10-8x11-0

open to below

plant shelf

62'-0"

58'-0"

Deck

sitting

MBr
13-0x20-0

Brk
12-0x9-6

Living
13-8x17-0
vaulted

Family
15-0x17-6

Kit
11-8x 11-8

raised clg

D W

Dn

Up

Dining
11-0x 13-6

Entry
vaulted

Br 4
11-0x 10-4

Garage
21-4x22-0

Porch depth 5-0

First Floor
1,933 sq. ft.

Flexible Design Is Popular

Features

- 1,440 total square feet of living area
- Open floor plan with access to covered porches in front and back
- Lots of linen, pantry and closet space throughout
- Laundry/mud room between kitchen and garage is a convenient feature
- 2 bedrooms, 2 baths, 2-car side entry garage
- Basement foundation

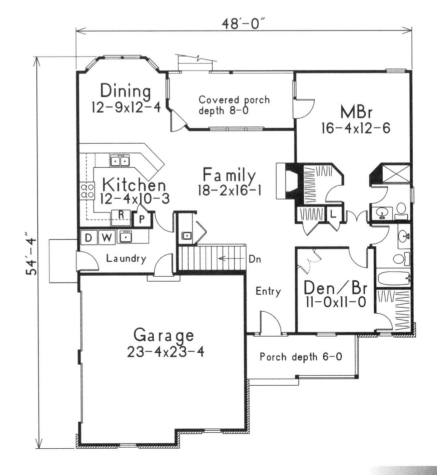

Spectacular Five Bedroom Home

Features

- 2,801 total square feet of living area
- 9' ceilings on the first floor
- Full view dining bay with elegant circle-top windows
- Wrap-around porches provide outdoor exposure in all directions
- Secluded master bedroom with double vanities and walk-in closets
- Convenient game room
- 5 bedrooms, 3 baths, 2-car side entry garage
- Slab foundation

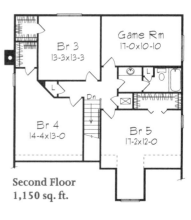

Second Floor
1,150 sq. ft.

First Floor
1,651 sq. ft.

Open Floor Plan With Extra Amenities

Features

- 1,680 total square feet of living area
- Compact and efficient layout in an affordable package
- Second floor has three bedrooms all with oversized closets
- All bedrooms are on the second floor for privacy
- 3 bedrooms, 2 1/2 baths, 2-car garage
- Basement foundation

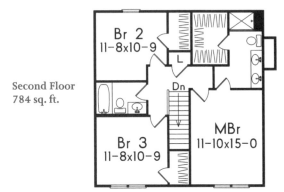

Second Floor
784 sq. ft.

Br 2
11-8x10-9

MBr
11-10x15-0

Br 3
11-8x10-9

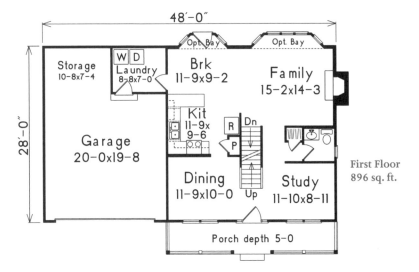

48'-0"

28'-0"

Storage
10-8x7-4

W D Laundry
8-8x7-0

Brk
11-9x9-2

Family
15-2x14-3

Kit
11-9x 9-6

Garage
20-0x19-8

Dining
11-9x10-0

Study
11-10x8-11

First Floor
896 sq. ft.

Porch depth 5-0

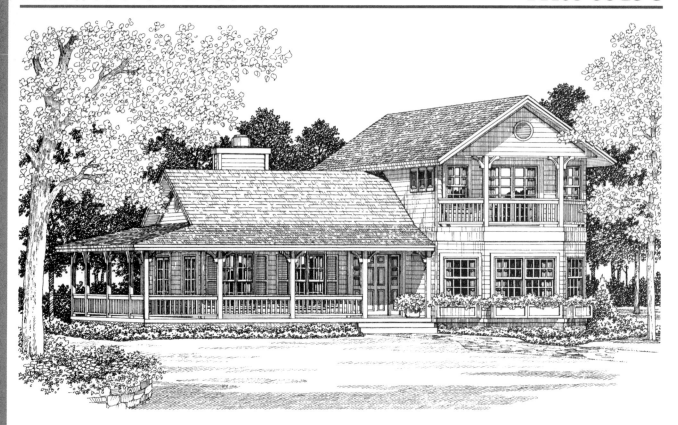

Wrap-Around Porch Adds Warmth To Home

Features

- 1,974 total square feet of living area

- Sunny bayed nook invites casual dining and shares its natural light with a snack counter and kitchen

- Spacious master bedroom occupies a bay window and offers a sumptuous bath

- Both second floor bedrooms have private balconies

- 3 bedrooms, 2 1/2 baths

- Basement or crawl space foundation, please specify when ordering

Second Floor
600 sq. ft.

First Floor
1,374 sq. ft.

Great Recreation Room On The Second Floor

Features

- 2,750 total square feet of living area
- Oversized rooms throughout
- 9' ceilings on the first floor
- Unique utility bay workshop off garage
- Spacious master bedroom is adorned with a luxurious bath
- Optional six bedroom plan is also included
- 5 bedrooms, 3 1/2 baths, 2-car side entry garage
- Basement foundation, drawings also include crawl space and slab foundations

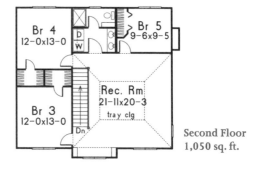

Second Floor
1,050 sq. ft.

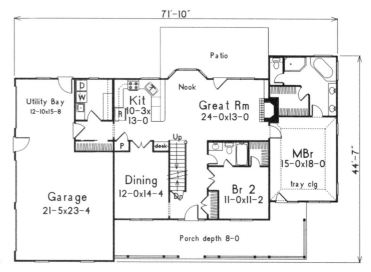

First Floor
1,700 sq. ft.

Open Floor Plan With Plenty Of Light

Features

- 2,475 total square feet of living area
- Country feeling with wrap-around porch and dormered front
- Open floor plan with living and dining areas combined has access to a sundeck
- First floor master bedroom features many luxuries
- Bonus room on the second floor has an additional 384 square feet of living area
- 3 bedrooms, 2 1/2 baths, 2-car side entry garage
- Walk-out basement foundation

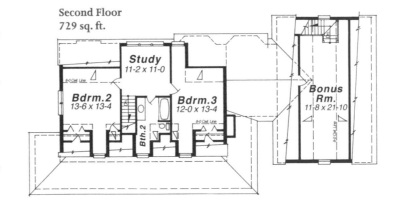

Second Floor
729 sq. ft.

Study
11-2 x 11-0

Bdrm.2
13-6 x 13-4

Bdrm.3
12-0 x 13-4

Bth.2

Bonus Rm.
11-8 x 21-10

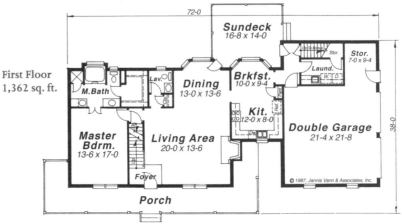

First Floor
1,362 sq. ft.

Sundeck
16-8 x 14-0

Brkfst.
10-0 x 9-4

Laund.

Stor.
7-0 x 9-4

Dining
13-0 x 13-6

M.Bath

Lav.

Kit.
12-0 x 8-0

Double Garage
21-4 x 21-8

38-0

72-0

Master Bdrm.
13-6 x 17-0

Living Area
20-0 x 13-6

Foyer

Porch

© 1987, Jannis Vann & Associates, Inc.

Victorian Turret Provides Dramatic Focus

Features

- 2,214 total square feet of living area
- Victorian accents dominate facade
- Covered porches and decks fan out to connect front and rear entries and add to outdoor living space
- Elegant master bedroom suite features a five-sided windowed alcove and private deck
- Corner kitchen with a sink-top peninsula
- 4 bedrooms, 2 1/2 baths, 2-car drive under garage
- Basement foundation

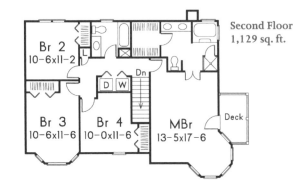

Second Floor
1,129 sq. ft.

Br 2
10-6x11-2

Br 3
10-6x11-6

Br 4
10-0x11-6

MBr
13-5x17-6

Deck

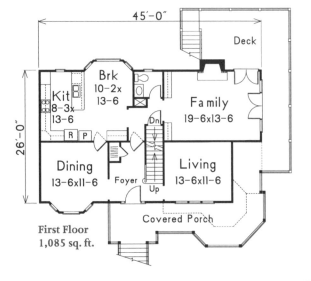

45'-0"

Deck

Brk
10-2x
13-6

Kit
8-3x
13-6

Family
19-6x13-6

26'-0"

Dining
13-6x11-6

Foyer

Living
13-6x11-6

Up

Covered Porch

First Floor
1,085 sq. ft.

Inviting Covered Verandas

Features

- 1,830 total square feet of living area

- Inviting covered verandas in the front and rear of the home

- Great room has a fireplace and cathedral ceiling

- Handy service porch allows easy access

- Master bedroom has a vaulted ceiling and private bath

- 3 bedrooms, 2 baths, 3-car side entry garage

- Basement, crawl space or slab foundation, please specify when ordering

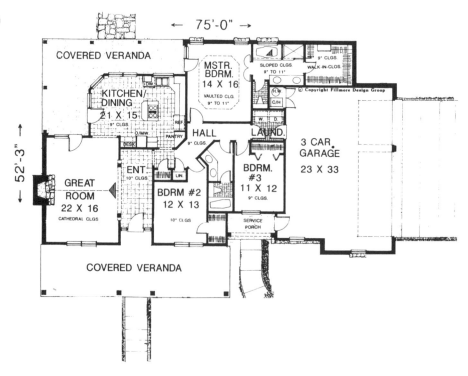

To order call toll-free 1-800-DREAM HOME or visit www.houseplansandmore.com

Country Comfort

Features

- 2,636 total square feet of living area
- Master bedroom has a generous walk-in closet, luxurious bath and a vaulted sitting area
- Spacious kitchen has an island cooktop and vaulted breakfast nook
- Bonus room above garage has an additional 389 square feet of living area
- 4 bedrooms, 3 1/2 baths, 2-car side entry garage, 1-car drive under garage
- Basement foundation

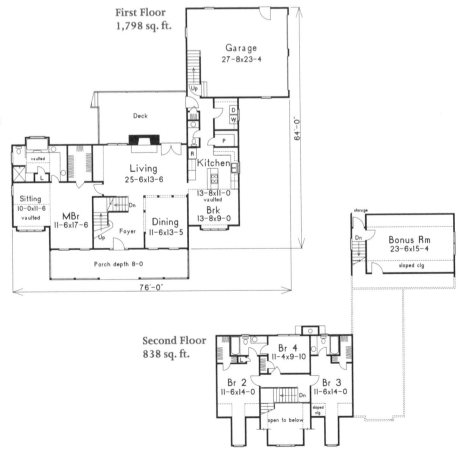

First Floor
1,798 sq. ft.

Garage
27-8x23-4

64'-0"

Deck

Living
25-6x13-6

Kitchen

vaulted

Sitting
10-0x11-6
vaulted

MBr
11-6x17-6

Foyer

Dining
11-6x13-5

Brk
13-8x9-0

13-8x11-0
vaulted

Porch depth 8-0

76'-0"

storage

Bonus Rm
23-6x15-4

sloped clg

Second Floor
838 sq. ft.

Br 4
11-4x9-10

Br 2
11-6x14-0

Br 3
11-6x14-0

sloped clg

open to below

A Welcoming Farmhouse Style

Features

- 2,629 total square feet of living area
- 9' ceilings on the first floor of this home
- Kitchen, breakfast and hearth rooms connect creating one large living space ideal for family living
- Master suite has its own wing with large private bath and walk-in closet
- Wrap-around porch in the front of the home makes a lasting impression
- Future playroom on the second floor has an additional 327 square feet of living area
- 3 bedrooms, 2 1/2 baths, 2-car side entry garage
- Slab foundation

Separate Living Areas Lend Privacy

Features

- 2,562 total square feet of living area
- Large, open foyer creates a grand entrance
- Convenient open breakfast area includes peninsula counter, bay window and easy access to the deck
- Dining and living rooms flow together for expanded entertaining space
- Bonus room above the garage is included in the square footage
- 3 bedrooms, 2 1/2 baths, 2-car side entry garage
- Basement foundation, drawings also include slab and crawl space foundations

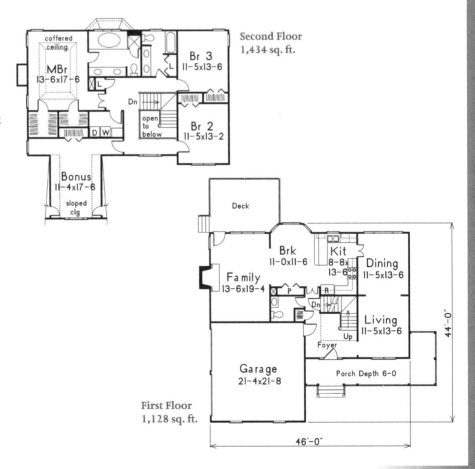

Second Floor 1,434 sq. ft.

coffered ceiling

MBr 13-6x17-6

Br 3 11-5x13-6

Br 2 11-5x13-2

Dn

open to below

D | W

Bonus 11-4x17-6

sloped clg

First Floor 1,128 sq. ft.

Deck

Brk 11-0x11-6

Kit 8-8x 13-6

Dining 11-5x13-6

Family 13-6x19-4

Living 11-5x13-6

Foyer

Up

Dn

Garage 21-4x21-8

Porch Depth 6-0

44'-0"

46'-0"

Wrap-Around Porch Offers A Warm Welcome

Features

- 2,764 total square feet of living area

- A balcony leads to a small study area while offering a dramatic view to the family room and fireplace

- Master bedroom provides convenience and comfort with its whirlpool tub, double-bowl vanity, shower and large walk-in closet

- Delightful library is a nice quiet place to relax

- 4 bedrooms, 2 1/2 baths, 2-car side entry garage

- Basement foundation

Second Floor
821 sq. ft.

First Floor
1,943 sq. ft.

Porch Creates A Comfortable Feel

Features

- 2,266 total square feet of living area

- Great room includes a fireplace flanked by built-in bookshelves and a dining nook with bay window

- Unique media room includes a double-door entrance, walk-in closet and access to a full bath

- Master bedroom has a lovely sitting area and private bath with a walk-in closet, step-up tub and double vanity

- 3 bedrooms, 3 baths, 2-car side entry garage

- Basement foundation, drawings also include crawl space foundation

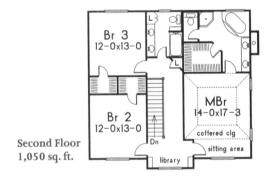

Br 3
12-0x13-0

Br 2
12-0x13-0

MBr
14-0x17-3

coffered clg

sitting area

library

Second Floor
1,050 sq. ft.

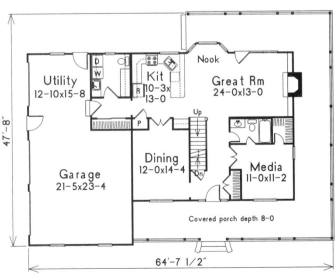

Utility
12-10x15-8

Kit
10-3x13-0

Nook

Great Rm
24-0x13-0

Garage
21-5x23-4

Dining
12-0x14-4

Media
11-0x11-2

Up

Dn

Covered porch depth 8-0

47'-8"

64'-7 1/2"

First Floor
1,216 sq. ft.

Two-Story Has A Farmhouse Feel

Features

- 3,444 total square feet of living area
- Lavish master bath has double vanities and walk-in closets
- Kitchen has a wonderful food preparation island that doubles as extra dining space
- Computer/library area on the second floor has double-door access onto the second floor balcony
- Future gameroom on the second floor has an additional 318 square feet of living area
- 5 bedrooms, 4 baths, 2-car detached garage
- Crawl space foundation

First Floor
2,236 sq. ft.

Width: 42'-6"
Depth: 71'-4"

Porch

Master Bath

Family
17'8"x 21'2"

Master Bedroom
14'4"x 16'10"

Kitchen

Breakfast

Hall

Utility

Dining
14'2"x 12'3"

Bath

Porch

Study
14'4"x 14'6"

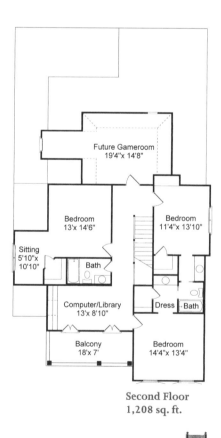

Future Gameroom
19'4"x 14'8"

Bedroom
13'x 14'6"

Bedroom
11'4"x 13'10"

Sitting
5'10"x 10'10"

Bath

Computer/Library
13'x 8'10"

Dress | Bath

Balcony
18'x 7'

Bedroom
14'4"x 13'4"

Second Floor
1,208 sq. ft.

Secluded Master Suite

Features

- 1,937 total square feet of living area
- Upscale great room offers a sloped ceiling, fireplace with extended hearth and built-in shelves for an entertainment center
- Gourmet kitchen includes a cook-top island counter and a quaint morning room
- Master suite has a sloped ceiling, cozy sitting room, walk-in closet and a private bath with whirlpool tub
- 3 bedrooms, 2 baths, 2-car side entry garage
- Crawl space foundation

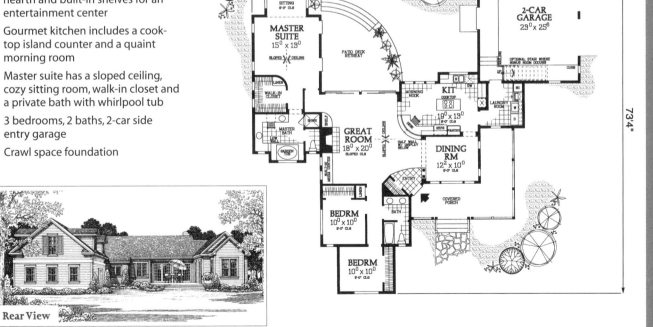

Rear View

Unique Side Grilling Porch

Features

- 1,922 total square feet of living area
- Master bath has whirlpool tub, split vanities and an attractive glass shower
- Great room features cozy fireplace
- Convenient built-in computer desk in hall
- 3 bedrooms, 2 1/2 baths, 2-car rear entry garage
- Crawl space or slab foundation, please specify when ordering

First Floor
1,298 sq. ft.

© 2001 NELSON DESIGN GROUP, LLC

36' 4"

64' 10"

M.BATH 14'-8" X 10'-4"
WHP TUB
LIN
GLASS SHWR
MASTER SUITE 14'-8" X 16'-0"
GARAGE 20'-8" X 20'-0"
W.I.C.
FRENCH DOORS
GRILLING PORCH 11'-2" X 10'-2"
BRKFAST ROOM 10'-0" X 10'-0"
UP
KITCHEN 10'-0" X 12'-4"
PAN
REF
DW
OPT. COURT YARD
GREAT ROOM 14'-8" X 16'-5"
DINING 9'-8" X 12'-0"
8" COLUMNS
COVERED PORCH 16'-4" X 8'-0"

Second Floor
624 sq. ft.

ATTIC STORAGE
DN
LIN
BATH
COMPUTER DESK
LIN
BEDROOM 2 12'-8" X 14'-1"
BEDROOM 3 12'-0" X 16'-1"
BALCONY PORCH 16'-6" X 8'-0"

Plan #578-068D-0006

Price Code A

Covered Porch Surrounds Home

Features

- 1,399 total square feet of living area
- Living room overlooks the dining area through arched columns
- Laundry room contains a handy half bath
- Spacious master bedroom includes a sitting area, walk-in closet and plenty of sunlight
- 3 bedrooms, 1 1/2 baths, 1-car garage
- Basement foundation, drawings also include crawl space and slab foundations

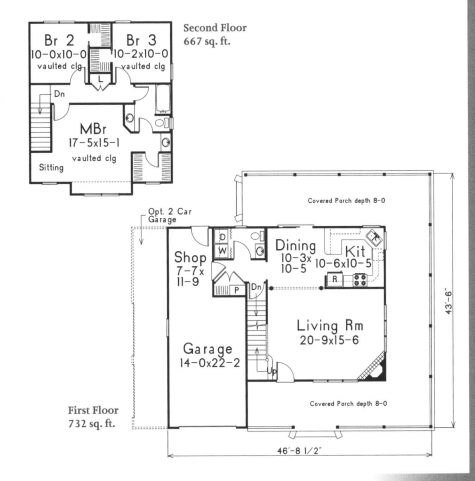

Second Floor
667 sq. ft.

First Floor
732 sq. ft.

Facade Is Pleasing To The Eye

Features

- 2,562 total square feet of living area
- Plenty of outdoor living areas including a screen porch, extra-wide covered porch and a sundeck
- Open living is created with columns separating the great room from the breakfast room
- The master bedroom on the second floor has its own private deck and luxurious bath
- 4 bedrooms, 2 1/2 baths, 2-car drive under garage
- Basement foundation

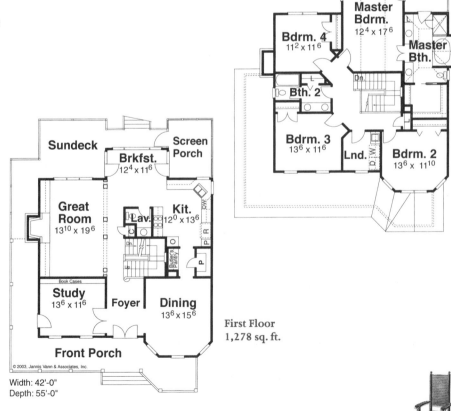

Second Floor
1,284 sq. ft.

Deck

Master Bdrm.
12^4 x 17^6

Bdrm. 4
11^2 x 11^6

Master Bth.

Bth. 2

Bdrm. 3
13^6 x 11^6

Lnd.

Bdrm. 2
13^6 x 11^{10}

Dn.

Sundeck

Brkfst.
12^4 x 11^6

Screen Porch

Great Room
13^{10} x 19^6

Lav.

Kit.
12^0 x 13^6

Book Cases

Study
13^6 x 11^6

Foyer

Dining
13^6 x 15^6

Front Porch

© 2003, Jannis Vann & Associates, Inc.

First Floor
1,278 sq. ft.

Width: 42'-0"
Depth: 55'-0"

Graceful Southern Hospitality

Features

- 1,771 total square feet of living area
- Efficient country kitchen shares space with a bayed eating area
- Two-story family/great room is warmed by a fireplace in winter and open to outdoor country comfort in the summer with double French doors
- First floor master suite offers a bay window and access to the porch through French doors
- 3 bedrooms, 2 1/2 baths, optional 2-car detached garage
- Basement foundation

Second Floor
600 sq. ft.

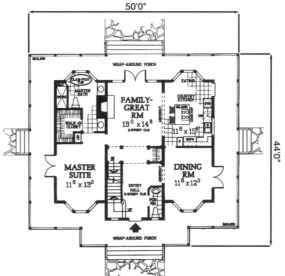

First Floor
1,171 sq. ft.

Spectacular Two-Story Victorian

Features

- 2,406 total square feet of living area

- Master bedroom has a beautiful fireplace, private balcony, enormous walk-in closet and private bath with dressing area

- Unique kitchen-in-a-bay attaches to the breakfast area and beyond to the formal dining area that has a covered porch and fireplace

- First floor activity area has a see-through fireplace, bookcases and covered veranda nearby

- 3 bedrooms, 2 1/2 baths

- Basement foundation

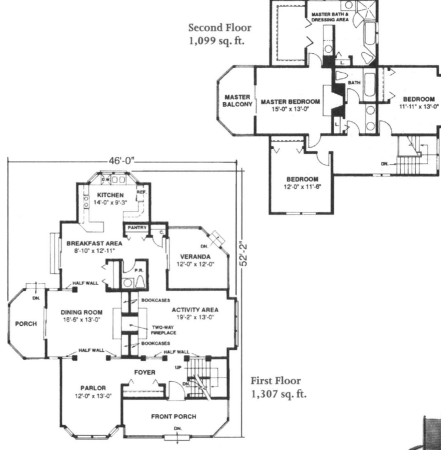

Second Floor
1,099 sq. ft.

First Floor
1,307 sq. ft.

Dormers Accent Country Home

Features

- 1,818 total square feet of living area

- Breakfast room is tucked behind the kitchen and has a laundry closet and deck access

- Living and dining areas share a vaulted ceiling and fireplace

- Master bedroom has two closets, a large double-bowl vanity and a separate tub and shower

- Large front porch wraps around the home

- 4 bedrooms, 2 1/2 baths, 2-car drive under garage

- Basement foundation

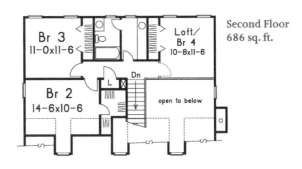

Second Floor
686 sq. ft.

Br 3
11-0x11-6

Loft/
Br 4
10-8x11-6

Br 2
14-6x10-6

open to below

Dn

First Floor
1,132 sq. ft.

38'-0"

32'-0"

Deck

Brk
8-2x
8-2

Kit
9-4x
13-6

Dining
13-6x11-6

Living
13-6x15-6

vaulted

MBr
14-6x13-6

Up

Dn

W D

Porch depth 6-0

Timeless Design Offers Prestige

Features

- 1,973 total square feet of living area
- This country home offers a grand-sized living room with views to the front and rear of the home
- Living room features a cozy fireplace and accesses the master bedroom complete with a walk-in closet and compartmented bath
- Laundry room with half bath and coat closet is convenient to the garage
- Second floor is comprised of two large bedrooms and a full bath
- 3 bedrooms, 2 1/2 baths, 2-car garage
- Partial basement/crawl space foundation

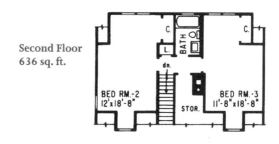

Second Floor
636 sq. ft.

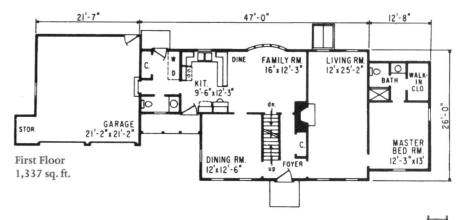

First Floor
1,337 sq. ft.

Wrap-Around Porch And Turret Accent Design

Features

- 3,556 total square feet of living area
- Jack and Jill bath is located between two of the bedrooms on the second floor
- Second floor features three bedrooms and overlooks the great room
- Formal entrance and additional family entrance from covered porch to laundry/mud room
- First floor master bedroom features a coffered ceiling, double walk-in closets, luxury bath and direct access to the study
- 4 bedrooms, 3 1/2 baths, 3-car side entry garage
- Basement foundation

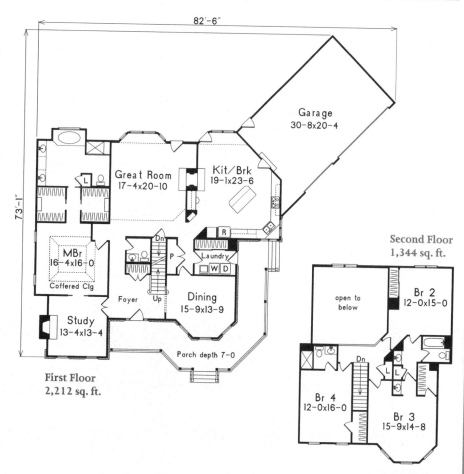

First Floor
2,212 sq. ft.

Second Floor
1,344 sq. ft.

#578-068D-0013

Price Code E

A Perfect Family Home

Features

- 2,645 total square feet of living area

- Second floor has a second washer and dryer area for convenience

- Second floor casual family room is ideal for a children's play area with adjacent computer room

- First floor master bedroom has a luxurious private bath with corner tub and walk-in closet

- Bonus room on the second floor has an additional 438 square feet of living area

- 3 bedrooms, 2 1/2 baths, 2-car side entry garage

- Basement foundation, drawings also include crawl space and slab foundations

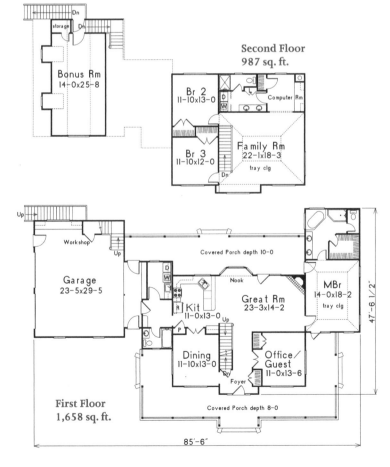

To order call toll-free 1-800-DREAM HOME or visit www.houseplansandmore.com

KE0134
ND7820
Megan K

Grand Staircase Is The Focal Point

Features

- 2,083 total square feet of living area
- Breakfast nook is a sunny bay window
- Half wall with columns creates a lovely entry into the living room
- Second floor landing has a cozy window seat surrounded on both sides by built-in bookshelves
- 3 bedrooms, 2 1/2 baths, 2-car side entry garage
- Basement or crawl space foundation, please specify when ordering

Second Floor
970 sq. ft.

Br 2
12-0 x 12-5

Master Br
12-0 x 15-4

Br 3
12-0 x 11-9

First Floor
1,113 sq. ft.

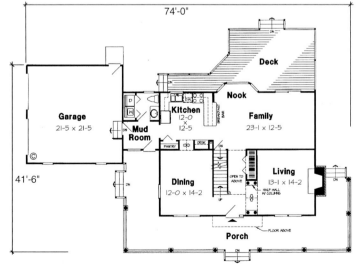

74'-0"

41'-6"

Deck

Garage
21-5 x 21-5

Mud Room

Kitchen
12-0 x 12-5

Nook

Family
23-1 x 12-5

Dining
12-0 x 14-2

Living
13-1 x 14-2

Porch

n #578-004D-0002   Price Code C

Well-Designed Ranch With Wrap-Around Porch

Features

- 1,823 total square feet of living area
- Vaulted living room is spacious and easily accesses the dining area
- The master bedroom boasts a tray ceiling, large walk-in closet and a private bath with a corner whirlpool tub
- Cheerful dining area is convenient to the U-shaped kitchen and also enjoys patio access
- Centrally located laundry room connects the garage to the living areas
- 3 bedrooms, 2 baths, 2-car garage
- Basement foundation

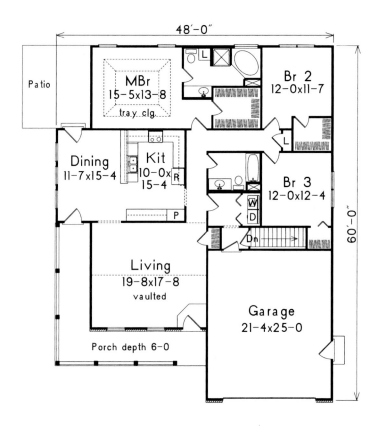

To order call toll-free 1-800-DREAM HOME or visit www.houseplansandmore.com

Country Home With Front Orientation

Features

- 2,029 total square feet of living area

- Stonework, gables, roof dormer and double porches create a country flavor

- Kitchen enjoys extravagant cabinetry and counterspace in a bay, island snack bar, built-in pantry and cheery dining area with multiple tall windows

- Angled stair descends from large entry with wood columns and is open to a vaulted great room with corner fireplace

- Master bedroom boasts two walk-in closets, a private bath with double-door entry and a secluded porch

- 4 bedrooms, 2 baths, 2-car side entry garage

- Basement foundation, drawings also include crawl space and slab foundations

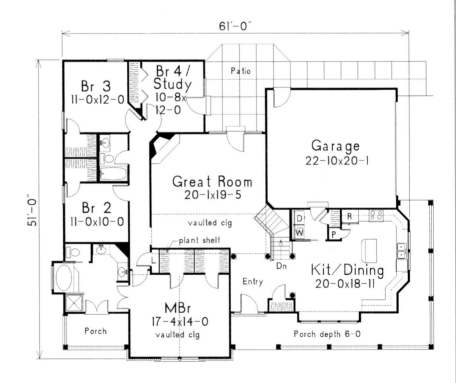

61'-0"

51'-0"

Br 3
11-0x12-0

Br 4 /
Study
10-8x
12-0

Patio

Garage
22-10x20-1

Great Room
20-1x19-5

vaulted clg

plant shelf

Br 2
11-0x10-0

Dn

Kit/Dining
20-0x18-11

Entry

MBr
17-4x14-0
vaulted clg

Porch

Porch depth 6-0

Traditional Home For A Small Lot

Features

- 1,635 total square feet of living area
- Large wrap-around front porch
- Open living and dining rooms are separated only by columns for added openness
- Kitchen includes a large work island and snack bar
- Master bedroom with tray ceiling has three closets
- 3 bedrooms, 2 1/2 baths, 2-car garage
- Basement, crawl space or slab foundation, please specify when ordering

First Floor
880 sq. ft.

Second Floor
755 sq. ft.

Handsome Columns And Trim Details

Features

- 1,575 total square feet of living area
- A half bath is tucked away in the laundry area for convenience
- Second floor hall has a handy desk
- Bonus area on the second floor has an additional 353 square feet of living area
- 3 bedrooms, 2 1/2 baths, 2-car garage
- Basement foundation

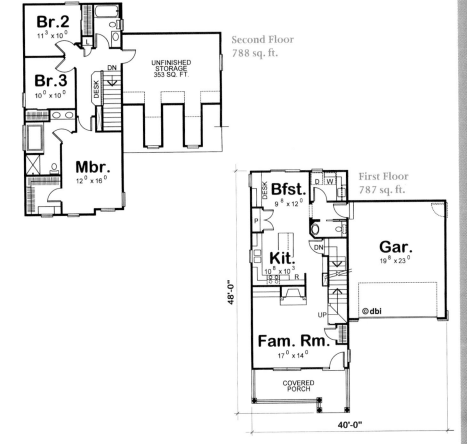

Second Floor
788 sq. ft.

First Floor
787 sq. ft.

Practical Two-Story, Full Of Features

Features

- 2,058 total square feet of living area
- Handsome two-story foyer with balcony creates a spacious entrance area
- Vaulted ceiling in the master bedroom with private dressing area and large walk-in closet
- Skylights furnish natural lighting in the hall and master bath
- Laundry closet is conveniently located on the second floor near the bedrooms
- 3 bedrooms, 2 1/2 baths, 2-car garage
- Basement foundation, drawings also include slab and crawl space foundations

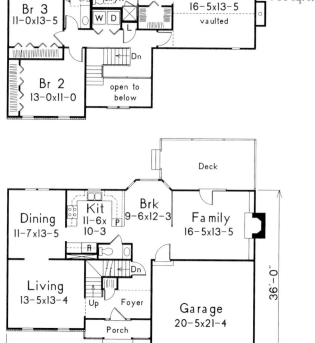

Second Floor
960 sq. ft.

Br 3
11-0x13-5

MBr
16-5x13-5
vaulted

Br 2
13-0x11-0

open to below

Dn

First Floor
1,098 sq. ft.

Deck

Dining
11-7x13-5

Kit
11-6x
10-3

Brk
9-6x12-3

Family
16-5x13-5

Living
13-5x13-4

Foyer

Garage
20-5x21-4

Porch

Up

Dn

36'-0"

50'-0"

Wonderful Two-Story Is Charming, Yet Practical

Features

- 2,280 total square feet of living area
- Laundry area is conveniently located on the second floor
- Compact, yet efficient kitchen
- Unique shaped dining room overlooks front porch
- Cozy living room is enhanced with a sloped ceiling and fireplace
- 4 bedrooms, 2 1/2 baths, 2-car side entry garage
- Basement foundation

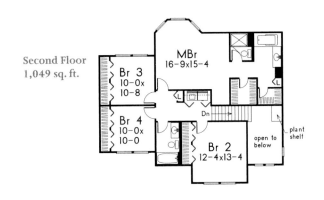

Second Floor
1,049 sq. ft.

MBr
16-9x15-4

Br 3
10-0x
10-8

Br 4
10-0x
10-0

Br 2
12-4x13-4

Dn

open to below

plant shelf

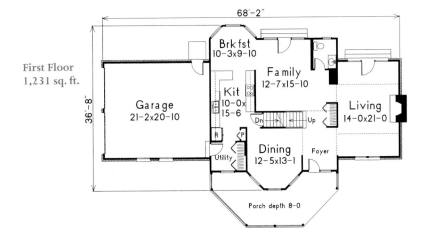

First Floor
1,231 sq. ft.

68'-2"

36'-8"

Garage
21-2x20-10

Brk fst
10-3x9-10

Family
12-7x15-10

Kit
10-0x
15-6

Living
14-0x21-0

Dining
12-5x13-1

Utility

Foyer

Dn

Up

Porch depth 8-0

Dining With A View

Features

- 1,524 total square feet of living area
- Delightful balcony overlooks two-story entry illuminated by oval window
- Roomy first floor master bedroom offers quiet privacy
- All bedrooms feature one or more walk-in closets
- 3 bedrooms, 2 1/2 baths, 2-car garage
- Basement foundation, drawings also include crawl space and slab foundations

Second Floor
573 sq. ft.

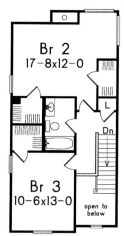

First Floor
951 sq. ft.

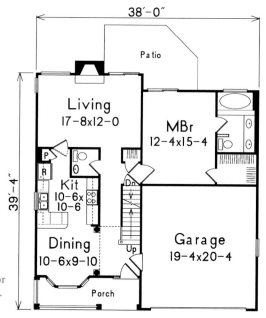

Great Looks Accentuated By Elliptical Brick Arches

Features

- 2,521 total square feet of living area
- Large living and dining rooms are a plus for formal entertaining or large family gatherings
- Informal kitchen, breakfast and family rooms feature a 37' vista and double bay windows
- Generously sized master bedroom and three secondary bedrooms grace the second floor
- 4 bedrooms, 2 1/2 baths, 2-car garage
- Basement foundation

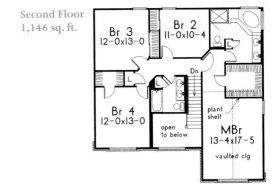

Second Floor
1,146 sq. ft.

Br 3
12-0x13-0

Br 2
11-0x10-4

Br 4
12-0x13-0

Dn

open to below

plant shelf

MBr
13-4x17-5

vaulted clg

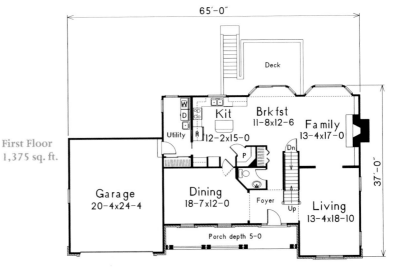

First Floor
1,375 sq. ft.

65'-0"

Deck

W D

Brk fst
11-8x12-6

Kit
12-2x15-0

Family
13-4x17-0

Utility

P

Dn

37'-0"

Garage
20-4x24-4

Dining
18-7x12-0

Foyer

Up

Living
13-4x18-10

Porch depth 5-0

Third Floor All-Purpose Room

Features

- 3,006 total square feet of living area

- Energy efficient home with 2" x 6" exterior walls

- Large all-purpose room and bath on third floor

- Efficient U-shaped kitchen includes a pantry and adjacent planning desk

- 4 bedrooms, 3 1/2 baths, 2-car side entry garage

- Basement foundation, drawings also include slab foundation

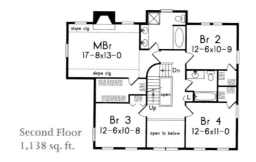

Second Floor
1,138 sq. ft.

MBr
17-8x13-0

Br 2
12-6x10-9

Br 3
12-6x10-8

Br 4
12-6x11-0

Third Floor
575 sq. ft.

All Purpose
Room
22-0x24-0

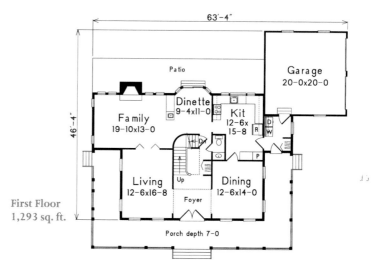

First Floor
1,293 sq. ft.

63'-4"

46'-4"

Patio

Garage
20-0x20-0

Dinette
9-4x11-0

Kit
12-6x
15-8

Family
19-10x13-0

Living
12-6x16-8

Dining
12-6x14-0

Foyer

Porch depth 7-0

Outdoor Covered Deck Warmed By Fireplace

Rear Deck

First Floor
3,171 sq. ft.

Features

- 3,171 total square feet of living area
- An enormous walk-in closet is located in the master bath and dressing area
- The great room, breakfast area and kitchen combine with 12' ceilings to create an open feel
- The optional lower level has an additional 1,897 square feet of living area and is designed for entertaining featuring a wet bar with seating, a billiards room, large media room, two bedrooms and a full bath
- 3 bedrooms, 2 1/2 baths, 3-car side entry garage
- Walk-out basement foundation

Distinctive Country Porch

Features

- 2,182 total square feet of living area
- Meandering porch creates an inviting look
- Generous great room has four double-hung windows and sliding doors to exterior
- Highly functional kitchen features island/breakfast bar, menu desk and convenient pantry
- Each secondary bedroom includes generous closet space and a private bath
- 3 bedrooms, 3 1/2 baths, 2-car side entry garage
- Basement foundation, drawings also include crawl space and slab foundations

Second Floor
1,070 sq. ft.

MBr
19-4x13-0
Vaulted

Br 2
14-0x11-0

Br 3
12-8x12-0
Vaulted

Great Rm
19-4x15-0

Breakfast
11-8x13-0

Kit
12-0x14-6

Entry

Dining
15-0x12-0

Porch Depth 7-8

48'-8"

57'-0"

Garage
21-4x21-10

First Floor
1,112 sq. ft.

Double Atrium Embraces The Sun

Rear View

Features

- 3,199 total square feet of living area

- Grand-scale kitchen features bay-shaped cabinetry built over an atrium that overlooks a two-story window wall

- A second atrium dominates the master bedroom that boasts a sitting area with bay window as well as a luxurious bath that has a whirlpool tub open to the garden atrium and lower level study

- 3 bedrooms, 2 1/2 baths, 3-car side entry garage

- Walk-out basement foundation

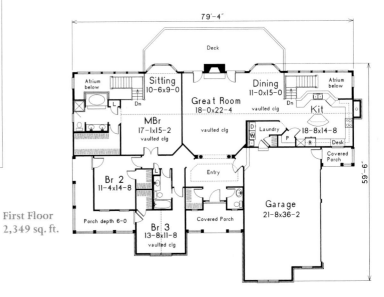

First Floor
2,349 sq. ft.

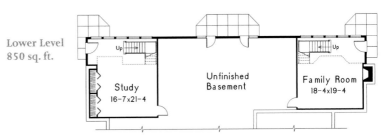

Lower Level
850 sq. ft.

Victorian Home With Panoramic Porch

Features

- 2,455 total square feet of living area
- The foyer is two stories high and opens to the living room
- 13' ceiling in living room
- Master bedroom includes bayed sitting area ideal for relaxing
- 4 bedrooms, 3 baths, 2-car side entry garage
- Basement, crawl space or slab foundation, please specify when ordering

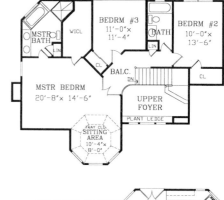

Second Floor
956 sq. ft.

BEDRM #3
11'-0" × 11'-4"

BEDRM #2
10'-0" × 13'-6"

MSTR BATH

WICL

BATH

LIN

BALC.

MSTR BEDRM
20'-8" × 14'-6"

UPPER FOYER

PLANT LEDGE

TRAY CLG.
SITTING AREA
10'-4" × 8'-0"

Kitchen

First Floor
1,499 sq. ft.

Width: 69'-0"
Depth: 47'-0"

SUNKEN
FAMILY RM
21'-4" × 15'-0"

BKFST RM
9'-0" × 14'-0"

KITCHEN
11'-0" × 14'-0"

VAULTED
DINING RM
13'-8" × 11'-0"

BATH

DN TO
OPT.
BSMT

REF

PANT

WET BAR

HIGH CEIL
FOYER

VAULTED
LIVING RM
15'-8" × 16'-0"

UTIL

LAUN RM

W D

CL

STOR

DEN/
GUEST RM
13'-4" × 11'-8"

COV. PORCH

COV. PORCH

TWO CAR GARAGE
20'-0" × 20'-6"

© Jerold Axelrod, Architect

COV. PORCH

Unique Style With Corner Entry

Rear View

Features

- 1,763 total square feet of living area
- Dining room has a large box-bay window and a recessed ceiling
- Living room includes a large fireplace
- Kitchen has plenty of workspace, a pantry and a double sink overlooking the deck
- Master bedroom features a large bath with walk-in closet
- 3 bedrooms, 2 1/2 baths, 2-car garage
- Basement foundation

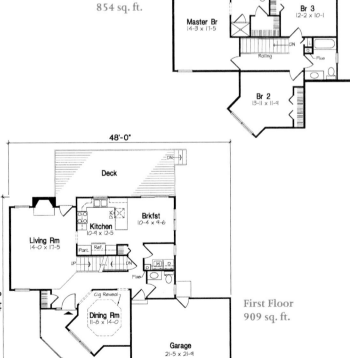

Second Floor
854 sq. ft.

Master Br
14-3 x 17-5

Br 3
12-2 x 10-1

Railing

Br 2
13-11 x 11-9

Line of Floor Below

48'-0"

Deck

Brkfst
10-4 x 9-6

Kitchen
10-4 x 12-5

Living Rm
14-0 x 17-5

44'-0"

Dining Rm
11-8 x 14-0

Garage
21-5 x 21-4

Covered Porch

First Floor
909 sq. ft.

Quaint Exterior, Full Front Porch

Features

- 1,657 total square feet of living area
- Stylish pass-through between living and dining areas
- Master bedroom is secluded from living area for privacy
- Large windows in breakfast and dining areas
- 3 bedrooms, 2 1/2 baths, 2-car drive under garage
- Basement foundation

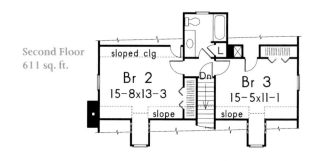

Second Floor
611 sq. ft.

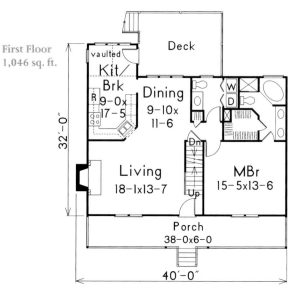

First Floor
1,046 sq. ft.

Picture Perfect For A Country Setting

Features

- 2,967 total square feet of living area
- An exterior with charm graced with country porch and multiple arched projected box windows
- Dining area is oversized and adjoins a fully equipped kitchen with walk-in pantry
- Two bay windows light up the enormous informal living area to the rear
- 4 bedrooms, 3 1/2 baths, 3-car side entry garage
- Basement foundation

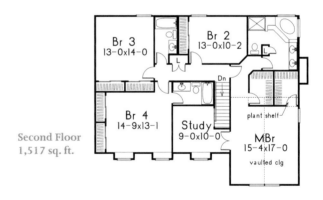

Second Floor
1,517 sq. ft.

Br 3
13-0x14-0

Br 2
13-0x10-2

Br 4
14-9x13-1

Study
9-0x10-0

MBr
15-4x17-0

vaulted clg

plant shelf

Dn

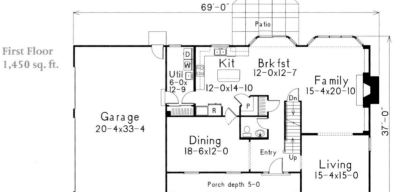

First Floor
1,450 sq. ft.

69'-0"

Patio

Kit
12-0x14-10

Brkfst
12-0x12-7

Util
6-0x
12-9

Family
15-4x20-10

Garage
20-4x33-4

Dining
18-6x12-0

Living
15-4x15-0

Entry

Dn

Up

37'-0"

Porch depth 5-0

Cozy Cottage Living Achieved

Features

- 1,375 total square feet of living area
- Den can easily convert to a second bedroom
- A center island in the kitchen allows extra space for organizing and food preparation
- Centrally located laundry room
- 1 bedroom, 2 baths, 2-car rear entry garage
- Basement foundation

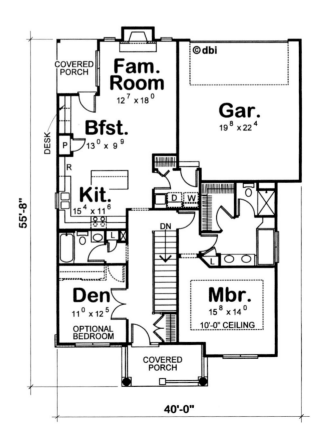

Beautiful Entrance Is Graced With Southern Charm

Features

- 3,266 total square feet of living area
- Screen porch has double-door entrances from the living room
- Sunny breakfast room has lots of windows for a cheerful atmosphere
- All bedrooms on the second floor have spacious walk-in closets
- Multimedia room makes a great casual family room
- 5 bedrooms, 3 1/2 baths, 2-car drive under garage
- Two-story pier foundation

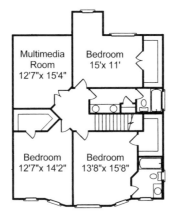

Second Floor
1,230 sq. ft.

Multimedia Room 12'7"x 15'4"
Bedroom 15'x 11'
Bedroom 12'7"x 14'2"
Bedroom 13'8"x 15'8"

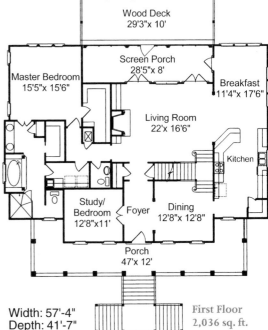

Wood Deck 29'3"x 10'
Screen Porch 28'5"x 8'
Master Bedroom 15'5"x 15'6"
Breakfast 11'4"x 17'6"
Living Room 22'x 16'6"
Kitchen
Study/Bedroom 12'8"x11'
Foyer
Dining 12'8"x 12'8"
Porch 47'x 12'

Width: 57'-4"
Depth: 41'-7"

First Floor
2,036 sq. ft.

Rear View

Sculptured Roof Line And Facade Add Charm

Features

- 1,674 total square feet of living area
- Vaulted great room, dining area and kitchen all enjoy a central fireplace and log bin
- Convenient laundry/mud room is located between the garage and family area with handy stairs to the basement
- Easily expandable screened porch and adjacent patio access the dining area
- Master bedroom features a full bath with tub, separate shower and walk-in closet
- 3 bedrooms, 2 baths, 2-car garage
- Basement foundation, drawings also include crawl space and slab foundations

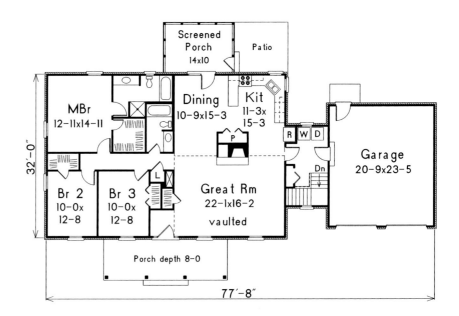

Arched Accents Enhance Facade

Features

- 1,704 total square feet of living area
- Open living and dining areas combine for added spaciousness
- Master bedroom features a private bath and walk-in closet
- Sunny kitchen/nook has space for dining
- Cabinet bar in hallway leading to the living area is designed for entertaining
- 3 bedrooms, 2 baths, 2-car garage
- Basement foundation

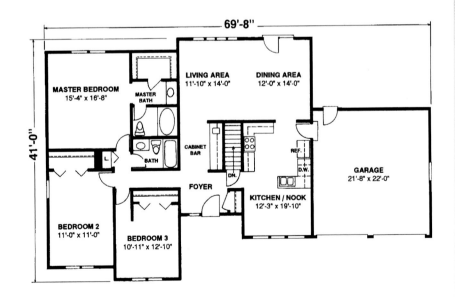

Attractive Entry Created By Full-Length Porch

Features

- 2,357 total square feet of living area
- 9' ceilings on the first floor
- Secluded master bedroom includes a private bath with double walk-in closets and vanity
- Balcony overlooks living room with large fireplace
- The future game room on the second floor has an additional 303 square feet of living area
- 4 bedrooms, 3 1/2 baths, 2-car side entry garage
- Slab foundation, drawings also include crawl space foundation

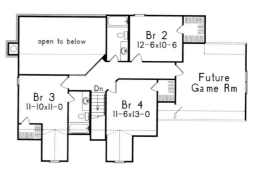

Second Floor
865 sq. ft.

open to below

Br 2
12-6x10-6

Future Game Rm

Br 3
11-10x11-0

Dn

Br 4
11-6x13-0

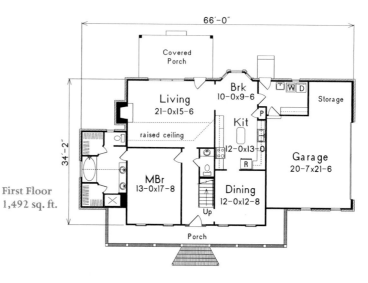

66'-0"

First Floor
1,492 sq. ft.

34'-2"

Covered Porch

Brk
10-0x9-6

W D

Storage

Living
21-0x15-6

raised ceiling

Kit
12-0x13-0

P

Garage
20-7x21-6

MBr
13-0x17-8

R

Dining
12-0x12-8

Up

Porch

Country-Style Home With Large Front Porch

Features

- 1,501 total square feet of living area
- Spacious kitchen with dining area is open to the outdoors
- Convenient utility room is adjacent to garage
- Master bedroom features a private bath, dressing area and access to the large covered porch
- Large family room creates openness
- 3 bedrooms, 2 baths, 2-car side entry garage
- Basement foundation, drawings also include crawl space and slab foundations

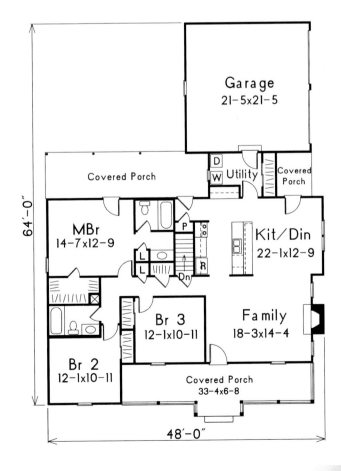

Splendid Master Bedroom

Features

- 2,041 total square feet of living area
- Great room accesses directly onto the covered rear deck with ceiling fan above
- Private master bedroom has a beautiful octagon-shaped sitting area that opens and brightens the space
- Two secondary bedrooms share a full bath
- 3 bedrooms, 2 baths, 2-car side entry garage
- Walk-out basement foundation

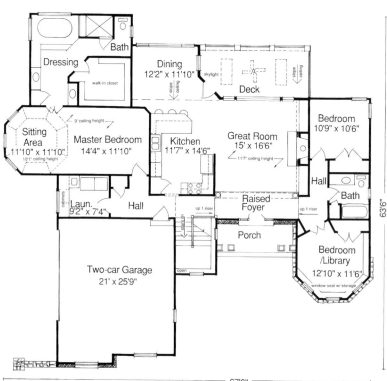

Great Room

To order call toll-free **1-800-DREAM HOME** or visit **www.houseplansandmore.com**

Country-Style Home Has A Lovely Screened Porch

Great Room

Features

- 1,595 total square feet of living area
- Large great room features a tray ceiling and French doors to a screened porch
- Dining room and bedroom #2 have bay windows
- Master bedroom has a tray ceiling and a bay window
- 3 bedrooms, 2 baths, 2-car side entry garage
- Basement, crawl space, slab or walk-out basement foundation, please specify when ordering

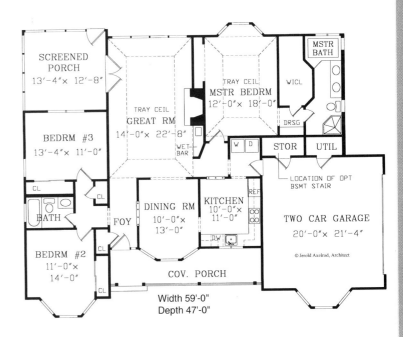

SCREENED PORCH
13'-4" x 12'-8"

MSTR BATH

TRAY CEIL
MSTR BEDRM
12'-0" x 18'-0"

WICL

DRSG

TRAY CEIL
GREAT RM
14'-0" x 22'-8"

BEDRM #3
13'-4" x 11'-0"

WET-BAR

W   D

STOR

UTIL

CL

BATH

CL

FOY

DINING RM
10'-0" x 13'-0"

KITCHEN
10'-0" x 11'-0"

REF

LOCATION OF OPT BSMT STAIR

TWO CAR GARAGE
20'-0" x 21'-4"

© Jerold Axelrod, Architect

BEDRM #2
11'-0" x 14'-0"

CL

DW

CL

COV. PORCH

Width 59'-0"
Depth 47'-0"

Dramatic Layout Created By Victorian Turret

Features

- 2,050 total square feet of living area
- Large kitchen and dining area have access to garage and porch
- Master bedroom features a unique turret design, private bath and large walk-in closet
- Laundry facilities are conveniently located near the bedrooms
- 3 bedrooms, 2 1/2 baths, 2-car side entry garage
- Basement foundation, drawings also include crawl space and slab foundations

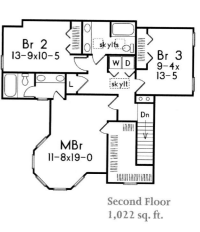

Second Floor
1,022 sq. ft.

Br 2
13-9x10-5

Br 3
9-4x
13-5

W D

skylts

skylt

L

MBr
11-8x19-0

Dn

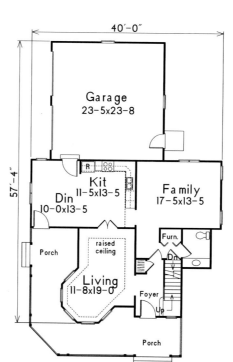

40'-0"

Garage
23-5x23-8

Kit
11-5x13-5

Din
10-0x13-5

Family
17-5x13-5

57'-4"

Porch

raised ceiling

Furn.

Dn

Living
11-8x19-0

Foyer

Up

Porch

First Floor
1,028 sq. ft.

A Special Home For Views

Features

- 1,684 total square feet of living area
- Delightful wrap-around porch is anchored by a full masonry fireplace
- The vaulted great room includes a large bay window, fireplace, dining balcony and atrium window wall
- Double walk-in closets, large luxury bath and sliding doors to exterior balcony are a few fantastic features of the master bedroom
- Atrium opens to 611 square feet of optional living area on the lower level
- 3 bedrooms, 2 baths, 2-car drive under garage
- Walk-out basement foundation

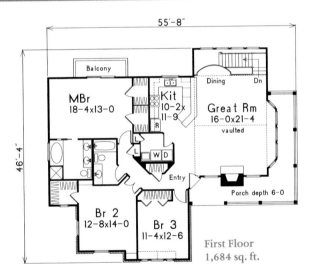

55'-8"

46'-4"

Balcony

MBr
18-4x13-0

Kit
10-2x
11-9

Dining   Dn

Great Rm
16-0x21-4
vaulted

Entry

Br 2
12-8x14-0

Br 3
11-4x12-6

Porch depth 6-0

First Floor
1,684 sq. ft.

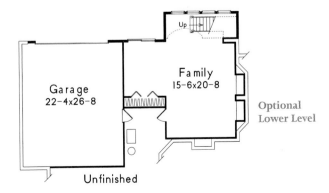

Up

Garage
22-4x26-8

Family
15-6x20-8

Optional
Lower Level

Unfinished

Rear View

Massive Ranch With Classy Features

Features

- 2,874 total square feet of living area
- Large family room with sloped ceiling and wood beams adjoins the kitchen and breakfast area with windows on two walls
- Large foyer opens to the family room with massive stone fireplace and open stairs to the basement
- Private master bedroom includes a raised tub under the bay window, dramatic dressing area and a huge walk-in closet
- 4 bedrooms, 2 1/2 baths, 2-car side entry garage
- Basement foundation

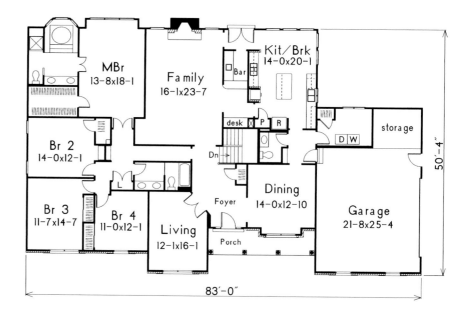

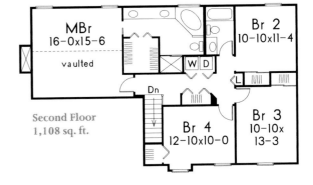

Open Breakfast/Family Room Combination

Features

- 2,135 total square feet of living area
- Family room features extra space, an impressive fireplace and full wall of windows that joins the breakfast room creating a spacious entertainment area
- Washer and dryer are conveniently located on the second floor near the bedrooms
- The kitchen features an island counter and pantry
- 4 bedrooms, 2 1/2 baths, 2-car garage
- Basement foundation

Second Floor
1,108 sq. ft.

MBr
16-0x15-6
vaulted

Br 2
10-10x11-4

Br 4
12-10x10-0

Br 3
10-10x
13-3

Dn

W D

L

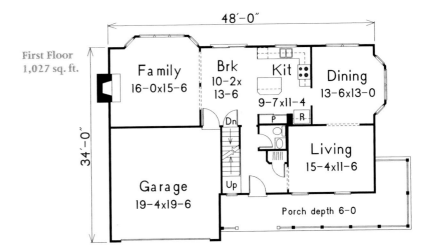

First Floor
1,027 sq. ft.

48'-0"

34'-0"

Family
16-0x15-6

Brk
10-2x
13-6

Kit
9-7x11-4

Dining
13-6x13-0

Living
15-4x11-6

Garage
19-4x19-6

Dn

Up

P   R

Porch depth 6-0

Plan #578-040D-0003

Price Code B

Rambling Country Bungalow

Features

- 1,475 total square feet of living area
- Family room features a high ceiling and prominent corner fireplace
- Kitchen with island counter and garden window makes a convenient connection between the family and dining rooms
- Hallway leads to three bedrooms all with large walk-in closets
- Covered breezeway joins main house and garage
- Full-width covered porch entry lends a country touch
- 3 bedrooms, 2 baths, 2-car detached side entry garage
- Slab foundation, drawings also include crawl space foundation

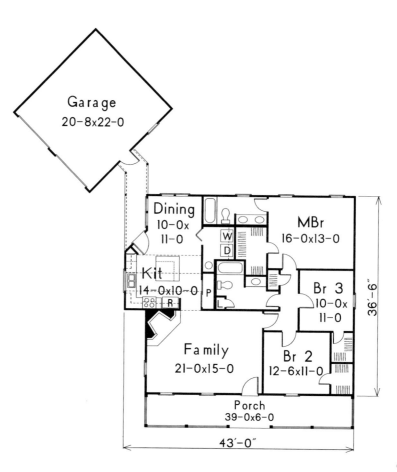

Garage
20-8x22-0

Dining
10-0x11-0

MBr
16-0x13-0

Kit
14-0x10-0

Br 3
10-0x11-0

Family
21-0x15-0

Br 2
12-6x11-0

Porch
39-0x6-0

36'-6"

43'-0"

Fireplaces Add Warm And Cozy Feeling

Features

- 2,932 total square feet of living area
- 9' ceilings throughout home
- Rear stairs create convenient access to second floor from living area
- Spacious kitchen has pass-through to the family room, a convenient island and pantry
- Cozy built-in table in breakfast area
- Secluded master bedroom has a luxurious bath and patio access
- 4 bedrooms, 3 1/2 baths, 2-car side entry garage
- Slab foundation

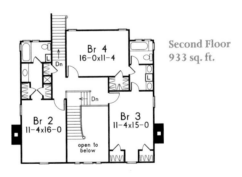

Second Floor
933 sq. ft.

First Floor
1,999 sq. ft.

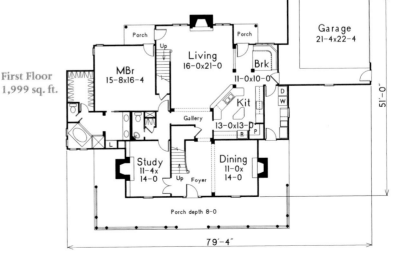

Grand-Scale Design

Features

- 4,237 total square feet of living area
- Grand entrance has a vaulted two-story foyer
- Fireplaces in formal living room and master bedroom
- Second floor bedrooms have their own window seats
- Bonus room above the garage has an additional 497 square feet of living area
- 4 bedrooms, 3 1/2 baths, 3-car side entry garage
- Basement, crawl space or slab foundation, please specify when ordering

Second Floor
1,586 sq. ft.

Rear View

First Floor
2,651 sq. ft.

To order call toll-free 1-800-DREAM HOME or visit www.houseplansandmore.com

Plan #578-001D-0018

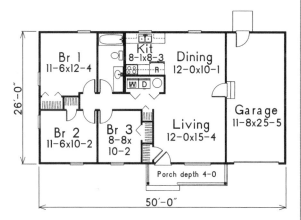

Front Porch And Center Gable

Features

- 988 total square feet of living area
- Pleasant covered porch entry
- The kitchen, living and dining areas are combined to maximize space
- Entry has convenient coat closet
- Laundry closet is located adjacent to bedrooms
- 3 bedrooms, 1 bath, 1-car garage
- Basement foundation, drawings also include crawl space foundation

Plan #578-043D-0005

Price Code B

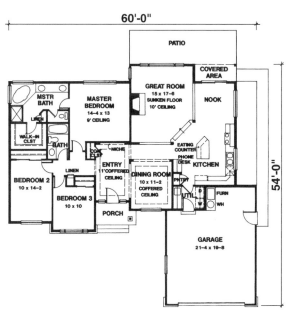

Private Bedrooms

Features

- 1,734 total square feet of living area
- Large entry boasts a coffered ceiling and display niches
- Sunken great room has 10' ceiling
- 9' ceiling in the master bedroom
- 3 bedrooms, 2 baths, 2-car garage
- Crawl space foundation

To order call toll-free 1-800-DREAM HOME or visit www.houseplansandmore.com

Private Master Suite

Features

- 1,458 total square feet of living area
- A divider wall allows for some privacy in the formal dining area while maintaining openness
- Two secondary bedrooms share a full bath
- Covered front and rear porches create enjoyable outdoor living spaces
- 3 bedrooms, 2 baths, 2-car garage
- Slab or crawl space foundation, please specify when ordering

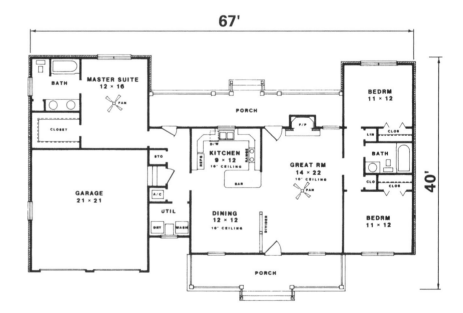

Plan #578-020D-0015

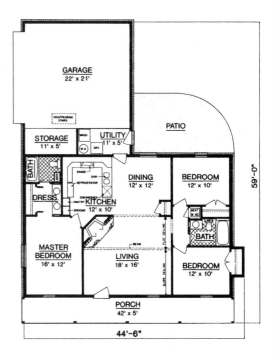

Quaint And Cozy

Features

- 1,191 total square feet of living area
- Energy efficient home with 2" x 6" exterior walls
- Master bedroom is located near living areas for maximum convenience
- Living room has a cathedral ceiling and stone fireplace
- 3 bedrooms, 2 baths, 2-car side entry garage
- Slab foundation, drawings also include crawl space foundation

Plan #578-069D-0001

Price Code AA

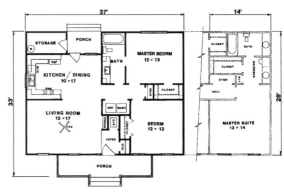

Inviting Victorian Details

Features

- 947 total square feet of living area
- Efficiently designed kitchen/dining area accesses the outdoors onto a rear porch
- Future expansion plans included which allow the home to become 392 square feet larger with 3 bedrooms and 2 baths
- 2 bedrooms, 1 bath
- Crawl space or slab foundation, please specify when ordering

Dormers Add Southern Accent

Features

- 2,651 total square feet of living area
- Vaulted family room has a corner fireplace and access to the breakfast room and outdoor patio
- Dining room has a double-door entry from the covered front porch and a beautiful built-in corner display area
- Master bedroom has a 10' tray ceiling, private bath and two walk-in closets
- Kitchen has an enormous amount of counterspace with plenty of eating area and overlooks a cheerful breakfast room
- 3 bedrooms, 2 baths, 2-car side entry garage
- Basement foundation, drawings also include crawl space and slab foundations

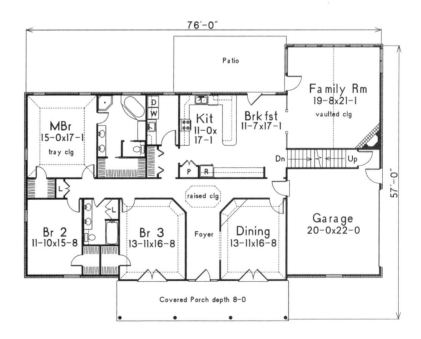

Plan #578-021D-0008

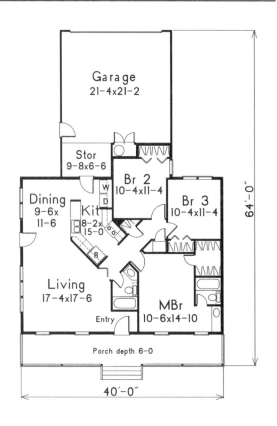

Convenient And Charming

Features

- 1,266 total square feet of living area
- Narrow frontage is perfect for small lots
- Energy efficient home with 2" x 6" exterior walls
- Design incorporates full-size master bedroom complete with dressing room, bath and walk-in closet
- Angled kitchen includes handy laundry facilities and is adjacent to an oversized storage area
- 3 bedrooms, 2 baths, 2-car rear entry garage
- Crawl space foundation, drawings also include slab foundation

Plan #578-037D-0016

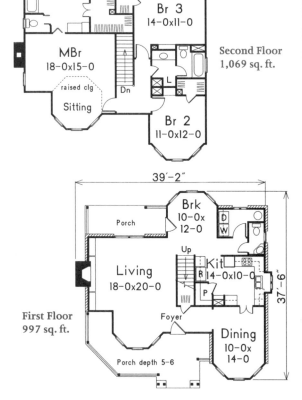

Home Features Double Bays

Features

- 2,066 total square feet of living area
- Large master bedroom includes sitting area and private bath
- Open living room features a fireplace with built-in bookshelves
- Spacious kitchen accesses formal dining area and breakfast room
- 3 bedrooms, 2 1/2 baths, optional 2-car side entry garage
- Slab foundation

Three-Season Room Links With Surroundings

Features

- 2,351 total square feet of living area
- Coffered ceiling in dining room adds elegant appeal
- Wrap-around porch creates a pleasant escape
- Cozy study features a double-door entry and extra storage
- Double walk-in closets balance and organize the master bedroom
- 3 bedrooms, 2 1/2 baths, 2-car garage
- Basement foundation

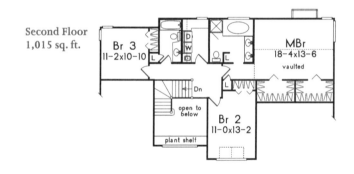

Second Floor
1,015 sq. ft.

Br 3
11-2x10-10

MBr
18-4x13-6
vaulted

Dn

open to below

Br 2
11-0x13-2

plant shelf

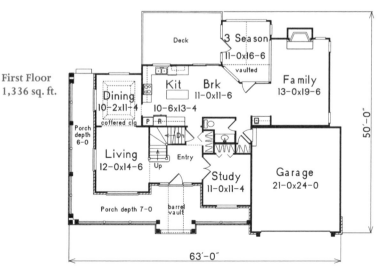

First Floor
1,336 sq. ft.

Deck

3 Season
11-0x16-6
vaulted

Kit
10-6x13-4

Brk
11-0x11-6

Family
13-0x19-6

Dining
10-2x11-4
coffered clg

Living
12-0x14-6

Entry

Study
11-0x11-4

Garage
21-0x24-0

Porch depth 6-0

Porch depth 7-0

barrel vault

50'-0"

63'-0"

Plan #578-001D-0025

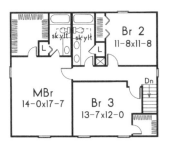

Second Floor
938 sq. ft.

Br 2
11-8x11-8

MBr
14-0x17-7

Br 3
13-7x12-0

Dn

Large Living Areas

Features

- 1,998 total square feet of living area
- Large family room features a fireplace and access to the kitchen and dining area
- Utility room is conveniently located near the garage and kitchen
- Kitchen/breakfast area includes a pantry, island workspace and easy access to the patio
- 3 bedrooms, 2 1/2 baths, 2-car side entry garage
- Basement foundation, drawings also include crawl space and slab foundations

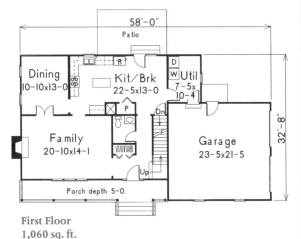

58'-0"

Patio

Dining
10-10x13-0

Kit/Brk
22-5x13-0

Util
7-5x
10-4

W D

Family
20-10x14-1

Garage
23-5x21-5

32'-8"

Dn

Up

Porch depth 5-0

First Floor
1,060 sq. ft.

Plan #578-056D-0001

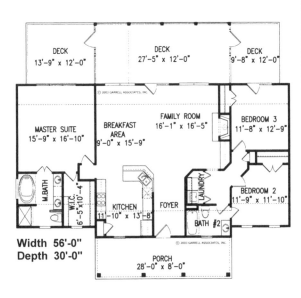

DECK
13'-9" x 12'-0"

DECK
27'-5" x 12'-0"

DECK
9'-8" x 12'-0"

© 2003 GARRELL ASSOCIATES, INC.

MASTER SUITE
15'-9" x 16'-10"

BREAKFAST
AREA
9'-0" x 15'-9"

FAMILY ROOM
16'-1" x 16'-5"

BEDROOM 3
11'-8" x 12'-9"

M.BATH

W.I.C.
6'-5"x10'-4"

KITCHEN
11'-10" x 13'-8"

LAUNDRY

FOYER

BATH #2

BEDROOM 2
11'-9" x 11'-10"

Width 56'-0"
Depth 30'-0"

© 2003 GARRELL ASSOCIATES, INC.

PORCH
28'-0" x 8'-0"

Country Cottage

Features

- 1,624 total square feet of living area
- Large covered deck leads to two uncovered decks accessible by the master bedroom and bedroom #3
- Kitchen overlooks into the breakfast area and family room
- Laundry closet is located near the secondary bedrooms
- 3 bedrooms, 2 baths
- Crawl space or slab foundation, please specify when ordering

To order call toll-free 1-800-DREAM HOME or visit www.houseplansandmore.com

Victorian Styling Makes This A Charming Home

Features

- 2,645 total square feet of living area
- First floor activity area has a wall of windows creating a cheerful atmosphere
- Formal living room has a box-bay window and cozy fireplace
- Master bedroom and bedroom #2 have distinctive sloped ceilings
- 3 bedrooms, 2 1/2 baths, 2-car side entry garage
- Basement foundation

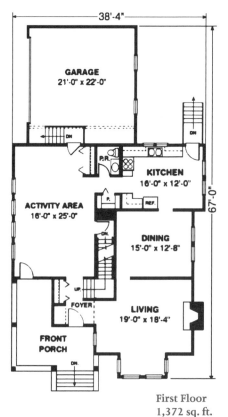

38'-4"

GARAGE
21'-0" x 22'-0"

KITCHEN
16'-0" x 12'-0"

P.R.

ACTIVITY AREA
16'-0" x 25'-0"

REF.

DINING
15'-0" x 12'-8"

67'-0"

UP.

FOYER

LIVING
19'-0" x 18'-4"

FRONT PORCH

DN.

First Floor
1,372 sq. ft.

Second Floor
1,273 sq. ft.

MASTER BATH

UP

BEDROOM 3
13'-10" x 12'-0"

BATH

COFFERED CEILING

MASTER BEDROOM
16'-0" x 14'-0"

DN.

LAUNDRY

W.

D.

OPEN TO BELOW

BEDROOM 2
16'-6" x 14'-0"

FLAT CEILING

SLOPED CEILING

Plan #578-037D-0017

Welcoming Front Porch

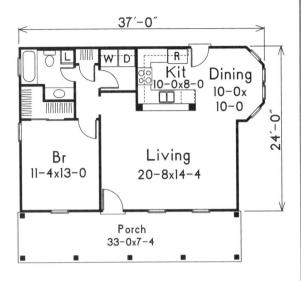

Features

- 829 total square feet of living area
- U-shaped kitchen opens into living area by a 42" high counter
- Oversized bay window and French door accent dining room
- Gathering space is created by the large living room
- Convenient utility room and linen closet
- 1 bedroom, 1 bath
- Slab foundation

Plan #578-047D-0035

Ranch Has A Lot To Offer

Features

- 2,077 total square feet of living area
- Lots of storage space throughout
- Enormous covered patio adds a lot of space when entertaining
- Angled walls add appeal throughout this home
- 3 bedrooms, 2 baths, 2-car side entry garage
- Slab foundation

Popular Plan Offers Attractive Exterior

Features

- 2,212 total square feet of living area
- Louvered shutters, turned posts with railing and garage door detailing are a few inviting features
- Dining room is spacious and borders a well-planned U-shaped kitchen and breakfast room
- Colossal walk-in closet and an oversized private bath are part of a gracious master bedroom
- 3 bedrooms, 2 1/2 baths, 2-car garage
- Partial basement/crawl space foundation, drawings also include crawl space foundation

Second Floor
952 sq. ft.

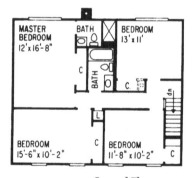

Second Floor
4 Bedroom Option

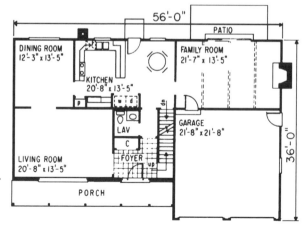

First Floor
1,260 sq. ft.

To order call toll-free 1-800-DREAM HOME or visit www.houseplansandmore.com

Plan #578-015D-0030

Width: 66'-0"
Depth: 50'-0"

Fabulous Curb Appeal

Features

- 1,588 total square feet of living area
- Workshop in garage is ideal for storage and projects
- 12' vaulted master suite has double closets as well as a lovely bath with bayed tub and compartmentalized shower and toilet area
- Lovely arched entry to 14' vaulted great room flows into the dining room and sky-lit kitchen
- 3 bedrooms, 2 baths, 2-car garage
- Basement foundation

Plan #578-065D-0017

Price Code C

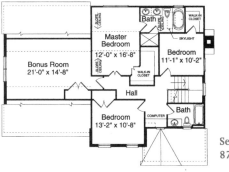

Second Floor
876 sq. ft.

Functional Family Home

Features

- 1,856 total square feet of living area
- The roomy kitchen offers an abundance of cabinets and counterspace as well as a convenient pantry
- Bonus room on the second floor has an additional 325 square feet of living area
- 3 bedrooms, 2 1/2 baths, 2-car garage
- Basement foundation

First Floor
980 sq. ft.

To order call toll-free 1-800-DREAM HOME **or visit** www.houseplansandmore.com

Terrific Custom-Style Victorian Makes An Impression

Features

- 2,562 total square feet of living area
- Numerous bay windows create a design unlike any other
- Enormous master bedroom has a private bath with step-up tub-in-a-bay
- Second floor laundry room is located near all the bedrooms
- Cheerful breakfast room extends onto the covered private porch
- 4 bedrooms, 2 1/2 baths, 2-car garage
- Basement foundation

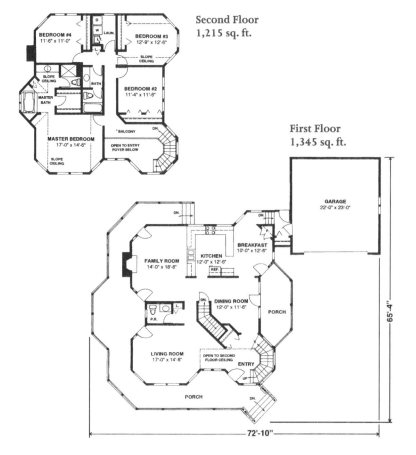

Second Floor
1,215 sq. ft.

First Floor
1,345 sq. ft.

Plan #578-040D-0013

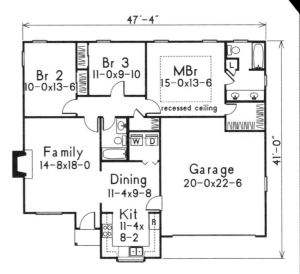

Gable Facade Adds Appeal

Features

- 1,304 total square feet of living area
- Covered entrance leads into the family room with a cozy fireplace
- 10' ceilings in kitchen, dining and family rooms
- Master bedroom features a coffered ceiling, walk-in closet and private bath
- Efficient kitchen includes large window over the sink
- 3 bedrooms, 2 baths, 2-car garage
- Slab foundation

Plan #578-053D-0001

Price Code B

Colonial For Practical Living

Features

- 1,582 total square feet of living area
- Large fireplace and windows enhance the living area
- Rear door in garage is convenient to the garden and kitchen
- Dormers add light to the foyer and bedrooms
- 3 bedrooms, 2 1/2 baths, 1-car garage
- Slab foundation, drawings also include crawl space foundation

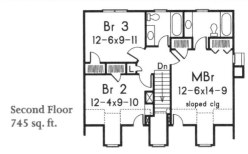

Second Floor
745 sq. ft.

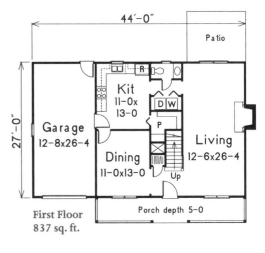

First Floor
837 sq. ft.

To order call toll-free 1-800-DREAM HOME or visit www.houseplansandmore.com

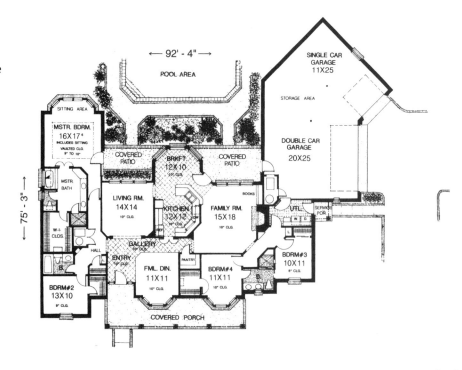

Double Bays Accent Front

Features

- 2,529 total square feet of living area

- Kitchen and breakfast area are located between the family and living rooms for easy access

- Master bedroom includes a sitting area, private bath and access to the covered patio

- 4 bedrooms, 3 baths, 3-car side entry garage

- Slab foundation

Plan #578-049D-0007

Modern Rustic Design

Features

- 1,118 total square feet of living area
- Convenient kitchen has direct access into garage and looks out onto front covered porch
- The covered patio is enjoyed by the living room and master suite
- Octagon-shaped dining room adds interest to the front exterior while the interior is sunny and bright
- 2 bedrooms, 2 baths, 2-car garage
- Slab foundation

Plan #578-053D-0041

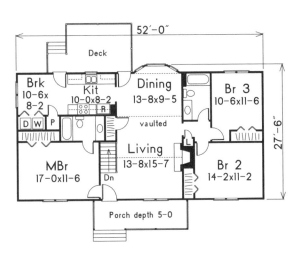

Central Living Space

Features

- 1,364 total square feet of living area
- Pass-through kitchen opens into breakfast room with laundry closet and access to deck
- Adjoining dining and living rooms with vaulted ceilings and a fireplace create an open living area
- 3 bedrooms, 2 baths, 2-car drive under garage
- Basement foundation

To order call toll-free 1-800-DREAM HOME or visit www.houseplansandmore.com

Large Porch And Balcony Create An Impressive Exterior

Features

- 2,352 total square feet of living area
- Separate family and living rooms for casual and formal entertaining
- Master bedroom features a private dressing area and bath
- Bedrooms are located on the second floor for privacy
- 4 bedrooms, 2 1/2 baths, 2-car rear entry garage
- Crawl space foundation, drawings also include basement and slab foundations

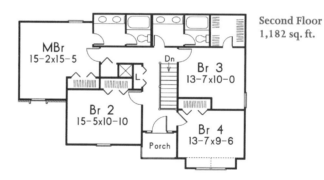

Second Floor
1,182 sq. ft.

MBr
15-2x15-5

Br 3
13-7x10-0

Br 2
15-5x10-10

Br 4
13-7x9-6

Dn

L

Porch

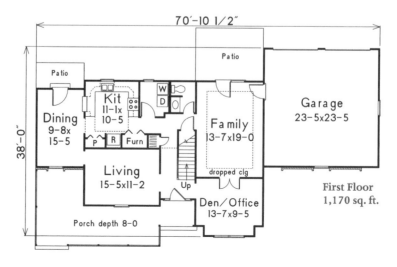

70'-10 1/2"

38'-0"

Patio

Patio

Dining
9-8x
15-5

Kit
11-1x
10-5

W
D

Family
13-7x19-0

Garage
23-5x23-5

P   R   Furn

Living
15-5x11-2

Up

dropped clg

Den/Office
13-7x9-5

Porch depth 8-0

First Floor
1,170 sq. ft.

Plan #578-040D-0014

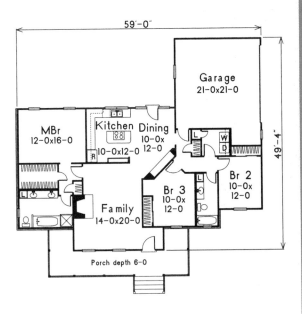

Welcoming Front Porch

Features

- 1,595 total square feet of living area
- Dining room has a convenient built-in desk
- L-shaped kitchen features an island cooktop
- Family room has a high ceiling and fireplace
- Private master bedroom includes a large walk-in closet and bath with separate tub and shower units
- 3 bedrooms, 2 baths, 2-car side entry garage
- Slab foundation, drawings also include crawl space foundation

Plan #578-068D-0003

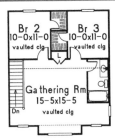

Outdoor Living

Features

- 1,784 total square feet of living area
- Living area features a corner fireplace and large windows
- The second floor gathering room is great for a children's play area
- Secluded master bedroom has separate porch entrances and a large master bath with walk-in closet
- 3 bedrooms, 2 1/2 baths, 1-car garage
- Basement foundation, drawings also include crawl space foundation

To order call toll-free 1-800-DREAM HOME or visit www.houseplansandmore.com

Triple Dormers

Features

- 2,360 total square feet of living area
- First floor master bedroom has a private bath with step-up tub
- Living area fireplace is flanked by double French doors that lead to a spacious deck
- Dormers accentuate second floor bedrooms and bath
- 4 bedrooms, 2 1/2 baths, 2-car side entry garage
- Slab foundation

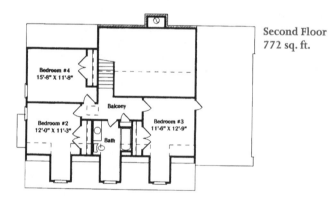

Second Floor
772 sq. ft.

Bedroom #4
15'-8" X 11'-8"

Bedroom #2
12'-0" X 11'-3"

Balcony

Bath

Bedroom #3
11'-6" X 12'-9"

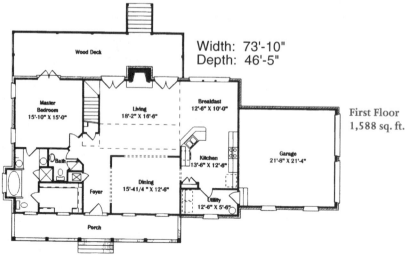

Width: 73'-10"
Depth: 46'-5"

First Floor
1,588 sq. ft.

Wood Deck

Master Bedroom
15'-10" X 15'-0"

Living
18'-2" X 16'-6"

Breakfast
12'-6" X 10'-0"

Bath

Kitchen
13'-6" X 12'-6"

Garage
21'-8" X 21'-4"

Foyer

Dining
15'-41/4" X 12'-6"

Utility
12'-6" X 5'-6"

Porch

Plan #578-001D-0043

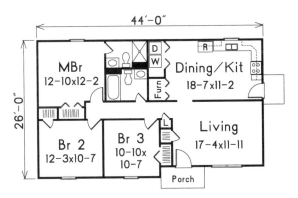

Spacious Living Areas

Features

- 1,104 total square feet of living area
- Master bedroom includes a private bath
- Convenient side entrance to the dining area/kitchen
- Laundry area is located near the kitchen
- Large living area creates a comfortable atmosphere
- 3 bedrooms, 2 baths
- Crawl space foundation, drawings also include basement and slab foundations

Plan #578-045D-0014

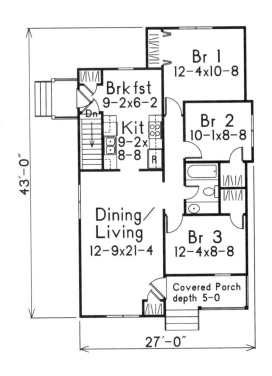

Small Home Maximizes Space

Features

- 987 total square feet of living area
- Galley kitchen opens into the cozy breakfast room
- Dining/living room offers an expansive open area
- Front porch is great for enjoying outdoor living
- 3 bedrooms, 1 bath
- Basement foundation

To order call toll-free 1-800-DREAM HOME or visit www.houseplansandmore.com

Study Has Direct Access Outdoors

Features

- 2,397 total square feet of living area

- Pleasant morning room off the kitchen looks out onto the patio

- Second floor master bedroom has a cozy feel with a fireplace and its own private bath

- Bonus room on the second floor has an additional 406 square feet of living area

- 3 bedrooms, 2 1/2 baths, 2-car garage

- Basement foundation

Second Floor
1,099 sq. ft.

First Floor
1,298 sq. ft.

Width: 57'-6"
Depth: 43'-2"

Plan #578-001D-0072

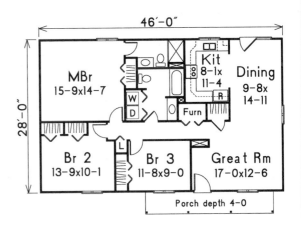

Peaceful Shaded Front Porch

Features

- 1,288 total square feet of living area
- Kitchen, dining area and great room join to create open living spaces
- Master bedroom includes private bath
- Hall bath features convenient laundry closet
- Dining room accesses the outdoors
- 3 bedrooms, 2 baths
- Crawl space foundation, drawings also include basement and slab foundations

Plan #578-045D-0017

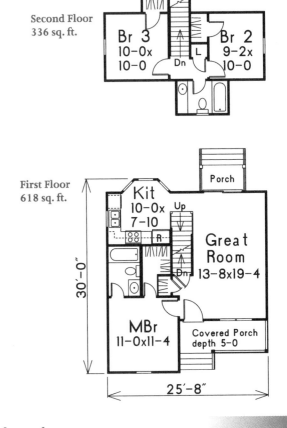

Covered Porch Adds Charm

Features

- 954 total square feet of living area
- Kitchen has a cozy bayed eating area
- Master bedroom has a walk-in closet and private bath
- Large great room has access to the back porch
- 3 bedrooms, 2 baths
- Basement foundation

To order call toll-free 1-800-DREAM HOME or visit www.houseplansandmore.com

Easy Living

Features

- 1,753 total square feet of living area
- Kitchen with breakfast bar over-looks morning room and accesses covered porch
- Master suite has amenities such as a private bath, spacious closets and sunny bay window
- 3 bedrooms, 2 baths
- Slab or crawl space foundation, please specify when ordering

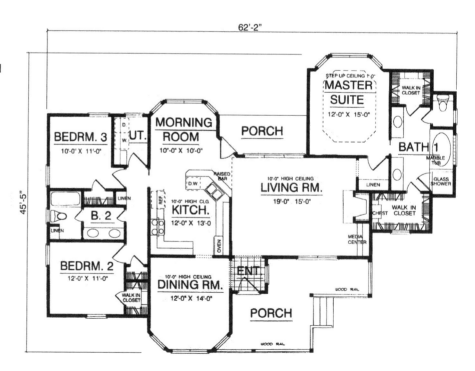

To order call toll-free **1-800-DREAM HOME** or visit www.houseplansandmore.com

Plan #578-051D-0059

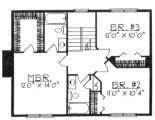

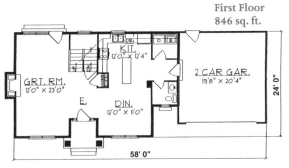

Second Floor
707 sq. ft.

BR. #3
12'0" X 10'0"

MBR
12'0" X 14'0"

BR. #2
11'0" X 10'4"

First Floor
846 sq. ft.

GRT. RM.
12'0" X 23'0"

KIT.
12'0" X 12'4"

2 CAR GAR.
19'8" X 20'4"

DIN.
12'0" X 11'0"

24'0"

58'0"

Compact, Yet Stunning Home

Features

- 1,553 total square feet of living area
- First floor laundry conveniently located
- Spacious and efficient kitchen
- Triple window French door in great room leads to the outdoors
- 3 bedrooms, 2 1/2 baths, 2-car garage
- Crawl space foundation

Plan #578-060D-0019

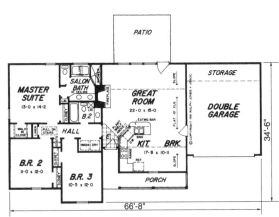

PATIO

STORAGE

MASTER SUITE
13-0 x 14-2

SALON BATH

B.2

GREAT ROOM
22-0 x 15-0

DOUBLE GARAGE

HALL

EATING BAR

KIT
17-8 x 10-11

BRK

B.R. 2
11-0 x 12-0

B.R. 3
10-5 x 12-0

PORCH

34'-6"

66'-8"

Great Family Plan

Features

- 1,382 total square feet of living area
- An appealing open feel with kitchen, breakfast room and great room combining for the ultimate use of space
- All bedrooms are separate from living areas for privacy
- Extra storage in garage
- 3 bedrooms, 2 baths, 2-car garage
- Slab or crawl space foundation, please specify when ordering

To order call toll-free 1-800-DREAM HOME or visit www.houseplansandmore.com

Convenient First Floor Master Suite

Features

- 2,504 total square feet of living area
- Efficient kitchen boasts a peninsula counter adding workspace as well as an eating bar
- The nook and kitchen blend nicely into the great room for family gathering
- The utility room has a soaking sink, extra counterspace and plenty of room for an additional refrigerator
- The bonus room on the second floor has 391 square feet of living area and is included in the total square footage
- 4 bedrooms, 2 1/2 baths, 3-car garage
- Basement foundation

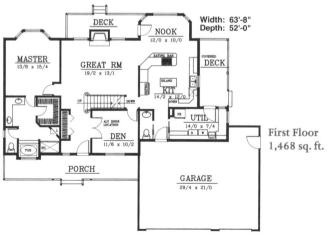

Second Floor
1,036 sq. ft.

Width: 63'-8"
Depth: 52'-0"

First Floor
1,468 sq. ft.

Plan #578-015D-0046

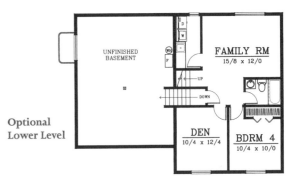

First Floor
1,224 sq. ft.

Width: 42'-0"
Depth: 32'-0"

PATIO

KIT
9/0 x 11/0

VAULTED
DINING
11/6 x 11/0

VAULTED
MASTER
12/2 x 12/0

PANTRY   DESK

DOWN

UP

LINEN

VAULTED
LIVING RM
17/2 x 11/6

BDRM 2
10/4 x 11/0

BDRM 3
10/4 x 11/0

COVERED
PORCH

W SEAT   W SEAT

Optional
Lower Level

UNFINISHED
BASEMENT

FAMILY RM
15/8 x 12/0

UP

DOWN

DEN
10/4 x 12/4

BDRM 4
10/4 x 10/0

Split-Level Has Charming Style

Features

- 1,224 total square feet of living area
- Energy efficient home with 2" x 6" exterior walls
- Charming window seats are featured in bedrooms #2 and #3
- Optional lower level has an additional 682 square feet of living area
- 3 bedrooms, 2 baths
- Partial basement/slab foundation

Plan #578-065D-0022

Master Bedroom
15'3" x 12
9' ceiling height

Great Room
18'2" x 17

Dining
12'4" x 12

Porch
11'4" x 10'9"

Kitchen
17'4" x 9'6"

Storage
7' x 14'8"

Bath

Hall

walk in
closet

Bath

Foyer

Laun.

Two-car Garage
20' x 22'

pantry

Bedroom
11' x 10'2"

Bedroom
10'6" x 11'

slope
ceiling

slope
ceiling

Porch

48'10"

60'

Spacious Foyer Welcomes Guests

Features

- 1,593 total square feet of living area
- The rear porch is a pleasant surprise and perfect for enjoying the outdoors
- A large island separates the kitchen from the dining area
- 3 bedrooms, 2 baths, 2-car garage
- Basement foundation

Trio Of Dormers Adds Curb Appeal

Features

- 1,806 total square feet of living area
- Covered porch in the rear of the home adds an outdoor living area
- Private and formal living room
- Kitchen has snack counter that extends into family room
- 3 bedrooms, 2 baths, 2-car garage
- Slab foundation

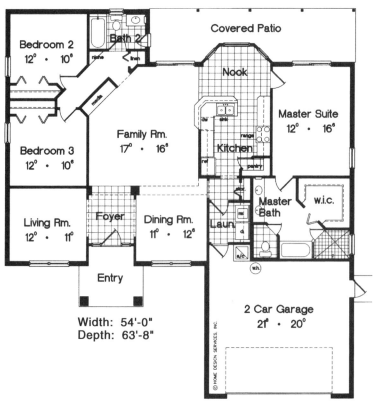

Bedroom 2
12⁰ · 10⁸

Bath 2

Covered Patio

Nook

Master Suite
12⁰ · 16⁸

Family Rm.
17⁰ · 16⁸

Kitchen

Bedroom 3
12⁰ · 10⁸

Master Bath

w.i.c.

Living Rm.
12⁰ · 11⁰

Foyer

Dining Rm.
11⁰ · 12⁸

Laun.

Entry

Width: 54'-0"
Depth: 63'-8"

2 Car Garage
21⁶ · 20⁰

© HOME DESIGN SERVICES, INC.

Plan #578-051D-0021

Impressive Country Home

Features

- 1,739 total square feet of living area
- The living room features a cathedral ceiling and fireplace that also warms adjoining rooms
- Kitchen with center island provides an abundance of counterspace and connects with the dining area
- The laundry area serves as the home entrance from the garage
- 3 bedrooms, 2 1/2 baths, 2-car garage
- Basement foundation

Plan #578-036D-0013

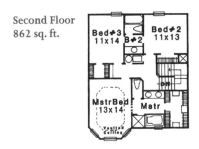

Second Floor
862 sq. ft.

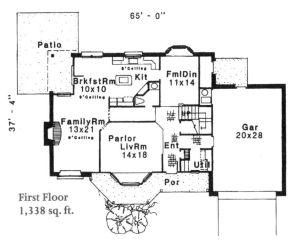

First Floor
1,338 sq. ft.

Comfortable Family Living

Features

- 2,200 total square feet of living area
- Master bedroom has vaulted ceiling, spacious bath and an enormous walk-in closet
- Spacious kitchen has a center island which adds extra workspace
- Parlor/living room features a gorgeous bay window
- 3 bedrooms, 2 1/2 baths, 2-car garage
- Crawl space or slab foundation, please specify when ordering

To order call toll-free 1-800-DREAM HOME or visit www.houseplansandmore.com

Covered Porches All Around

Features

- 1,725 total square feet of living area
- Spectacular arches when entering foyer
- Dining room has a double-door entry leading to the kitchen
- Unique desk area off kitchen is ideal for a computer work station
- 3 bedrooms, 2 baths, 2-car side entry garage
- Crawl space foundation, drawings also include slab foundation

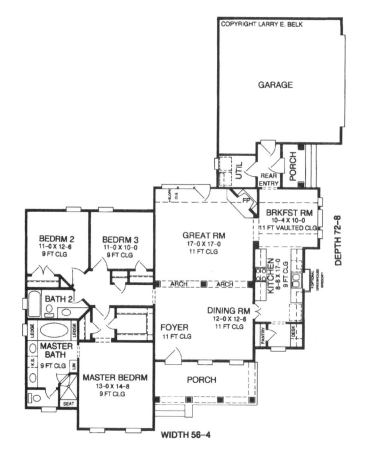

Plan #578-001D-0074

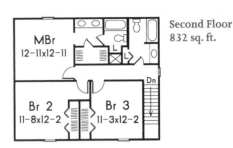

Second Floor
832 sq. ft.

MBr
12-11x12-11

Br 2
11-8x12-2

Br 3
11-3x12-2

Dn

Porch Adds Welcoming Appeal

Features

- 1,664 total square feet of living area
- L-shaped country kitchen includes pantry and cozy breakfast area
- Bedrooms are located on the second floor for privacy
- Master bedroom includes a walk-in closet, dressing area and bath
- 3 bedrooms, 2 1/2 baths, 2-car garage
- Crawl space foundation, drawings also include basement and slab foundations

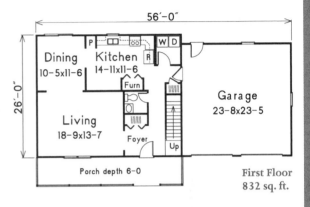

56'-0"

26'-0"

Dining
10-5x11-6

Kitchen
14-11x11-6

W D

P

R

Furn

Living
18-9x13-7

Garage
23-8x23-5

Foyer

Up

Porch depth 6-0

First Floor
832 sq. ft.

Plan #578-047D-0003

2 Car Port

Utility

Storage

Nook

Kitchen

Bedroom 2
12⁰ · 11⁴

Bath

Master Bath

Bedroom 3
10⁰ · 11⁴

Family
22⁰ · 15⁰

Master Bedroom
17⁴ · 12⁰

W.I.C.

Foyer

Covered Porch

Entry

Width: 51'-0"
Depth: 70'-8"

Bayed Breakfast Nook

Features

- 1,442 total square feet of living area
- Utility room includes extra counterspace and a closet for storage
- Kitchen has a useful center island creating extra workspace
- Vaulted master bedroom has unique double-door entry, private bath and a walk-in closet
- 3 bedrooms, 2 baths, 2-car side entry carport
- Slab foundation

To order call toll-free 1-800-DREAM HOME or visit www.houseplansandmore.com

Enhanced By Columned Porch

Features

- 1,887 total square feet of living area
- Enormous great room is the heart of this home with an overlooking kitchen and dining room
- Formal dining room has a lovely bay window
- Master bedroom has spacious bath with corner step-up tub, double vanity and walk-in closet
- 3 bedrooms, 2 1/2 baths, 2-car garage
- Basement foundation

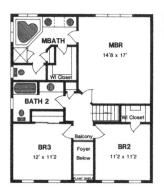

Second Floor
926 sq. ft.

MBATH

MBR
14'8 x 17'

WI Closet

BATH 2

WI Closet

BR3
12' x 11'2

Balcony
Foyer
Below

BR2
11'2 x 11'2

PLANT SHELF

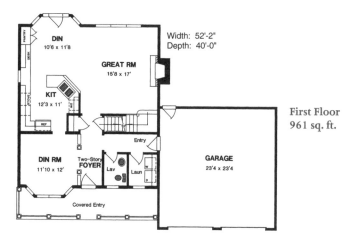

PANTRY

DIN
10'6 x 11'8

GREAT RM
15'8 x 17'

KIT
12'3 x 11'

REF

DIN RM
11'10 x 12'

Two-Story
FOYER

Lav

Laun

Entry

GARAGE
23'4 x 23'4

Covered Entry

Width: 52'-2"
Depth: 40'-0"

First Floor
961 sq. ft.

Plan #578-040D-0028

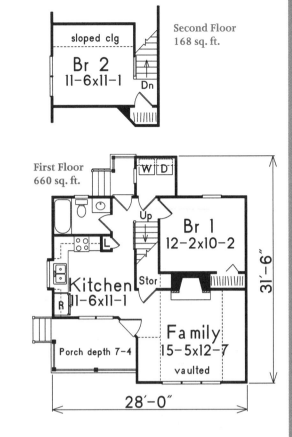

Second Floor
168 sq. ft.

sloped clg

Br 2
11-6x11-1

Dn

First Floor
660 sq. ft.

W D

Up

Stor

Br 1
12-2x10-2

Kitchen
11-6x11-1

Porch depth 7-4

Family
15-5x12-7

vaulted

31'-6"

28'-0"

Appealing And Cozy Cottage

Features

- 828 total square feet of living area
- Vaulted ceiling in living area enhances space
- Sloped ceiling creates unique style in bedroom #2
- Efficient storage space under the stairs
- Covered entry porch provides cozy sitting area and plenty of shade
- 2 bedrooms, 1 bath
- Crawl space foundation

Plan #578-053D-0056

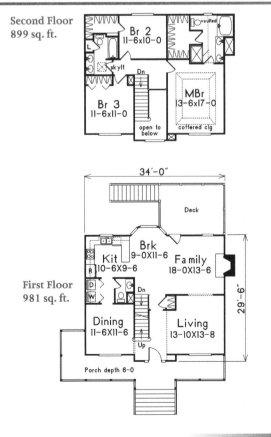

Second Floor
899 sq. ft.

Br 2
11-6x10-0

vaulted

skylt

Dn

Br 3
11-6x11-0

MBr
13-6x17-0

open to
below

coffered clg

34'-0"

Deck

Brk
9-0x11-6

Kit
10-6x9-6

Family
18-0x13-6

First Floor
981 sq. ft.

Dining
11-6x11-6

Dn

Living
13-10x13-8

Up

29'-6"

Porch depth 6-0

Charming Extras Add Character

Features

- 1,880 total square feet of living area
- Master bedroom is enhanced with a coffered ceiling
- Generous family and breakfast areas are modern and functional
- The front porch complements the front facade
- 3 bedrooms, 2 1/2 baths, 2-car drive under garage
- Basement foundation

Ranch With A Country Feel

Features

- 2,355 total square feet of living area
- A double-door entry leads into a private den perfect for a home office
- Vaulted ceilings and a fireplace make the family room a terrific gathering spot
- Cheerful nook off kitchen makes an ideal breakfast area
- 9' ceilings throughout home
- 3 bedrooms, 3 baths, 3-car side entry garage
- Crawl space foundation

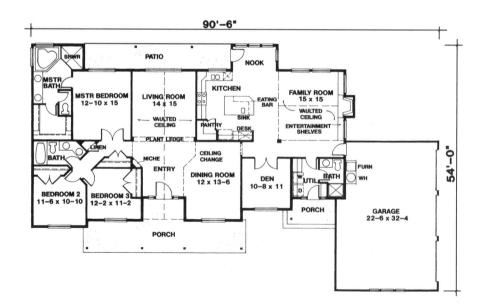

Traditional Exterior Boasts Exciting Interior

Rear View

Features

- 2,531 total square feet of living area
- Charming porch with dormers leads into vaulted great room with atrium
- Well-designed kitchen and breakfast bar adjoin extra-large laundry/mud room
- Double sinks, tub with window above and plant shelf complete vaulted master bath
- 4 bedrooms, 2 1/2 baths, 2-car side entry garage
- Walk-out basement foundation

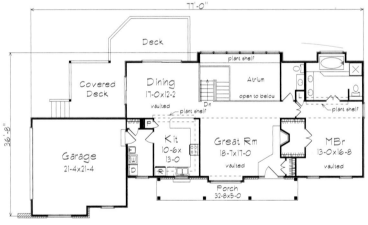

First Floor
1,297 sq. ft.

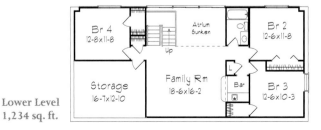

Lower Level
1,234 sq. ft.

Country-Style Comfort

Features

- 2,826 total square feet of living area
- Wrap-around covered porch is accessible from family and breakfast rooms in addition to front entrance
- Bonus room, which is included in the square footage, has a separate entrance and is suitable for an office or private accommodations
- Large, full-windowed breakfast room
- 4 bedrooms, 2 1/2 baths, 2-car side entry garage
- Basement foundation

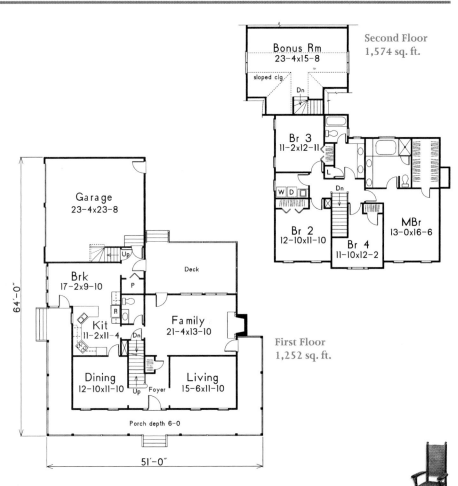

Second Floor
1,574 sq. ft.

First Floor
1,252 sq. ft.

To order call toll-free 1-800-DREAM HOME or visit www.houseplansandmore.com

Plan #578-072D-0004

Master Suite Is Hard To Resist

Features

- 1,926 total square feet of living area
- A breathtaking wall of windows brightens the great room
- A double-door entry leads to the master suite which features a large bath and walk-in closet
- An island cooktop in the kitchen makes mealtime a breeze
- 3 bedrooms, 3 baths, 2-car garage
- Basement foundation

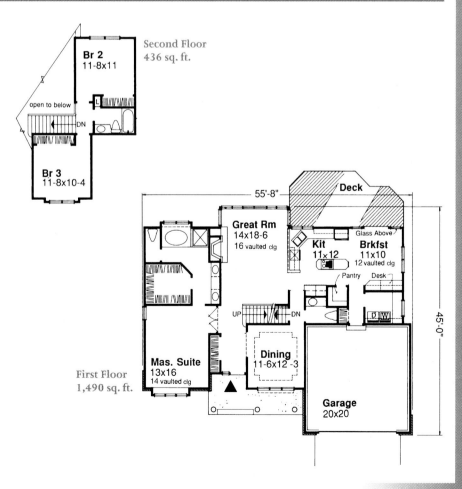

Second Floor
436 sq. ft.

Br 2
11-8x11

open to below

DN

Br 3
11-8x10-4

Deck

55'-8"

Great Rm
14x18-6
16 vaulted clg

Kit
11x12

Brkfst
11x10
12 vaulted clg

Glass Above

Pantry   Desk

UP   DN

Mas. Suite
13x16
14 vaulted clg

First Floor
1,490 sq. ft.

Dining
11-6x12-3

D W

45'-0"

Garage
20x20

Charming Facade

Features

- 1,643 total square feet of living area
- An attractive front entry porch gives this ranch a country accent
- Spacious family/dining room is the focal point of this design
- Kitchen and utility room are conveniently located near gathering areas
- Formal living room in the front of the home provides area for quiet and privacy
- Master bedroom has view to the rear of the home and a generous walk-in closet
- 3 bedrooms, 2 baths, 2-car garage
- Basement foundation, drawings also include crawl space and slab foundations

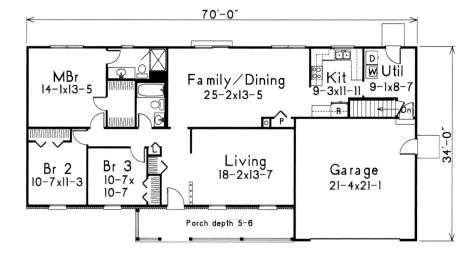

70'-0"

MBr
14-1x13-5

Family/Dining
25-2x13-5

Kit
9-3x11-11

Util
9-1x8-7

Br 2
10-7x11-3

Br 3
10-7x
10-7

Living
18-2x13-7

Garage
21-4x21-1

34'-0"

Porch depth 5-6

Country Charm Wrapped In A Veranda

Features

- 2,059 total square feet of living area
- Octagon-shaped breakfast room offers plenty of windows and creates a view to the veranda
- First floor master bedroom has a large walk-in closet and deluxe bath
- 9' ceilings throughout the home
- Secondary bedrooms and bath feature dormers and are adjacent to the cozy sitting area
- 3 bedrooms, 2 1/2 baths, 2-car detached garage
- Slab foundation, drawings also include basement and crawl space foundations

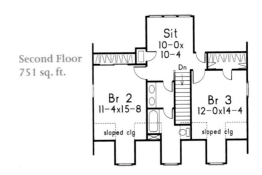

Second Floor
751 sq. ft.

Sit
10-0x
10-4

Dn

Br 2
11-4x15-8

Br 3
12-0x14-4

sloped clg   sloped clg

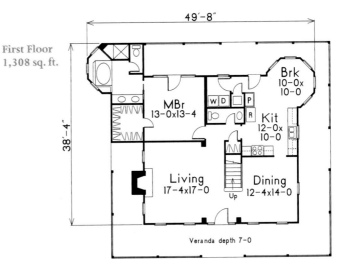

First Floor
1,308 sq. ft.

49'-8"

38'-4"

MBr
13-0x13-4

W D   P

Brk
10-0x
10-0

Kit
12-0x
10-0

R

Living
17-4x17-0

Up

Dining
12-4x14-0

Veranda depth 7-0

Ranch Offers Country Elegance

Features

- 1,787 total square feet of living area
- Large great room with fireplace and vaulted ceiling features three large skylights and windows galore
- Cooking is sure to be a pleasure in this L-shaped well-appointed kitchen which includes a bayed breakfast area with access to the rear deck
- Every bedroom offers a spacious walk-in closet with a convenient laundry room just steps away
- 415 square feet of optional living area available on the lower level
- 3 bedrooms, 2 baths, 2-car drive under garage
- Walk-out basement foundation

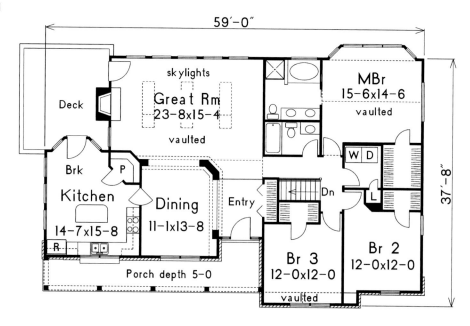

Perfect Home For Family Living

Features

- 1,700 total square feet of living area
- Oversized laundry room has a large pantry and storage area as well as access to the outdoors
- Master bedroom is separated from other bedrooms for privacy
- Raised snack bar in kitchen allows extra seating for dining
- 3 bedrooms, 2 baths
- Crawl space or slab foundation, please specify when ordering

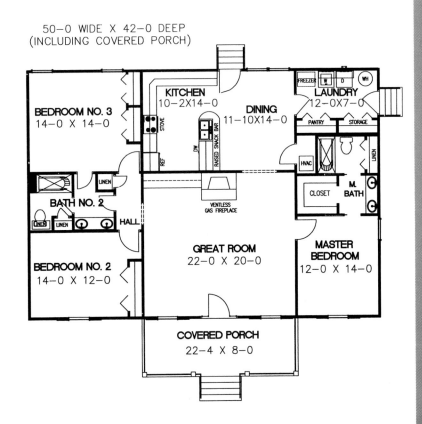

50-0 WIDE X 42-0 DEEP
(INCLUDING COVERED PORCH)

BEDROOM NO. 3
14-0 X 14-0

KITCHEN
10-2X14-0

DINING
11-10X14-0

LAUNDRY
12-0X7-0

FREEZER W D WH

PANTRY STORAGE

RAISED SNACK BAR

DW

REF

STOVE

HVAC

LINEN

BATH NO. 2

LINEN LINEN HALL

CLOSET

M. BATH

VENTLESS GAS FIREPLACE

GREAT ROOM
22-0 X 20-0

MASTER BEDROOM
12-0 X 14-0

BEDROOM NO. 2
14-0 X 12-0

COVERED PORCH
22-4 X 8-0

Plan #578-065D-0043

Price Code F

A French Country Delight

Features

- 3,816 total square feet of living area
- Beautifully designed master bedroom enjoys a lavish dressing area as well as access to the library
- Second floor computer loft is centrally located and includes plenty of counterspace
- The two-story great room has an impressive arched opening and a beautiful beamed ceiling
- The outdoor covered deck has a popular fireplace
- 4 bedrooms, 3 1/2 baths, 3-car side entry garage
- Basement foundation

Second Floor
1,091 sq. ft.

Great Room

First Floor
2,725 sq. ft.

To order call toll-free **1-800-DREAM HOME** or visit **www.houseplansandmore.com**

Modern Inside, Old-Fashioned Outside

Master Bedroom

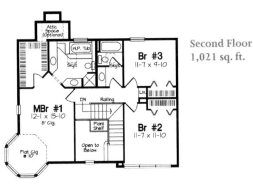

Second Floor
1,021 sq. ft.

MBr #1
12-1 x 15-10
8' Clg

Br #3
11-7 x 9-10

Br #2
11-7 x 11-10

Features

- 2,281 total square feet of living area
- Dramatic raised hearth in family room
- Kitchen is conveniently designed and features a large pantry closet
- Unique parlor offers privacy and quiet from the other more open living areas
- 3 bedrooms, 2 1/2 baths, 3-car side entry garage
- Basement, crawl space or slab foundation, please specify when ordering

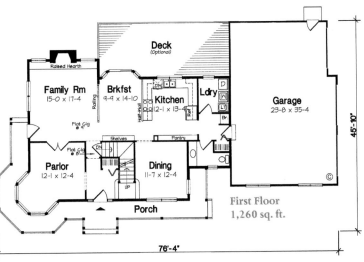

Deck
(Optional)

Raised Hearth

Family Rm
15-0 x 17-4

Brkfst
9-9 x 14-10

Kitchen
12-1 x 13-4

Ldry

Garage
23-8 x 35-4

Shelves

Pantry

Parlor
12-1 x 12-4

Dining
11-7 x 12-4

UP

Porch

First Floor
1,260 sq. ft.

45'-10"

76'-4"

Country Appeal For A Small Lot

Features

- 1,299 total square feet of living area
- Large porch for enjoying relaxing evenings
- First floor master bedroom has a bay window, walk-in closet and roomy bath
- Two generous bedrooms with lots of closet space, a hall bath, linen closet and balcony overlook comprise the second floor
- 3 bedrooms, 2 1/2 baths
- Basement foundation

First Floor
834 sq. ft.

Second Floor
465 sq. ft.

Impressive Home For Country Living

Features

- 1,991 total square feet of living area
- A large porch with roof dormers and flanking stonework creates a distinctive country appeal
- The highly functional U-shaped kitchen is open to the dining and living rooms defined by a colonnade
- Large bay windows are enjoyed by both the living room and master bedroom
- Every bedroom features spacious walk-in closets and its own private bath
- 3 bedrooms, 3 1/2 baths, 2-car side entry garage
- Basement foundation

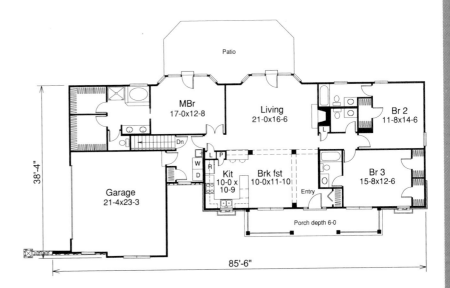

Nice Style With Room To Grow

Features

- 2,718 total square feet of living area
- The two-story foyer opens into the central kitchen which enjoys an island work station
- The vaulted master bedroom offers two walk-in closets and a private bath with garden tub
- An optional loft easily converts into a fourth bedroom and has an additional 223 square feet of living area
- 4 bedrooms, 2 1/2 baths, 2-car side entry garage
- Basement, crawl space or slab foundation, please specify when ordering

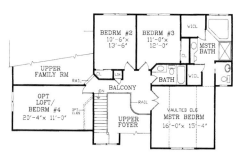

Second Floor
1,203 sq. ft.

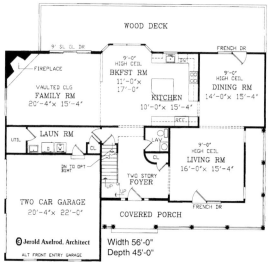

First Floor
1,515 sq. ft.

Width 56'-0"
Depth 45'-0"

Kitchen

To order call toll-free 1-800-DREAM HOME or visit www.houseplansandmore.com

Spacious Design With A Luxurious Appeal

Features

- 2,789 total square feet of living area
- Master bedroom with large walk-in closets has a glass shower and whirlpool tub
- Great room has a sunny wall of windows creating a cheerful atmosphere
- Second floor includes bonus room with 286 square feet of living area
- 4 bedrooms, 3 baths, 2-car side entry garage
- Walk-out basement, basement, crawl space or slab foundation, please specify when ordering

Second Floor
812 sq. ft.

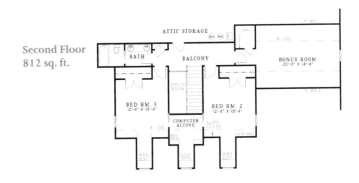

First Floor
1,977 sq. ft.

Duo Atrium For Fantastic Views

Features

- 2,125 total square feet of living area

- A cozy porch leads to the vaulted great room with fireplace through the entry which has a walk-in closet and bath

- Large and well-arranged kitchen offers spectacular views from its cantilevered sink cabinetry through a two-story atrium window wall

- Master bedroom boasts a sitting room, large walk-in closet and bath with garden tub overhanging a brightly lit atrium

- 1,047 square feet of optional living area on the lower level featuring a study and family room with walk-in bar and full bath below the kitchen

- 3 bedrooms, 2 1/2 baths, 2-car side entry garage

- Walk-out basement foundation

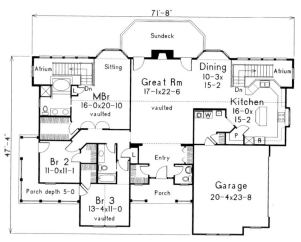

First Floor
2,125 sq. ft.

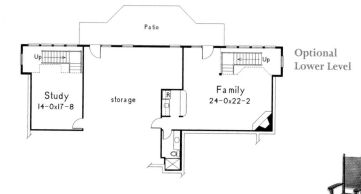

Optional
Lower Level

Atrium Living For Views On A Narrow Lot

Features

- 1,231 total square feet of living area
- Dutch gables and stone accents provide an enchanting appearance
- The spacious living room offers a masonry fireplace, atrium with window wall and is open to a dining area with bay window
- Kitchen has a breakfast counter, lots of cabinet space and glass sliding doors to a balcony
- 380 square feet of optional living area on the lower level
- 2 bedrooms, 2 baths, 1-car drive under garage
- Walk-out basement foundation

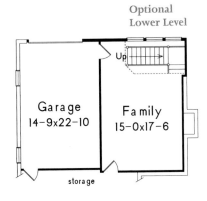

Optional
Lower Level

Garage
14-9x22-10

Family
15-0x17-6

Up

storage

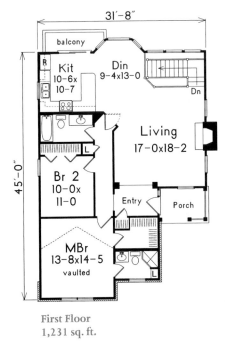

31'-8"

balcony

Kit
10-6x
10-7

Din
9-4x13-0

Dn

Living
17-0x18-2

45'-0"

Br 2
10-0x
11-0

Entry

Porch

MBr
13-8x14-5
vaulted

L

807

First Floor
1,231 sq. ft.

Beautiful Country Porch With Sundeck

Features

- 2,560 total square feet of living area
- Open two-story foyer adds charm to this elegant home
- Large great room features a fire-place, built-in cabinet and access to porch and sundeck
- First floor has 9' ceilings throughout
- Breakfast area has windows on all exterior walls with access to a sundeck and screen porch
- 4 bedrooms, 2 1/2 baths, 2-car drive under garage
- Basement foundation
- 144 square feet on the lower level

Second Floor
1,166 sq. ft.

Deck
8-10 x 11-8

Master Bdrm.
12-4 x 17-6

M.Bath

Bdrm.4
13-6 x 11-6

Bth.2

Balcony

Bdrm.3
13-6 x 11-6

Open To Foyer

Bdrm.2
13-6 x 11-6

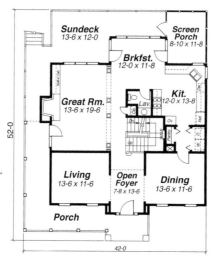

Sundeck
13-6 x 12-0

Screen Porch
8-10 x 11-8

Brkfst.
12-0 x 11-8

Kit.
12-0 x 13-8

Great Rm.
13-6 x 19-6

Lav.

52-0

Living
13-6 x 11-6

Open Foyer
7-8 x 13-6

Dining
13-6 x 11-6

Porch

42-0

First Floor
1,250 sq. ft.

Varied Exterior Finishes Enrich Facade

Features

- 2,696 total square feet of living area
- Magnificent master bedroom features a private covered porch and luxurious bath
- Second floor game room includes balcony access and adjacent loft
- Well-planned kitchen includes walk-in pantry, island cooktop and nearby spacious breakfast room
- 4 bedrooms, 3 baths, 2-car side entry garage
- Slab foundation, drawings also include crawl space foundation

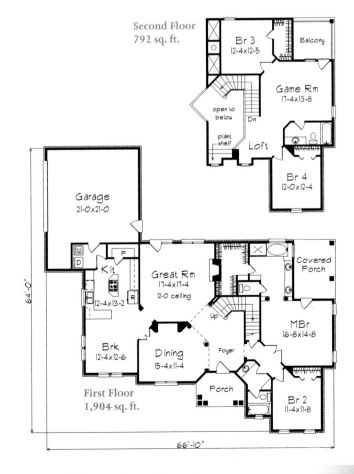

Rich With Victorian Details

Features

- 2,632 total square feet of living area
- Energy efficient home with 2" x 6" exterior walls
- Master bedroom has a cheerful octagon-shaped sitting area
- Arched entrances create a distinctive living room with a lovely tray ceiling and help define the dining room
- 4 bedrooms, 2 1/2 baths, 2-car garage
- Basement or crawl space foundation, please specify when ordering

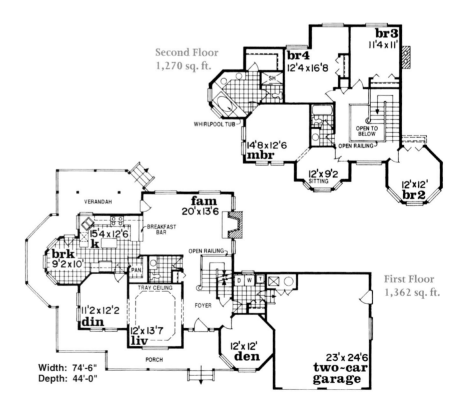

Second Floor
1,270 sq. ft.

First Floor
1,362 sq. ft.

Width: 74'-6"
Depth: 44'-0"

Dramatic U-Shaped Stairs

Features

- 2,287 total square feet of living area
- Wrap-around porch creates an inviting feeling
- First floor windows have transom windows above
- Den has a see-through fireplace into the family area
- 3 bedrooms, 2 1/2 baths, 2-car side entry garage
- Crawl space foundation

First Floor
1,371 sq. ft.

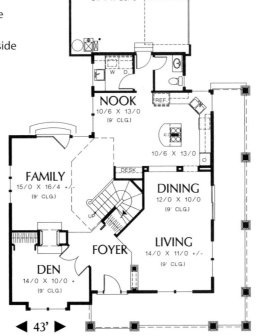

©Alan Mascord Design Associates, Inc.

GARAGE
21/4 X 20/0

NOOK
10/6 X 13/0
(9' CLG.)

REF.

10/6 X 13/0

FAMILY
15/0 X 16/4 +/-
(9' CLG.)

DESK

DINING
12/0 X 10/0
(9' CLG.)

UP

FOYER

LIVING
14/0 X 11/0 +/-
(9' CLG.)

DEN
14/0 X 10/0 +
(9' CLG.)

69'

43'

Second Floor
916 sq. ft.

©Alan Mascord Design Associates, Inc.

PLANT SHELF

BR. 3
10/6 X 13/0

FAMILY BELOW

LINEN

DN

BR. 2
12/4 X 11/0

VAULTED

MASTER
12/0 X 15/0 +

Stylish Retreat For A Narrow Lot

Features

- 1,084 total square feet of living area
- Delightful country porch for quiet evenings
- The living room offers a front feature window which invites the sun and includes a fireplace and dining area with private patio
- The U-shaped kitchen features lots of cabinets and a bayed breakfast room with built-in pantry
- Both bedrooms have walk-in closets and access to their own bath
- 2 bedrooms, 2 baths
- Basement foundation

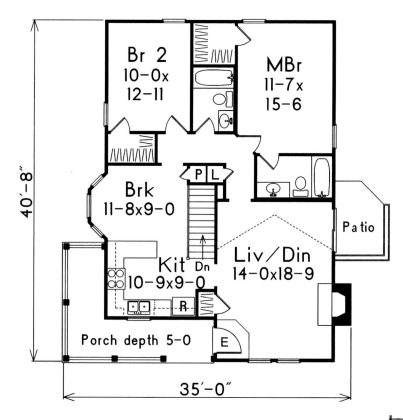

Compact Home For Functional Living

Features

- 1,220 total square feet of living area
- Vaulted ceilings add luxury to the living room and master bedroom
- Spacious living room is accented with a large fireplace and hearth
- Gracious dining area is adjacent to the convenient wrap-around kitchen
- Washer and dryer are handy to the bedrooms
- Covered porch entry adds appeal
- Rear deck adjoins dining area
- 3 bedrooms, 2 baths, 2-car drive under garage
- Basement foundation

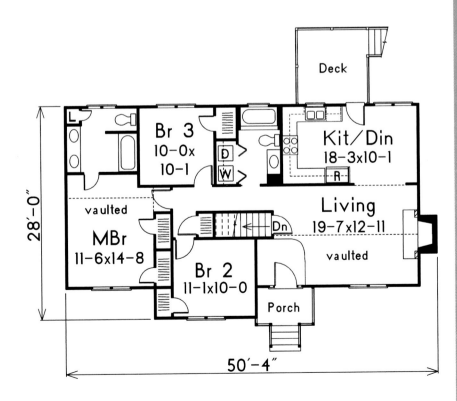

Home Has A Custom Feel

Features

- 3,072 total square feet of living area
- Charming window seats accent all the secondary bedrooms
- Master bedroom has a luxurious bath and an enormous walk-in closet
- Double-doors in both the study and the formal dining room lead to the covered front porch
- 4 bedrooms, 3 1/2 baths, 3-car side entry garage
- Slab foundation

Second Floor
956 sq. ft.

First Floor
2,116 sq. ft.

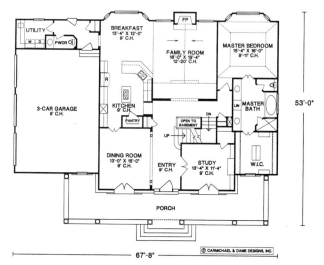

Victorian Ranch

Features

- 1,466 total square feet of living area
- The foyer flows into the great room which is warmed by a corner fireplace
- Sliding French doors open to the backyard from both the great room and adjoining formal dining room
- A turreted breakfast room overlooks the spacious front porch
- The master bedroom is separated for privacy and includes its own bath
- 3 bedrooms, 2 baths, 2-car side entry garage
- Basement, crawl space or slab foundation, please specify when ordering

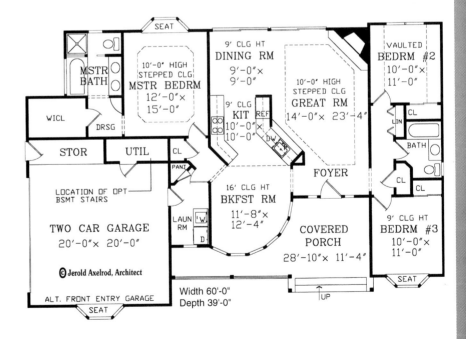

Enchanting Country Cottage

Features

- 1,140 total square feet of living area
- Open and spacious living and dining areas for family gatherings
- Well-organized kitchen with an abundance of cabinetry and a built-in pantry
- Roomy master bath features a double-bowl vanity
- 3 bedrooms, 2 baths, 2-car drive under garage
- Basement foundation

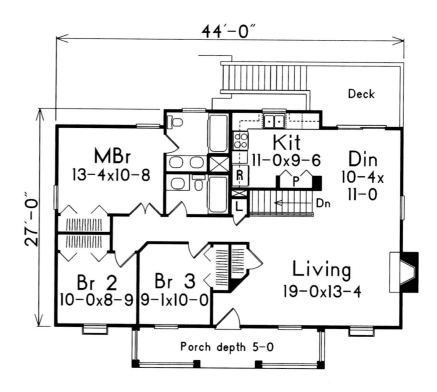

44'-0"

27'-0"

Deck

MBr
13-4x10-8

Kit
11-0x9-6

Din
10-4x
11-0

R

P

L

Dn

Br 2
10-0x8-9

Br 3
9-1x10-0

Living
19-0x13-4

Porch depth 5-0

Two-Story Atrium For Great Views

Features

- 2,900 total square feet of living area
- Elegant entry foyer leads to the second floor balcony overlook of the vaulted two-story atrium
- Spacious kitchen features an island breakfast bar, walk-in pantry, bayed breakfast room and adjoining screened porch
- Two large second floor bedrooms and stair balconies overlook a sun-drenched two-story vaulted atrium
- 4 bedrooms, 3 1/2 baths, 2-car side entry garage
- Basement foundation

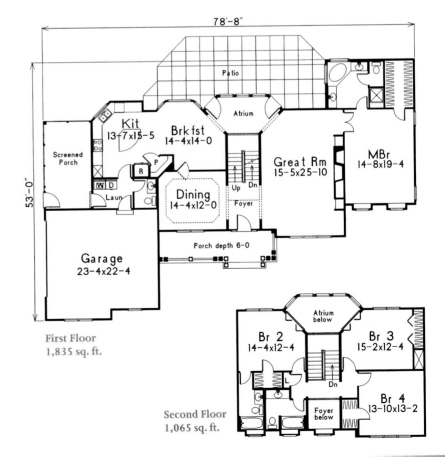

First Floor
1,835 sq. ft.

Second Floor
1,065 sq. ft.

Luxurious Log Home

Features

- 4,885 total square feet of living area
- Office includes cozy corner fireplace ideal for privacy
- Master bath is very special with whirlpool tub in a box bay window
- Second floor includes three bedrooms, a loft area and plenty of room for future expansion
- Future expansion on the second floor has an additional 1,180 square feet of living area
- 4 bedrooms, 4 1/2 baths, 3-car side entry garage
- Crawl space foundation

Second Floor
2,554 sq. ft.

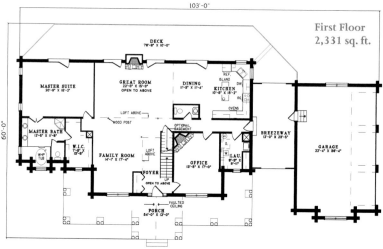

First Floor
2,331 sq. ft.

Large Built-In Desk

Features

- 1,815 total square feet of living area
- Second floor has a built-in desk in the hall that is ideal as a computer work station or mini office area
- Two doors into the laundry area make it handy from the master bedroom and the rest of the home
- Inviting covered porch
- Lots of counterspace and cabinetry in the kitchen
- 3 bedrooms, 2 1/2 baths, 2-car side entry garage
- Basement foundation

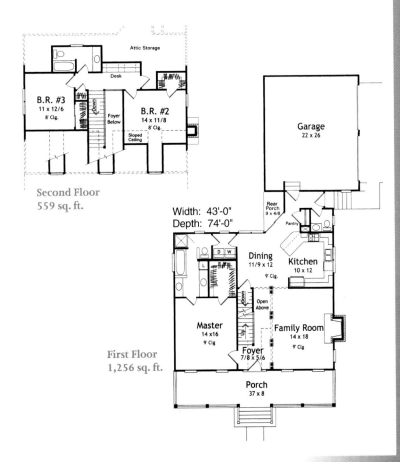

Second Floor
559 sq. ft.

Width: 43'-0"
Depth: 74'-0"

First Floor
1,256 sq. ft.

Compact Design Offers Privacy

Features

- 2,847 total square feet of living area
- Secluded first floor master bedroom includes an oversized window and a large walk-in closet
- Extensive attic storage and closet space
- Spacious second floor bedrooms, two of which share a private bath
- Great starter home with option to finish the second floor as needed
- 4 bedrooms, 3 1/2 baths, 2-car garage
- Basement foundation, drawings also include slab and crawl space foundations

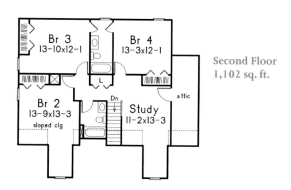

Br 3
13-10x12-1

Br 4
13-3x12-1

Second Floor
1,102 sq. ft.

Br 2
13-9x13-3

sloped clg

Dn

Study
11-2x13-3

attic

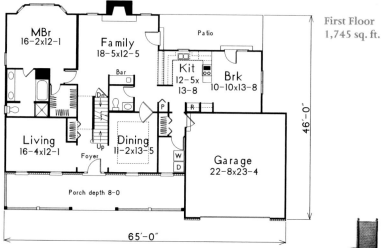

Second Floor
1,102 sq. ft.

MBr
16-2x12-1

Family
18-5x12-5

Patio

Bar

Kit
12-5x
13-8

Brk
10-10x13-8

First Floor
1,745 sq. ft.

Living
16-4x12-1

Dn

Up

Dining
11-2x13-5

Foyer

W
D

Garage
22-8x23-4

46-0"

Porch depth 8-0

65'-0"

Columned Entry And An Inviting Front Porch

Features

- 2,198 total square feet of living area
- Sunken living room has a vaulted ceiling, a corner fireplace and eye-catching windows with transoms
- A china hutch services the quiet dining room
- Well-planned and stylish, the kitchen offers a snack bar and a built-in desk
- 3 bedrooms, 2 1/2 baths, 2-car garage
- Basement foundation

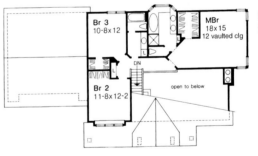

Second Floor
910 sq. ft.

Br 3
10-8x12

MBr
18x15
12 vaulted clg

Br 2
11-8x12-2

DN

open to below

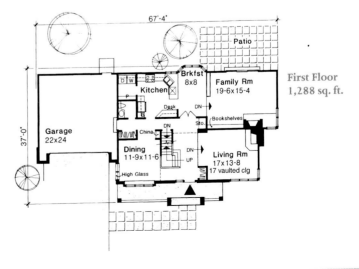

First Floor
1,288 sq. ft.

67'-4"

37'-0"

Patio

Brkfst
8x8

Family Rm
19-6x15-4

Kitchen

Desk

Bookshelves

Garage
22x24

China

Sto.

DN

DN

DN

UP

Dining
11-9x11-6

Living Rm
17x13-8
17 vaulted clg

High Glass

Trendsetting Appeal For A Narrow Lot

Features

- 1,294 total square feet of living area
- Great room features a fireplace and large bay with windows and patio doors
- Enjoy a laundry room immersed in light with large windows, an arched transom and attractive planter box
- Vaulted master bedroom features a bay window and two walk-in closets
- Bedroom #2 boasts a vaulted ceiling, plant shelf and half bath, perfect for a studio
- 2 bedrooms, 1 full bath, 2 half baths, 1-car rear entry garage
- Basement foundation

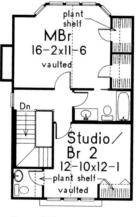

Second Floor
576 sq. ft.

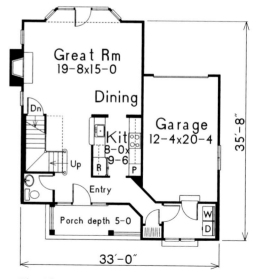

First Floor
718 sq. ft.

Classic Atrium Ranch With Rooms To Spare

Features

- 1,977 total square feet of living area
- Classic traditional exterior is always in style
- Spacious great room boasts a vaulted ceiling, dining area, atrium with elegant staircase and feature windows
- Atrium opens to 1,416 square feet of optional living area below which consists of a family room, two bedrooms, two baths and a study
- 4 bedrooms, 2 1/2 baths, 3-car side entry garage
- Walk-out basement foundation

First Floor
1,977 sq. ft.

76'-0"

45'-0"

MBr
14-6x15-5

Br 2
10-7x
10-0

Br 3
11-4x11x8

Br 4
11-8x12-8
vaulted

Brk
11-8x13-0

Deck

open to below   Dn

Great Rm
16-4x24-2
vaulted

Kit
11-3x
12-4

Dining

Garage
23-4x29-4

Porch

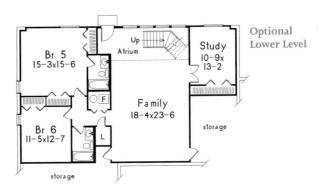

Optional
Lower Level

Up
Atrium

Br 5
15-3x15-6

Study
10-9x
13-2

Family
18-4x23-6

storage

Br 6
11-5x12-7

storage

Traditional Exterior, Handsome Accents

Features

- 1,882 total square feet of living area
- Wide, handsome entrance opens to the vaulted great room with fireplace
- Living and dining areas are conveniently joined but still allow privacy
- Private covered porch extends breakfast area
- Practical passageway runs through the laundry room from the garage to the kitchen
- Vaulted ceiling in master bedroom
- 3 bedrooms, 2 baths, 2-car garage
- Basement foundation

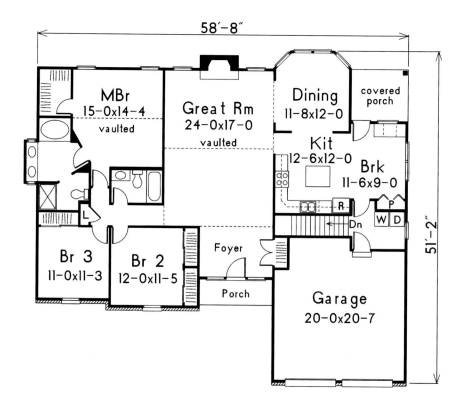

Plan #578-068D-0012

Plenty Of Seating At Breakfast Bar

Features

- 2,544 total square feet of living area
- Central family room becomes a gathering place
- Second floor recreation room is a great game room for children
- First floor master bedroom is secluded from main living areas
- 3 bedrooms, 2 1/2 baths, 2-car side entry garage
- Basement foundation, drawings also include crawl space and slab foundations

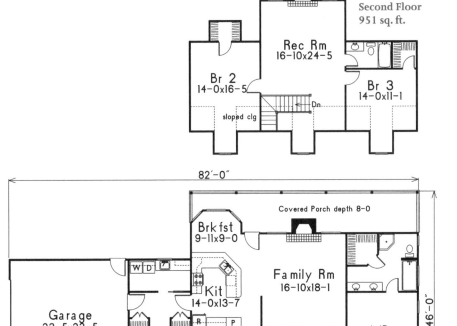

Second Floor 951 sq. ft.

Rec Rm 16-10x24-5
Br 2 14-0x16-5
Br 3 14-0x11-1
sloped clg

First Floor 1,593 sq. ft.

82'-0"
Covered Porch depth 8-0
Brkfst 9-11x9-0
Family Rm 16-10x18-1
Kit 14-0x13-7
Garage 23-5x23-5
Dining 14-0x11-0 tray clg
Foyer
MBr 14-0x18-0
46'-0"
Covered Porch depth 8-0

Inviting Porch Enhances Design

Features

- 1,389 total square feet of living area
- Formal living room has a warming fireplace and delightful bay window
- U-shaped kitchen shares a snack bar with the bayed family room
- Lovely master bedroom has its own private bath
- 3 bedrooms, 2 baths, 2-car garage
- Slab foundation

Distinctive Two-Level Porch

Features

- 2,605 total square feet of living area
- Master bedroom boasts a vaulted ceiling and transom picture window which lights sitting area
- Country kitchen features appliances set in between brick dividers and a beamed ceiling
- Living room features built-in book-cases, fireplace and a raised tray ceiling
- 4 bedrooms, 2 1/2 baths, 2-car side entry garage
- Slab foundation, drawings also include crawl space and basement foundations

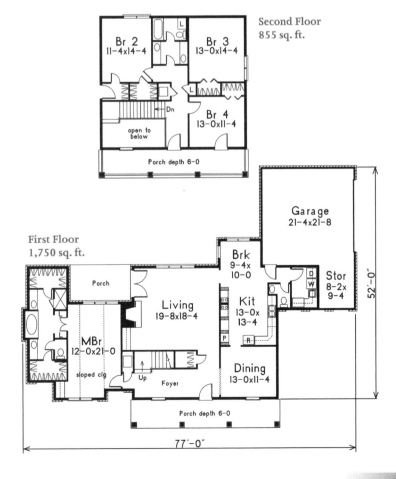

Second Floor
855 sq. ft.

Br 2
11-4x14-4

Br 3
13-0x14-4

Br 4
13-0x11-4

open to below

Dn

Porch depth 6-0

First Floor
1,750 sq. ft.

Garage
21-4x21-8

Brk
9-4x
10-0

Stor
8-2x
9-4

Porch

Living
19-8x18-4

Kit
13-0x
13-4

MBr
12-0x21-0

sloped clg

Up

Foyer

Dining
13-0x11-4

Porch depth 6-0

52'-0"

77'-0"

Dramatic Open Layout

Features

- 1,537 total square feet of living area
- Vaulted ceilings in the foyer and living room welcome guests
- Kitchen offers an eating bar and pantry
- Living room features a fireplace flanked by large windows
- 3 bedrooms, 2 baths, 2-car garage
- Basement foundation

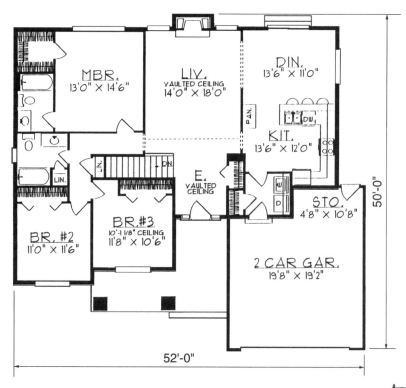

To order call toll-free 1-800-DREAM HOME or visit www.houseplansandmore.com

Plan #578-015D-0045

Ultimate Curb Appeal

Features

- 2,487 total square feet of living area
- Three second floor bedrooms and a convenient study loft share a hall bath
- Dining and living rooms feature French doors leading to a covered wrap-around porch
- First floor living spaces offer formal dining as well as a casual nook and kitchen with eating bar and pantry
- Bonus room on the second floor has an additional 338 square feet of living area
- 4 bedrooms, 2 1/2 baths, 2-car side entry garage
- Basement foundation

Second Floor
863 sq. ft.

DOWN
STORAGE DESK LINEN
STUDY LOFT
14/4 x 11/11
BOOKS
BDRM 3
11/9 x 11/11

UNFINISHED
BONUS
13/4 x 25/4

RAILING DOWN

BDRM 2
13/1 x 10/9

FOYER
BELOW

BDRM 4
11/0 x 10/9

DESK

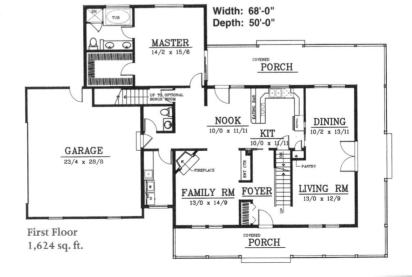

Width: 68'-0"
Depth: 50'-0"

SH. TUB

MASTER
14/2 x 15/6

COVERED
PORCH

UP TO OPTIONAL
BONUS ROOM

GARAGE
23/4 x 28/8

NOOK
10/0 x 11/11

EATING BAR

DINING
10/2 x 13/11

KIT
10/0 x 11/11

REFRIG.

FIREPLACE

ENT. CTR.

PANTRY

FAMILY RM
13/0 x 14/9

FOYER

LIVING RM
13/0 x 12/9

UP

First Floor
1,624 sq. ft.

COVERED
PORCH

Master Bedroom With Sitting Area

Features

- 2,188 total square feet of living area
- Master bedroom includes a private covered porch, sitting area and two large walk-in closets
- Spacious kitchen features a center island, snack bar and laundry access
- Great room has a 10' ceiling and a dramatic corner fireplace
- 3 bedrooms, 2 baths, 3-car side entry garage
- Basement foundation

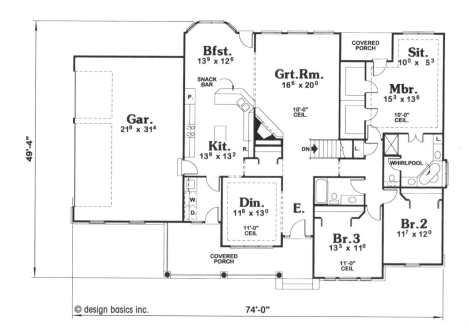

Bayed Sunroom Brightens Farmhouse

Features

- 2,491 total square feet of living area
- Entry is flanked by formal living and dining rooms
- Hallway between dining room and kitchen includes a butler's pantry to ease serving a party
- The kitchen, breakfast nook and family room combine for an expansive gathering space
- All bedrooms are located on the second floor for privacy
- 4 bedrooms, 2 1/2 baths, 2-car side entry garage
- Basement foundation

Second Floor
1,158 sq. ft.

First Floor
1,333 sq. ft.

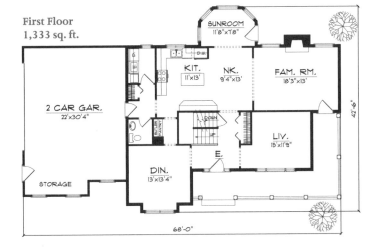

Impressive Gallery

Features

- 2,674 total square feet of living area
- First floor master bedroom has a convenient location
- Kitchen and breakfast area have an island and access to the covered front porch
- Second floor bedrooms have dormer window seats for added charm
- Optional future rooms on the second floor have an additional 520 square feet of living area
- 4 bedrooms, 3 baths, 3-car side entry garage
- Basement or slab foundation, please specify when ordering

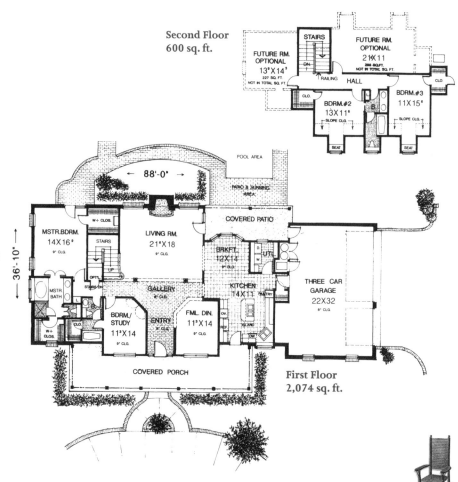

Second Floor
600 sq. ft.

First Floor
2,074 sq. ft.

To order call toll-free 1-800-DREAM HOME or visit www.houseplansandmore.com

Plan #578-062D-0044

Dormers Grace This Cozy Country Home

Features

- 2,044 total square feet of living area
- Second floor bonus room would make an ideal media room or home office area
- Country kitchen is oversized for large family gatherings
- Bonus room on the second floor has an additional 695 square feet of living area
- 3 bedrooms, 2 1/2 baths, 2-car garage
- Basement or crawl space foundation, please specify when ordering

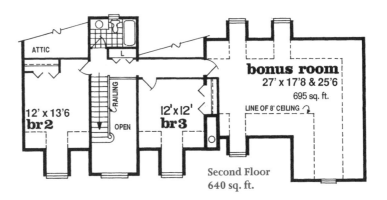

ATTIC

br 2
12' x 13'6

RAILING

OPEN

L

br 3
12' x 12'

bonus room
27' x 17'8 & 25'6
695 sq. ft.

LINE OF 8' CEILING

Second Floor
640 sq. ft.

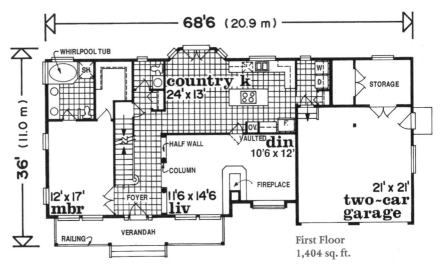

68'6 (20.9 m)

36' (11.0 m)

WHIRLPOOL TUB

SH

country k
24' x 13'

W
D

STORAGE

HALF WALL

OV.

F.

VAULTED

din
10'6 x 12'

COLUMN

12' x 17'
mbr

FOYER

11'6 x 14'6
liv

FIREPLACE

21' x 21'
two-car
garage

RAILING

VERANDAH

First Floor
1,404 sq. ft.

Porches Bring Outdoor Living In

Features

- 2,500 total square feet of living area

- Master bedroom has its own separate wing with front porch, double walk-in closets, private bath and access to back porch and patio

- Large unfinished gameroom on the second floor has an additional 359 square feet of living area

- Living area is oversized and has a fireplace

- 3 bedrooms, 3 baths

- Basement, slab or crawl space foundation, please specify when ordering

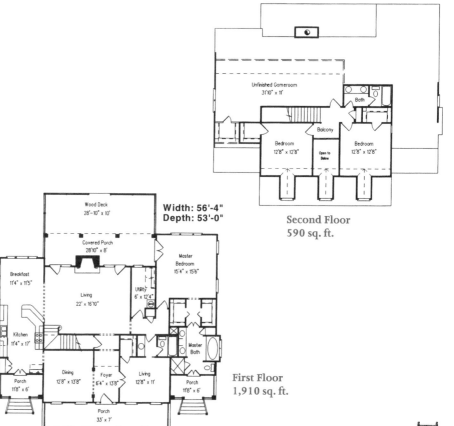

Width: 56'-4"
Depth: 53'-0"

Second Floor
590 sq. ft.

First Floor
1,910 sq. ft.

Wonderful Victorian Styling

Features

- 1,971 total square feet of living area
- Great room, kitchen and breakfast area unite to provide a central living space
- Unique parlor offers place for conversation off the dining area
- Deluxe master bedroom with walk-in closet and sunny master bath
- 3 bedrooms, 2 1/2 baths, optional 2-car garage
- Basement foundation

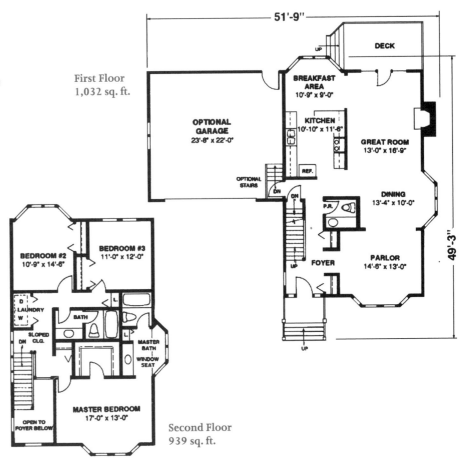

First Floor
1,032 sq. ft.

51'-9"

49'-3"

DECK

UP

BREAKFAST AREA
10'-9" x 9'-0"

OPTIONAL GARAGE
23'-8" x 22'-0"

KITCHEN
10'-10" x 11'-6"

GREAT ROOM
13'-0" x 16'-9"

REF.

OPTIONAL STAIRS

DN

DN

DINING
13'-4" x 10'-0"

P.R.

UP

FOYER

PARLOR
14'-6" x 13'-0"

UP

BEDROOM #2
10'-9" x 14'-6"

BEDROOM #3
11'-0" x 12'-0"

D
LAUNDRY
W

BATH

L

SLOPED CLG.
DN

L

MASTER BATH

WINDOW SEAT

MASTER BEDROOM
17'-0" x 13'-0"

OPEN TO FOYER BELOW

Second Floor
939 sq. ft.

Elaborate Stonework Adds Charm

Features

- 2,560 total square feet of living area
- See-through fireplace surrounded with shelving warms both the family and living rooms
- Tall ceilings in living areas
- Bedrooms maintain privacy
- 4 bedrooms, 3 baths, 3-car side entry garage
- Slab foundation

Width: 79'-3"
Depth: 60'-0"

© David C. Lutz

Comfortable Family Living

Features

- 2,097 total square feet of living area
- Formal living room connects with the dining room, perfect for entertaining
- Elegant two-story foyer
- Spacious entry off the garage is near the bath and laundry area
- Family room is warmed by a cozy fireplace
- 4 bedrooms, 2 1/2 baths, 2-car side entry garage
- Basement foundation

Width: 46'-0"
Depth: 49'-2"

First Floor
1,141 sq. ft.

GARAGE
21'8 x 21'4

DIN
10' x 11'

FAM RM
13'4 x 18'

SNACK BAR

DW

KIT
12' x 12'6

DIN RM
11' x 12'

PANTRY

Entry

LIV RM
14' x 13'6

Laun

Lav

two story
FOYER

Covered Entry

MBATH

WI Closet

MBR
13' x 13'6

BR 2
10' x 10'

BATH 2

BR 3
10' x 10'

Balcony

BR 4
14' x 9'9

Foyer Below

Second Floor
956 sq. ft.

Stylish Ranch With Rustic Charm

Features

- 1,344 total square feet of living area
- Family/dining room has sliding glass doors to the outdoors
- Master bedroom features a private bath
- Hall bath includes a double-bowl vanity for added convenience
- U-shaped kitchen features a large pantry and laundry area
- 3 bedrooms, 2 baths, 2-car garage
- Crawl space foundation, drawings also include basement and slab foundations

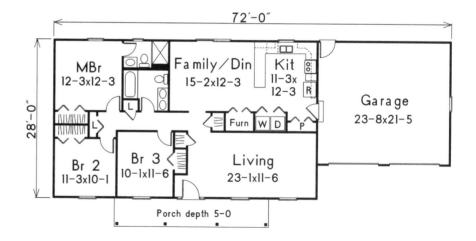

72'-0"

28'-0"

MBr
12-3x12-3

Family/Din
15-2x12-3

Kit
11-3x
12-3

Garage
23-8x21-5

Furn W D P

Br 2
11-3x10-1

Br 3
10-1x11-6

Living
23-1x11-6

Porch depth 5-0

Victorian Detailing Adds Interest

Features

- 1,662 total square feet of living area
- Activity area becomes an ideal place for family gatherings
- Well-organized kitchen includes lots of storage space, a walk-in pantry and plenty of cabinetry
- The rear of the home features a versatile back porch for dining or relaxing
- Master bedroom has a bay window and private balcony
- 2 bedrooms, 1 1/2 baths
- Basement foundation

Second Floor
570 sq. ft.

BEDROOM 2
10'-8" x 10'-0"

BATH

L

DN.

L

MASTER BEDROOM
13'-0" x 14'-7"

BALCONY

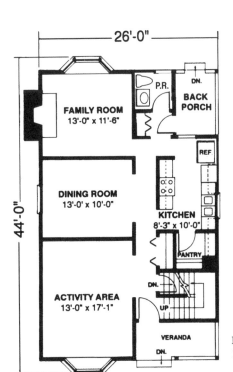

26'-0"

44'-0"

FAMILY ROOM
13'-0" x 11'-6"

P.R.

DN.

BACK PORCH

REF

DINING ROOM
13'-0" x 10'-0"

KITCHEN
8'-3" x 10'-0"

PANTRY

DN.

UP

ACTIVITY AREA
13'-0" x 17'-1"

VERANDA

DN.

First Floor
1,092 sq. ft.

Wrap-Around Country Porch

Features

- 1,875 total square feet of living area

- Country-style exterior with wrap-around porch and dormers

- Large second floor bedrooms share a dressing area and bath

- Master bedroom includes a bay window, walk-in closet, dressing area and bath

- 3 bedrooms, 2 baths, 2-car side entry garage

- Crawl space foundation, drawings also include basement and slab foundations

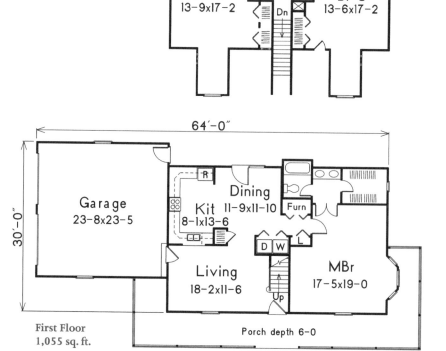

Second Floor
820 sq. ft.

Br 2
13-9x17-2

Br 3
13-6x17-2

Dn

64'-0"

30'-0"

Garage
23-8x23-5

Dining
11-9x11-10

Kit
8-1x13-6

Furn

Living
18-2x11-6

MBr
17-5x19-0

D W

Up

First Floor
1,055 sq. ft.

Porch depth 6-0

Well-Designed Home Makes Great Use Of Space

Features

- 1,948 total square feet of living area
- Family room offers warmth with an oversized fireplace and rustic beamed ceiling
- Fully-appointed kitchen extends into the family room
- Practical mud room is adjacent to the kitchen
- 3 bedrooms, 2 1/2 baths
- Basement foundation, drawings also include crawl space foundation

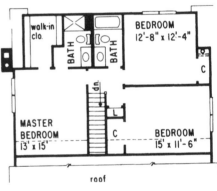

Second Floor
868 sq. ft.

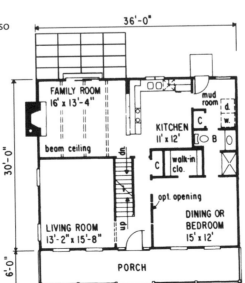

First Floor
1,080 sq. ft.

Inviting Porches On All Sides

Features

- 1,618 total square feet of living area
- Wrap-around porch offers a covered passageway to the garage
- Dramatic two-story entry, with balcony above and staircase provide an expansive feel with an added decorative oval window
- Dazzling kitchen features walk-in pantry, convenient laundry and covered rear porch
- 3 bedrooms, 2 1/2 baths, 1-car garage
- Basement foundation

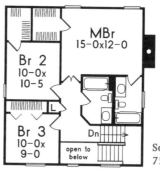

MBr 15-0x12-0

Br 2 10-0x 10-5

Br 3 10-0x 9-0

Dn

open to below

Second Floor 754 sq. ft.

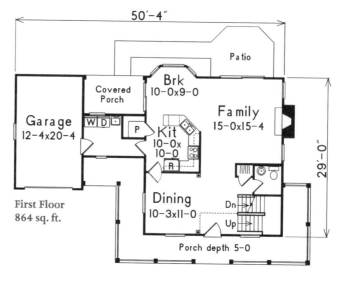

50'-4"

Patio

Garage 12-4x20-4

Covered Porch

W D

P

Brk 10-0x9-0

Kit 10-0x 10-0

Family 15-0x15-4

R

29'-0"

Dining 10-3x11-0

Dn

Up

First Floor 864 sq. ft.

Porch depth 5-0

Plantation-Style With Elegant Porch

Features

- 2,590 total square feet of living area
- Large formal entry adjacent to the dining room has a coffered ceiling
- Great room features skylights, a built-in bookcase and a corner fireplace
- Kitchen includes a large island eating bar adjacent to the bayed breakfast room
- 9' ceilings on the first floor
- Salon bath contains two walk-in closets, linen closet, double vanity, stepped tub and a separate shower
- Optional second floor has an additional 453 square feet of living area
- 3 bedrooms, 2 1/2 baths, 2-car side entry garage
- Slab or crawl space foundation, please specify when ordering

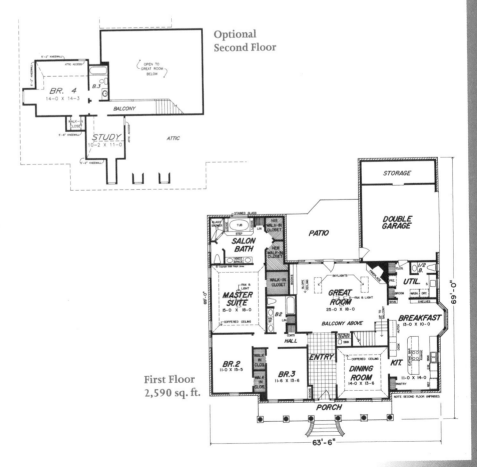

Optional
Second Floor

First Floor
2,590 sq. ft.

Dramatic Country Architecture In A Walk-Out Atrium

Features

- 2,100 total square feet of living area

- A large courtyard with stone walls, lantern columns and covered porch welcomes you into open spaces

- The great room features a stone fireplace, built-in shelves, vaulted ceiling and atrium with dramatic staircase and a two and a half story window wall

- Two walk-in closets, vaulted ceiling with plant shelf and a luxury bath adorn the master bedroom suite

- 1,391 square feet of optional living area on the lower level with family room, walk-in bar, sitting area, bedroom #3 and a bath

- 2 bedrooms, 2 baths, 3-car side entry garage

- Walk-out basement foundation

First Floor
2,100 sq. ft.

Optional
Lower Level

To order call toll-free 1-800-DREAM HOME or visit www.houseplansandmore.com

Open Format For Easy Living

Features

- 2,282 total square feet of living area

- Living and dining rooms combine to create a large, convenient entertaining area that includes a fireplace

- Comfortable covered porch allows access from secondary bedrooms

- Second floor game room overlooks foyer and includes a full bath

- Kitchen and breakfast areas are surrounded by mullioned windows

- 3 bedrooms, 3 baths, 2-car detached garage

- Slab foundation, drawings also include crawl space foundation

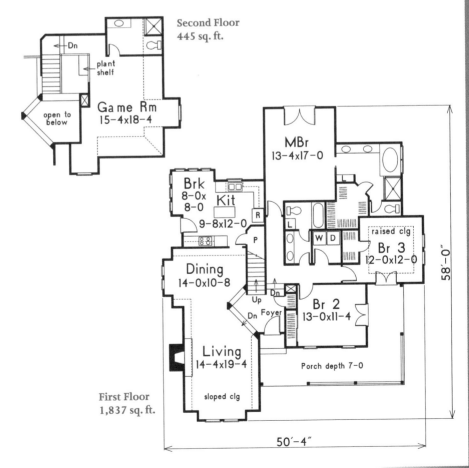

Second Floor
445 sq. ft.

Dn

plant shelf

Game Rm
15-4x18-4

open to below

MBr
13-4x17-0

Brk
8-0x 8-0

Kit
9-8x12-0

R

raised clg

Br 3
12-0x12-0

L

W D

Dining
14-0x10-8

P

Up Dn

58'-0"

Dn Foyer

Br 2
13-0x11-4

Living
14-4x19-4

Porch depth 7-0

First Floor
1,837 sq. ft.

sloped clg

50'-4"

Simply Country

Features

- 1,668 total square feet of living area
- Simple, but attractively styled ranch home is perfect for a narrow lot
- Front entry porch flows into the foyer which connects to the living room
- Garage entrance to home leads to the kitchen through the mud room/laundry area
- U-shaped kitchen opens to the dining area and family room
- Three bedrooms are situated at the rear of the home with two full baths
- Master bedroom has a walk-in closet
- 3 bedrooms, 2 baths, 2-car garage
- Partial basement/crawl space foundation, drawings also include crawl space and slab foundations

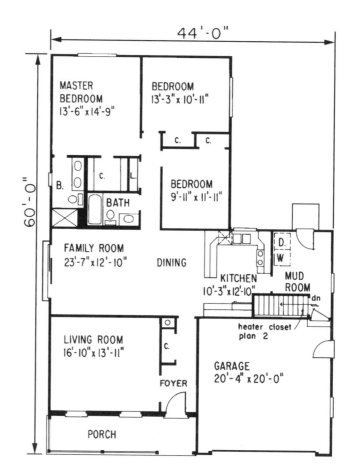

To order call toll-free 1-800-DREAM HOME or visit www.houseplansandmore.com

Spacious Styling For Gracious Living

Features

- 3,050 total square feet of living area

- Sunny garden room and two-way fireplace create a bright, airy living room

- Front porch is enhanced by arched transom windows and bold columns

- Sitting alcove, French door access to side patio, walk-in closets and abundant storage enhance the master bedroom

- 4 bedrooms, 3 1/2 baths, 2-car detached garage

- Slab foundation, drawings also include crawl space foundation

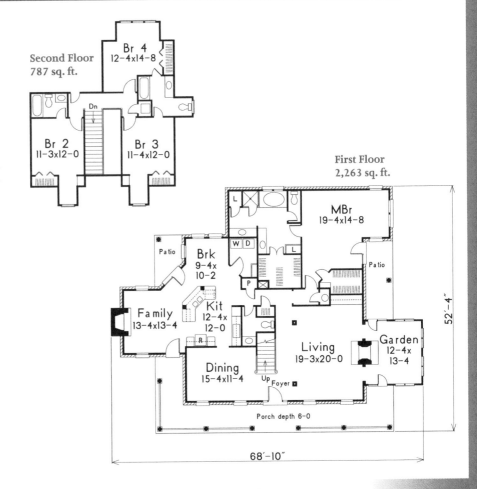

Second Floor 787 sq. ft.

Br 4 12-4x14-8

Br 2 11-3x12-0

Br 3 11-4x12-0

Dn

First Floor 2,263 sq. ft.

MBr 19-4x14-8

Patio

Patio

Brk 9-4x 10-2

W D

L

P

Family 13-4x13-4

Kit 12-4x 12-0

R

Dining 15-4x11-4

Up Foyer

Living 19-3x20-0

Garden 12-4x 13-4

Porch depth 6-0

52'-4"

68'-10"

Appealing Charming Porch

Features

- 1,643 total square feet of living area
- First floor master bedroom has a private bath, walk-in closet and easy access to the laundry closet
- Comfortable family room features a vaulted ceiling and a cozy fireplace
- Two bedrooms on the second floor share a bath
- 3 bedrooms, 2 1/2 baths, 2-car drive under garage
- Basement or crawl space foundation, please specify when ordering

Second Floor
579 sq. ft.

STORAGE

BEDROOM 3
15X12

BEDROOM 2
15X12

OPEN TO BELOW

DECK

SKYLIGHT

DINING
12x12

KITCHEN
10x12

34

MASTER BEDRM
15x13

FAMILY ROOM
18x15

First Floor
1,064 sq. ft.

38

Plan #578-053D-0007

Two-Story Foyer Adds To Country Charm

Features

- 1,922 total square feet of living area
- Varied front elevation features numerous accents
- Master bedroom suite is well-secluded with double-door entry and private bath
- Formal living and dining rooms located off the entry
- 3 bedrooms, 2 1/2 baths, 2-car garage
- Basement foundation

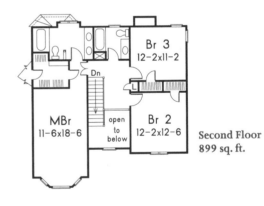

Second Floor
899 sq. ft.

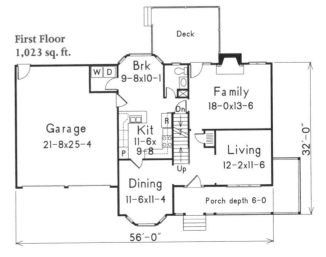

First Floor
1,023 sq. ft.

Corner Fireplace Warms The Family Room

Features

- 2,290 total square feet of living area
- Lovely master bedroom has a bayed sitting area, access to a private bath and a spacious walk-in closet
- View decorative columns upon entering the formal living and dining rooms
- Bonus room above the garage has an additional 234 square feet of living area
- 3 bedrooms, 2 1/2 baths, 2-car side entry garage
- Basement foundation

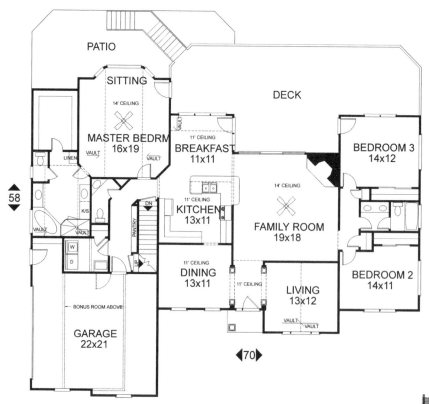

Plan #578-062D-0038

Fireplaces In Family And Living Rooms

Features

- 2,170 total square feet of living area
- Energy efficient home with 2" x 6" exterior walls
- Barrel vaulted two-story entrance foyer leads to an angled gallery
- Kitchen features a sunny bay window
- Bonus room with private staircase has an additional 390 square feet of living area
- 3 bedrooms, 2 1/2 baths, 2-car garage
- Basement foundation

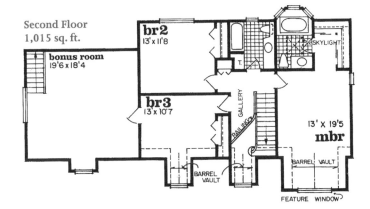

Second Floor
1,015 sq. ft.

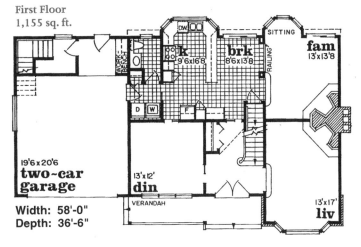

First Floor
1,155 sq. ft.

Width: 58'-0"
Depth: 36'-6"

To order call toll-free 1-800-DREAM HOME or visit www.houseplansandmore.com

187

Classic Rural Farmhouse

Features

- 2,363 total square feet of living area
- Covered porches provide outdoor seating areas
- Corner fireplace becomes focal point of family room
- Kitchen features island cooktop and adjoining nook
- Energy efficient home with 2" x 6" exterior walls
- 3 bedrooms, 2 1/2 baths, 2-car garage
- Partial basement/crawl space foundation

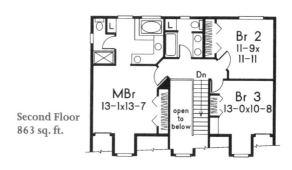

Second Floor
863 sq. ft.

MBr
13-1x13-7

Br 2
11-9x 11-11

Br 3
13-0x10-8

open to below

Dn

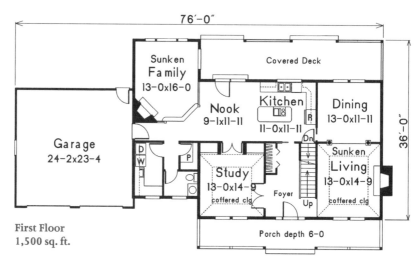

76'-0"

36'-0"

Sunken Family
13-0x16-0

Covered Deck

Nook
9-1x11-11

Kitchen
11-0x11-11

Dining
13-0x11-11

Garage
24-2x23-4

Study
13-0x14-9
coffered clg

Living
13-0x14-9
coffered clg

Sunken

Foyer

Up

Dn

First Floor
1,500 sq. ft.

Porch depth 6-0

To order call toll-free 1-800-DREAM HOME or visit www.houseplansandmore.com

Front Porch Creates Cozy Feeling

Features

- 1,786 total square feet of living area
- Galley-style kitchen is compact, but efficient
- Bay-shaped dining area is flooded with sunlight
- Living room is the center of this home making it an ideal gathering place
- Optional second floor has an additional 262 square feet of living area
- 3 bedrooms, 2 baths, 2-car garage
- Slab foundation

First Floor
1,786 sq. ft.

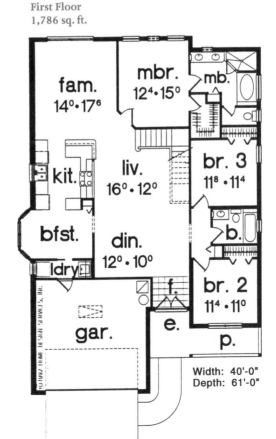

fam.
14⁰·17⁶

mbr.
12⁴·15⁰

mb.

kit.

liv.
16⁰·12⁰

br. 3
11⁸·11⁴

bfst.

din.
12⁰·10⁰

b.

ldry

br. 2
11⁴·11⁰

gar.

f.

e.

p.

Width: 40'-0"
Depth: 61'-0"

loft
11⁸·20⁰

Optional
Second Floor

© 1992 HOME DESIGN SERVICES, INC.

A Home With A Terrific Feeling

Features

- 2,202 total square feet of living area
- 9' ceilings on the first floor
- Guest bedroom located on the first floor for convenience could easily be converted to an office area
- Large kitchen with oversized island overlooks dining area
- 5 bedrooms, 3 full baths, 3 half baths, 2-car drive under garage
- Partial basement/crawl space foundation

Width: 34'-0"   Depth: 46'-0"

First Floor
1,174 sq. ft.

Second Floor
1,028 sq. ft.

Inviting, Cheerful Home

Features

- 2,554 total square feet of living area
- Dual fireplaces enhance family and living rooms
- All three bedrooms include spacious walk-in closets
- Double-bowl vanity in master bath for convenience
- 4 bedrooms, 2 1/2 baths, 2-car garage
- Basement foundation, drawings also include crawl space and slab foundations

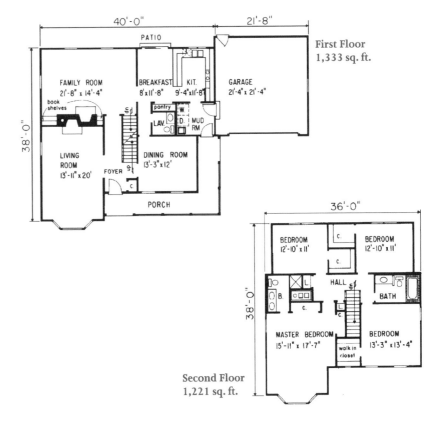

First Floor
1,333 sq. ft.

Second Floor
1,221 sq. ft.

Striking Double-Arched Entry

Features

- 3,494 total square feet of living area
- Majestic two-story foyer opens into the living and dining rooms, both framed by arched columns
- Balcony overlooks the large living area featuring French doors to a covered porch
- Luxurious master bedroom
- Convenient game room supports lots of activities
- 4 bedrooms, 3 1/2 baths, 3-car side entry garage
- Slab foundation, drawings also include crawl space foundation

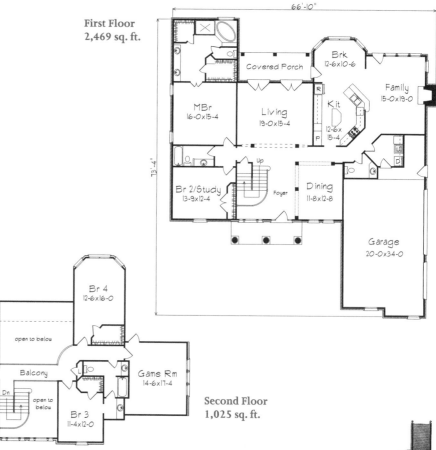

First Floor
2,469 sq. ft.

66'-10"

Covered Porch

Brk
12-6x10-6

Family
15-0x19-0

MBr
16-0x15-4

Living
19-0x15-4

Kit
12-6x
15-4

Br 2/Study
13-9x12-4

Foyer

Dining
11-8x12-8

Garage
20-0x34-0

13'-4"

Br 4
12-6x16-0

open to below

Balcony

Game Rm
14-6x17-4

Dn

open to below

Br 3
11-4x12-0

Second Floor
1,025 sq. ft.

Wrap-Around Country-Style Home

Features

- 2,449 total square feet of living area
- Striking living area features fireplace flanked with windows, cathedral ceiling and balcony
- First floor master bedroom has twin walk-in closets and large linen storage
- Dormers add space for desks or seats
- 3 bedrooms, 2 1/2 baths, 2-car detached garage
- Slab foundation, drawings also include crawl space foundation

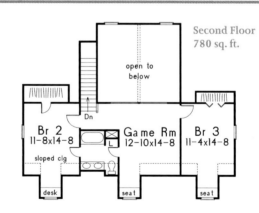

Second Floor
780 sq. ft.

open to below

Dn

Br 2
11-8x14-8
sloped clg
desk

Game Rm
12-10x14-8
seat

Br 3
11-4x14-8
seat

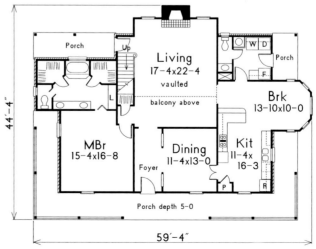

First Floor
1,669 sq. ft.

Porch

Up

Living
17-4x22-4
vaulted
balcony above

W D

Porch

F

Brk
13-10x10-0

44'-4"

MBr
15-4x16-8

Dining
11-4x13-0
Foyer

Kit
11-4x
16-3

P

R

Porch depth 5-0

59'-4"

Dramatic Interior With Country Charm

Features

- 2,409 total square feet of living area
- Double two-story bay windows adorn the wrap-around porch
- A grand-scale foyer features a 40' view through morning room
- An eating area, fireplace, palladian windows, vaulted ceiling and balcony overlook are among the many amenities of the spacious morning room
- Two large second floor bedrooms and an enormous third bedroom enjoy two walk-in closets, a bay window and access to hall bath
- 4 bedrooms, 2 1/2 baths, 2-car side entry garage with storage
- Basement foundation

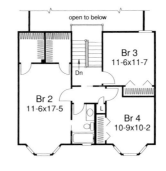

open to below

Br 3
11-6x11-7

Dn

Br 2
11-6x17-5

Br 4
10-9x10-2

Second Floor
799 sq. ft.

64'-4"

Morning Rm
25-4x14-8
vaulted

Patio

Laundry

Storage

Kit
13-8x12-8

W D

49'-0"

MBr
12-5x15-0
vaulted

Study
11-6x11-4

Entry

Dining
11-6x11-4
tray clg.

Garage
20-4x30-4

Dn   Up

Porch depth 6-0

First Floor
1,610 sq. ft.

To order call toll-free 1-800-DREAM HOME or visit www.houseplansandmore.com

Style Creates The Feel Of A Great Home

Features

- 2,920 total square feet of living area
- A large, cheerful and private sitting room connects the master bedroom to the master bath
- A cozy den features a unique angled entrance for interest
- The open kitchen flows into the breakfast nook for maximum convenience
- Second floor bonus room is included in the square footage
- 3 bedrooms, 2 1/2 baths, 3-car garage
- Crawl space foundation

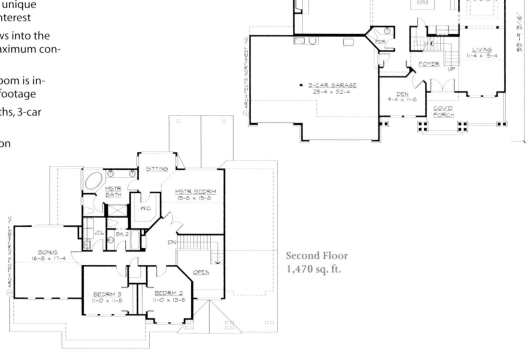

First Floor
1,450 sq. ft.

Second Floor
1,470 sq. ft.

An Enhancement To Any Neighborhood

Features

- 1,440 total square feet of living area
- Foyer adjoins massive-sized great room with sloping ceiling and tall masonry fireplace
- The kitchen connects to the spacious dining room and features a pass-through to the breakfast bar
- Master bedroom enjoys a private bath and two closets
- An oversized two-car side entry garage offers plenty of storage for bicycles, lawn equipment, etc.
- 3 bedrooms, 2 baths, 2-car side entry garage
- Basement foundation, drawings also include crawl space and slab foundations

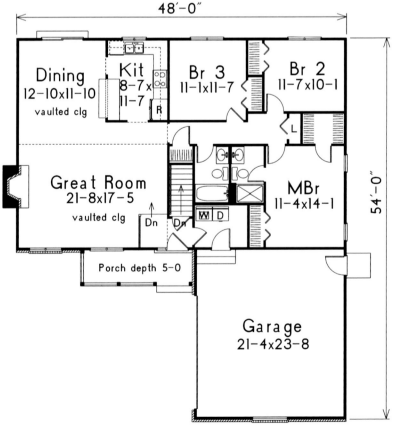

Affordable Two-Story Has It All

Features

- 1,308 total square feet of living area
- Multi-gabled facade and elongated porch create a pleasing country appeal
- Large dining room with bay window and view to rear patio opens to a full-functional kitchen with snack bar
- An attractive U-shaped stair with hall overlook leads to the second floor
- 3 bedrooms, 1 full bath, 2 half baths, 2-car garage
- Basement foundation

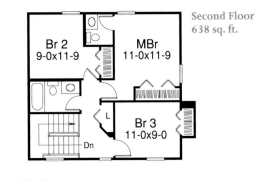

Second Floor 638 sq. ft.

Br 2 9-0x11-9

MBr 11-0x11-9

Br 3 11-0x9-0

Dn

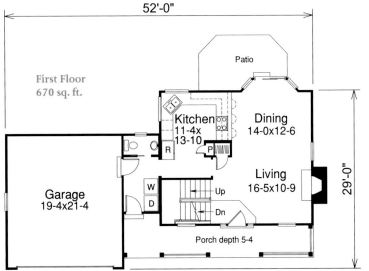

52'-0"

Patio

First Floor 670 sq. ft.

Kitchen 11-4x 13-10

Dining 14-0x12-6

Living 16-5x10-9

29'-0"

Garage 19-4x21-4

W D

Up

Dn

Porch depth 5-4

Cozy Front Porch

Features

- 1,328 total square feet of living area
- Wall of windows brightens the living room
- Open living is created on the first floor with the kitchen and dining area combining with the living room
- Master bedroom is located on the second floor for privacy
- 3 bedrooms, 2 baths
- Basement, crawl space or slab foundation, please specify when ordering

Second Floor
315 sq. ft.

Open to Living Room Below

Flat Clg @ 7'-6"
Master Br
12-0 x 13-4

DN

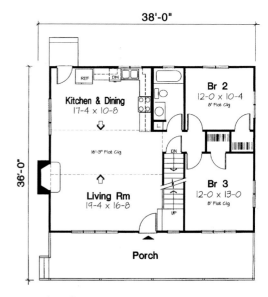

38'-0"

36'-0"

REF   DW

Kitchen & Dining
17-4 x 10-8

16'-3" Flat Clg

Living Rm
19-4 x 16-8

Br 2
12-0 x 10-4
8' Flat Clg

DN

UP

Br 3
12-0 x 13-0
8' Flat Clg

Porch

First Floor
1,013 sq. ft.

Rear View

Country-Style Home With Inviting Covered Porch

Features

- 2,567 total square feet of living area
- Breakfast room has a 12' cathedral ceiling and a bayed area full of windows
- Great room has a stepped ceiling, built-in media center and a corner fireplace
- Bonus room on the second floor has an additional 300 square feet of living area
- 4 bedrooms, 3 baths, 2-car side entry garage
- Basement, crawl space or slab foundation, please specify when ordering

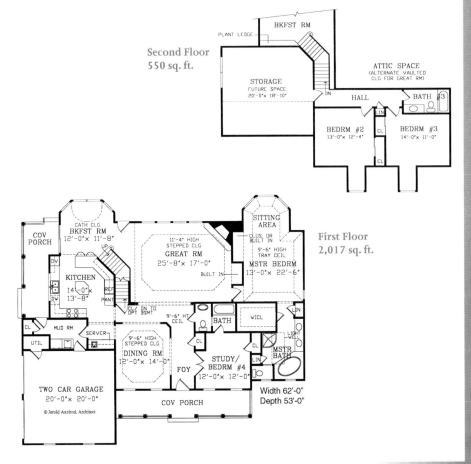

Second Floor
550 sq. ft.

First Floor
2,017 sq. ft.

Width 62'-0"
Depth 53'-0"

© Jerold Axelrod, Architect

Balcony Enjoys Spectacular Views In Atrium Home

Features

- 2,806 total square feet of living area
- Harmonious charm throughout
- Sweeping balcony and vaulted ceiling soar above spacious great room and walk-in bar
- Atrium with lower level family room is a unique touch, creating an open and airy feeling
- 4 bedrooms, 2 1/2 baths, 2-car garage
- Walk-out basement foundation

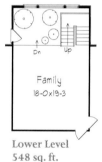

Lower Level
548 sq. ft.

First Floor
1,473 sq. ft.

Second Floor
785 sq. ft.

Rear View

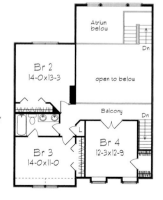

Stone Highlights This Victorian Home

Features

- 1,938 total square feet of living area
- Cozy office space on the first floor
- 9' ceilings on the first floor
- Energy efficient home with 2" x 6" exterior walls
- 3 bedrooms, 2 1/2 baths, 2-car side entry garage
- Basement foundation

Second Floor
894 sq. ft.

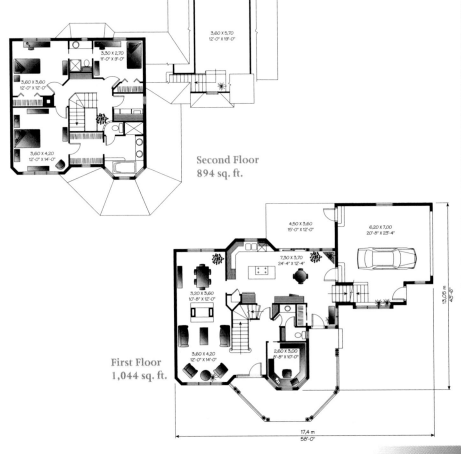

First Floor
1,044 sq. ft.

Victorian With First Floor Master Suite

Features

- 2,696 total square feet of living area
- Great room features a corner design fireplace
- Dining room has a 14' ceiling and beautiful sweeping views onto the curved front porch
- The second floor includes a turreted recreation room, two bedrooms and a full bath
- 4 bedrooms, 2 1/2 baths, 2-car side entry garage
- Basement, crawl space or slab foundation, please specify when ordering

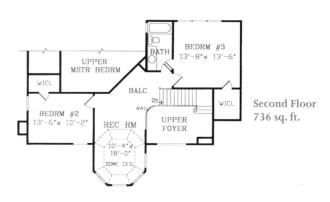

Second Floor
736 sq. ft.

Dining Room

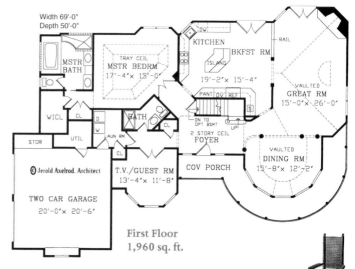

First Floor
1,960 sq. ft.

Large Corner Deck Lends Way To Outdoor Living Area

Features

- 1,283 total square feet of living area
- Vaulted breakfast room has sliding doors that open onto deck
- Kitchen features convenient corner sink and pass-through to dining room
- Open living atmosphere in dining area and great room
- Vaulted great room features a fireplace
- 3 bedrooms, 2 baths, 2-car garage
- Basement foundation

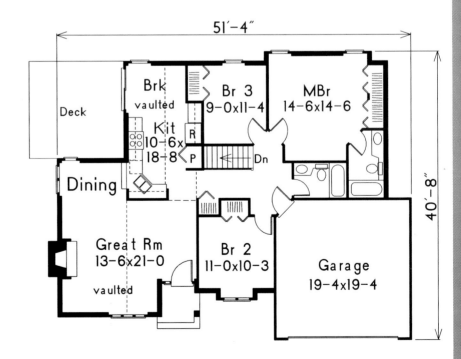

Distinct Country Look And Feel

Features

- 2,253 total square feet of living area
- Great room is joined by the rear covered porch
- Secluded parlor provides area for peace and quiet or a private office
- Sloped ceiling adds drama to the master bedroom
- Great room, kitchen and breakfast area combine for a large open living area
- 3 bedrooms, 2 1/2 baths, 2-car garage
- Basement foundation

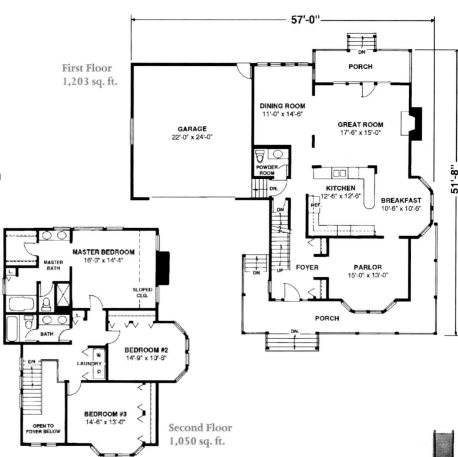

First Floor
1,203 sq. ft.

Second Floor
1,050 sq. ft.

Unique Features Create Style And Sophistication

Features

- 2,772 total square feet of living area
- 10' ceilings on the first floor and 9' ceilings on the second floor create a spacious atmosphere
- Large bay windows accent study and master bath
- Breakfast room features a dramatic curved wall with direct view and access onto porch
- 4 bedrooms, 3 1/2 baths, 2-car side entry garage
- Slab foundation

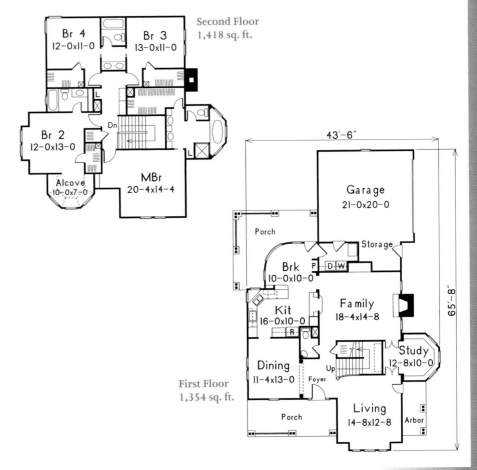

Second Floor
1,418 sq. ft.

Br 4
12-0x11-0

Br 3
13-0x11-0

Br 2
12-0x13-0

Dn

Alcove
10-0x7-0

MBr
20-4x14-4

First Floor
1,354 sq. ft.

43'-6"

65'-8"

Garage
21-0x20-0

Porch

Storage

Brk
10-0x10-0

P D W

Kit
16-0x10-0

Family
18-4x14-8

R

Dining
11-4x13-0

Up

Study
12-8x10-0

Foyer

Living
14-8x12-8

Porch

Arbor

Embracing The Sun

Features

- 1,850 total square feet of living area
- Large living room with fireplace is illuminated by three second story skylights
- Living and dining rooms are separated by a low wall while the dining room and kitchen are separated by a snack bar creating a spacious atmosphere
- Master bedroom has a huge bath with double vanity and large walk-in closet
- Two second floor bedrooms share a uniquely designed bath with skylight
- 3 bedrooms, 2 1/2 baths, 2-car garage
- Basement foundation

BEDROOM #2
10'-0" x 14'-7"

BATH 2 SKYLIGHT

BEDROOM #3
12'-0" x 14'-7"

DN.

Second Floor
630 sq. ft.

OPEN TO LIVING ROOM BELOW

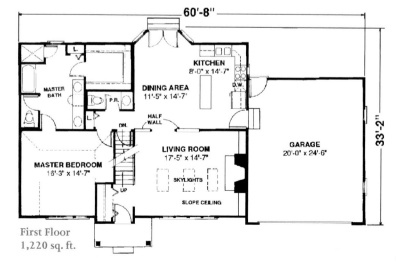

60'-8"

KITCHEN
8'-0" x 14'-7"

DINING AREA
11'-5" x 14'-7"

D.W.

MASTER BATH

P.R.

HALF WALL

DN.

33'-2"

LIVING ROOM
17'-5" x 14'-7"

GARAGE
20'-0" x 24'-6"

MASTER BEDROOM
16'-3" x 14'-7"

SKYLIGHTS

UP

SLOPE CEILING

First Floor
1,220 sq. ft.

To order call toll-free 1-800-DREAM HOME or visit www.houseplansandmore.com

Two-Story Living Room

Features

- 2,194 total square feet of living area
- Energy efficient home with 2" x 6" exterior walls
- A convenient laundry drop on the second floor leads to the centrally located utility room
- Both second floor bedrooms have large closets and their own bath
- Bonus room on the second floor has an additional 352 square feet of living space
- 3 bedrooms, 3 1/2 baths, 2-car side entry garage
- Crawl space foundation, drawings also include slab and basement foundations

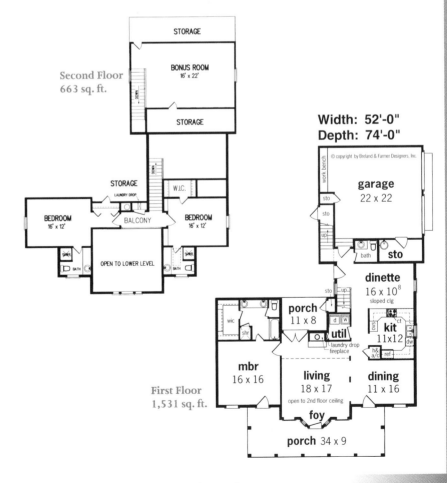

Second Floor
663 sq. ft.

Width: 52'-0"
Depth: 74'-0"

First Floor
1,531 sq. ft.

Five Bedroom Home Embraces Large Family

Features

- 2,828 total square feet of living area
- Popular wrap-around porch gives home country charm
- Secluded, oversized family room with vaulted ceiling and wet bar features many windows
- Any chef would be delighted to cook in this smartly designed kitchen with island and corner windows
- Spectacular master bedroom and bath
- 5 bedrooms, 3 1/2 baths, 2-car side entry garage
- Basement foundation, drawings also include crawl space and slab foundations

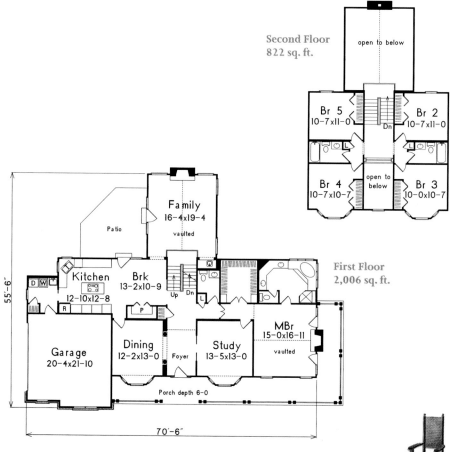

Second Floor
822 sq. ft.

open to below

Br 5
10-7x11-0

Br 2
10-7x11-0

Dn

open to below

Br 4
10-7x10-7

Br 3
10-0x10-7

First Floor
2,006 sq. ft.

Family
16-4x19-4
vaulted

Patio

Kitchen
12-10x12-8

Brk
13-2x10-9

Up

Dn

D W

R

P

MBr
15-0x16-11
vaulted

Garage
20-4x21-10

Dining
12-2x13-0

Foyer

Study
13-5x13-0

Porch depth 6-0

55'-6"

70'-6"

Comfortable Living At Its Finest

Features

- 3,013 total square feet of living area
- Oversized rooms throughout
- Kitchen features an island sink, large pantry and opens into the breakfast room with a sunroom feel
- Large family room with fireplace accesses the rear deck and front porch
- Master bedroom includes a large walk-in closet and private deluxe bath
- 4 bedrooms, 3 1/2 baths, 2-car side entry garage
- Basement foundation

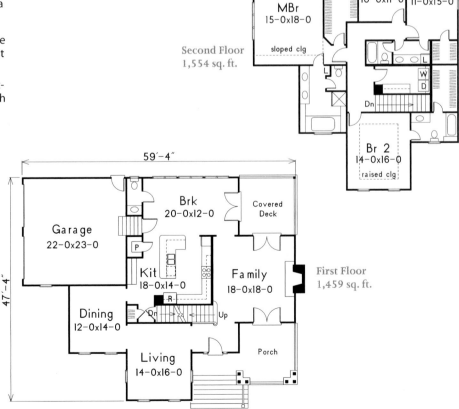

Second Floor
1,554 sq. ft.

MBr
15-0x18-0
sloped clg

Br 4
10-0x11-0

Br 3
11-0x15-0

W
D

Dn

Br 2
14-0x16-0
raised clg

First Floor
1,459 sq. ft.

59'-4"

47'-4"

Garage
22-0x23-0

Brk
20-0x12-0

Covered Deck

P

Kit
18-0x14-0

Family
18-0x18-0

R

Dining
12-0x14-0

Dn

Up

Living
14-0x16-0

Porch

Central Living Area Keeps Bedrooms Private

Features

- 1,546 total square feet of living area
- Spacious, open rooms create a casual atmosphere
- Master bedroom is secluded for privacy
- Dining room features a large bay window
- Kitchen and dinette combine for added space and include access to the outdoors
- Large laundry room includes a convenient sink
- 3 bedrooms, 2 baths, 2-car garage
- Basement foundation

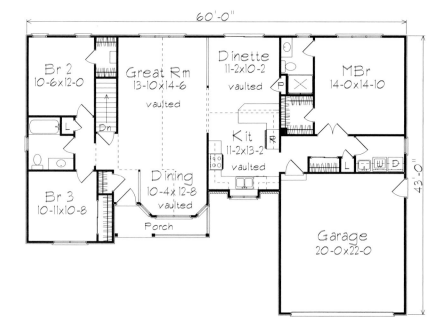

Fireplaces Accent Gathering Rooms

Features

- 2,659 total square feet of living area
- 9' ceilings throughout the first floor
- Balcony overlooks the large family room
- Private first floor master bedroom features two walk-in closets, a sloped ceiling and a luxury bath
- Double French doors in the dining room open onto the porch
- 4 bedrooms, 3 1/2 baths, 2-car garage
- Basement foundation

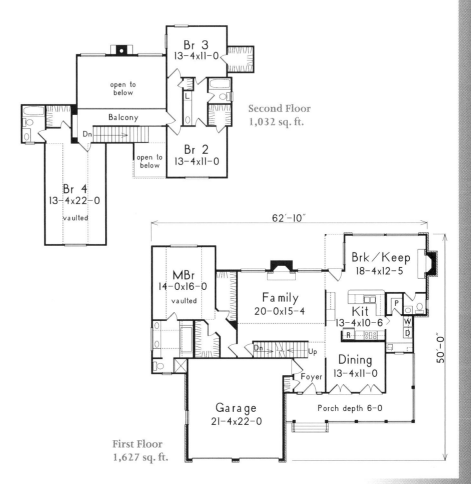

Br 3
13-4x11-0

open to below

Balcony

Dn

Br 2
13-4x11-0

open to below

Second Floor
1,032 sq. ft.

Br 4
13-4x22-0
vaulted

62'-10"

MBr
14-0x16-0
vaulted

Family
20-0x15-4

Brk/Keep
18-4x12-5

Kit
13-4x10-6

Dn   Up

Foyer

Dining
13-4x11-0

Garage
21-4x22-0

Porch depth 6-0

50'-0"

First Floor
1,627 sq. ft.

Cozy Front Porch Welcomes Guests

Features

- 1,393 total square feet of living area
- L-shaped kitchen features a walk-in pantry, island cooktop and is convenient to the laundry room and dining area
- Master bedroom features a large walk-in closet and private bath with separate tub and shower
- Convenient storage/coat closet in hall
- View to the patio from the dining area
- 3 bedrooms, 2 baths, 2-car detached garage
- Crawl space foundation, drawings also include slab foundation

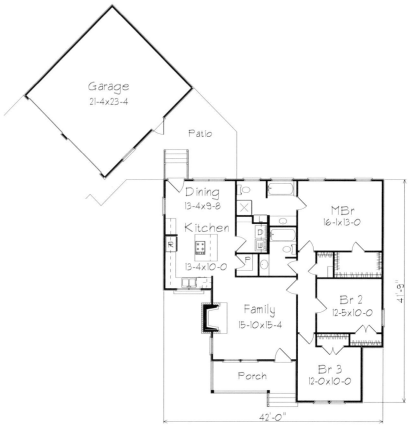

Large Great Room And Dining Area

Features

- 1,160 total square feet of living area
- U-shaped kitchen includes breakfast bar and convenient laundry area
- Master bedroom features private half bath and large closet
- Dining room has outdoor access
- Dining and great rooms combine to create an open living atmosphere
- 3 bedrooms, 1 1/2 baths
- Crawl space foundation, drawings also include basement and slab foundations

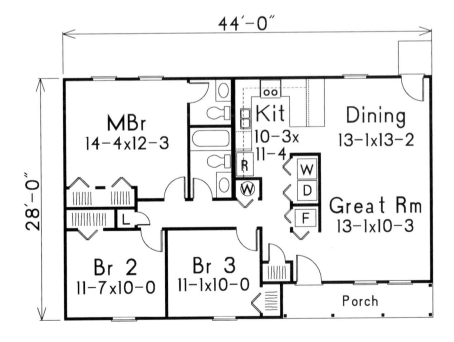

MBr 14-4x12-3

Kit 10-3x 11-4

Dining 13-1x13-2

Great Rm 13-1x10-3

Br 2 11-7x10-0

Br 3 11-1x10-0

Porch

44'-0"

28'-0"

Wonderful Family Home

Features

- 2,088 total square feet of living area
- A large and open foyer makes a welcoming entry into this home
- Vaulted master bath and a tray ceiling in the master bedroom add distinction
- A sunny bayed breakfast room is sure to be a popular place
- 3 bedrooms, 2 1/2 baths, 2-car garage
- Walk-out basement foundation

Second Floor
1,040 sq. ft.

First Floor
1,048 sq. ft.

Two-Story With Great Floor Plan

Features

- 2,460 total square feet of living area
- Living room has windows on three sides
- Kitchen contains island cooktop and built-in desk
- Enjoy a fireplace and a skylight in the spacious family room
- Bonus room on the second floor has an additional 597 square feet of living area
- 4 bedrooms, 2 1/2 baths, 3-car side entry garage
- Basement, crawl space or slab foundation, please specify when ordering

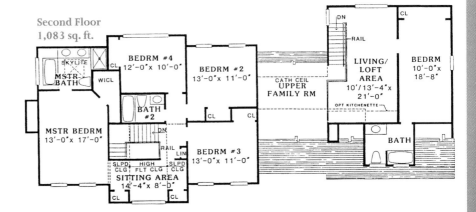

Second Floor
1,083 sq. ft.

SKYLITE
MSTR. BATH
WICL
BEDRM #4 12'-0" x 10'-0"
BEDRM #2 13'-0" x 11'-0"
BATH #2
CL
CL
MSTR BEDRM 13'-0" x 17'-0"
DN
RAIL
LIN
LIN
BEDRM #3 13'-0" x 11'-0"
SLPD CLG HIGH FLT CLG SLPD CLG
SITTING AREA 14'-4" x 8'-0"
CL
CL

DN
RAIL
CL
LIVING/ LOFT AREA 10'/13'-4" x 21'-0"
CATH CEIL UPPER FAMILY RM
OPT KITCHENETTE
BEDRM 10'-0" x 18'-8"
BATH

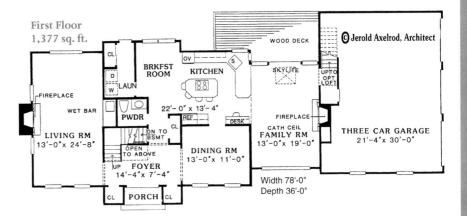

First Floor
1,377 sq. ft.

CL
FIREPLACE
WET BAR
LIVING RM 13'-0" x 24'-8"
D
W
LAUN
PWDR
OPEN TO ABOVE
UP
DN TO BSMT
FOYER 14'-4" x 7'-4"
CL
PORCH
CL
BRKFST ROOM
OV
KITCHEN 22'-0" x 13'-4"
S
REF
DESK
CL
DINING RM 13'-0" x 11'-0"
WOOD DECK
SKYLITE
FIREPLACE
CATH CEIL FAMILY RM 13'-0" x 19'-0"
UP TO OPT LOFT
© Jerold Axelrod, Architect
THREE CAR GARAGE 21'-4" x 30'-0"

Width 78'-0"
Depth 36'-0"

Surrounding Porch For Country Views

Features

- 1,428 total square feet of living area

- Large vaulted family room opens to dining area and kitchen with breakfast bar

- First floor master bedroom offers large bath, walk-in closet and nearby laundry facilities

- A spacious loft/bedroom #3 overlooking the family room and an additional bedroom and bath complement the second floor

- 3 bedrooms, 2 baths

- Basement foundation

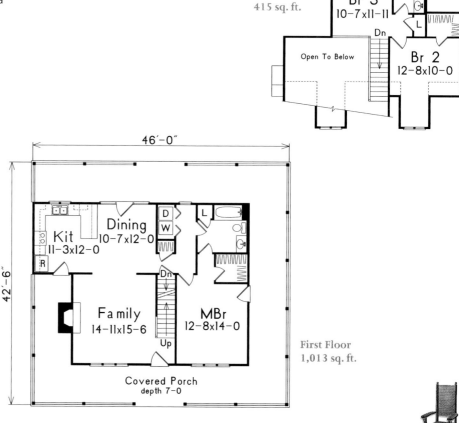

Second Floor
415 sq. ft.

Loft/ Br 3
10-7x11-11

Open To Below

Dn

Br 2
12-8x10-0

46'-0"

42'-6"

Kit
11-3x12-0

Dining
10-7x12-0

D
W

L

R

Dn

Family
14-11x15-6

Up

MBr
12-8x14-0

Covered Porch
depth 7-0

First Floor
1,013 sq. ft.

Covered Porch Highlights Home

Features

- 1,808 total square feet of living area
- Master bedroom has a walk-in closet, double vanities and a separate tub and shower
- Two second floor bedrooms share a study area and full bath
- Partially covered patio is complete with a skylight
- Side entrance opens to utility room with convenient counterspace and laundry sink
- 3 bedrooms, 2 1/2 baths, 2-car side entry garage
- Basement foundation

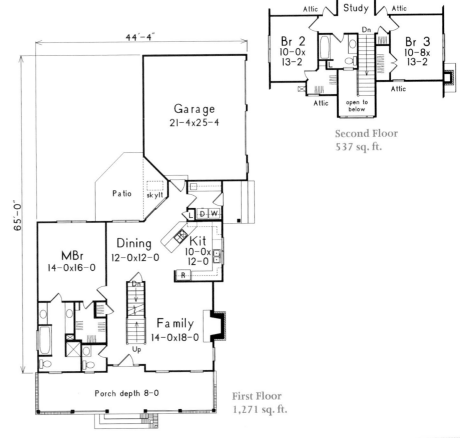

Second Floor
537 sq. ft.

First Floor
1,271 sq. ft.

Wrap-Around Porch Adds Curb Appeal

Features

- 1,840 total square feet of living area
- All bedrooms are located on the second floor for privacy
- Counter dining space is provided in the kitchen
- Formal dining room connects to the kitchen through French doors
- 4 bedrooms, 2 1/2 baths, 2-car side entry garage with shop/storage
- Basement, crawl space or slab foundation, please specify when ordering

Second Floor
826 sq. ft.

BEDROOM #3
11'-8"x11'-9"

HALL BATH   LIN   TUB/SHWR   TUB/SHWR   MSTR BATH   LIN   W.I.C.

BEDROOM #2
10'-8"x10'-0"

6'-7"

MASTER BEDROOM
11'-8"x16'-0"
(10' TRAY CLG)

SITTING AREA
(VAULTED)

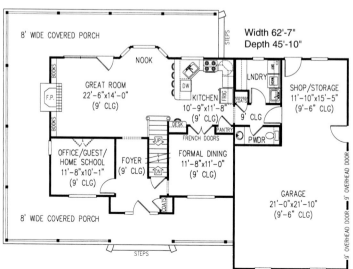

8' WIDE COVERED PORCH

NOOK

GREAT ROOM
22'-6"x14'-0"
(9' CLG)

KITCHEN
10'-9"x11'-8"
(9' CLG)

LNDRY

SHOP/STORAGE
11'-10"x15'-5"
(9'-6" CLG)

OFFICE/GUEST/
HOME SCHOOL
11'-8"x10'-1"
(9' CLG)

FOYER
(9' CLG)

FORMAL DINING
11'-8"x11'-0"
(9' CLG)

FRENCH DOORS

PWDR

GARAGE
21'-0"x21'-10"
(9'-6" CLG)

Width 62'-7"
Depth 45'-10"

8' WIDE COVERED PORCH

STEPS

First Floor
1,014 sq. ft.

Stylish And Functional

Features

- 3,046 total square feet of living area
- Secluded hearth room is tucked away from main living areas creating a cozy feeling
- Master suite maintains lots of privacy and has a luxurious feel
- Future playroom on the second floor has an additional 298 square feet of living area
- 4 bedrooms, 3 baths, 2-car side entry garage
- Slab foundation

Second Floor
754 sq. ft.

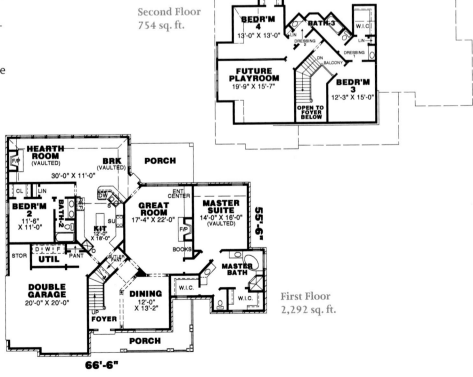

First Floor
2,292 sq. ft.

Plan #578-016D-0057

Price Code C

Angled Ranch Suited To Fit Any Lot

Features

- 1,709 total square feet of living area
- The fireplace is flanked by a media center for convenient relaxation
- Dining room features a beautiful built-in cabinet to hold fine collectibles and china
- Centrally located kitchen is a great gathering place
- 3 bedrooms, 2 1/2 baths, 2-car side entry garage
- Basement, crawl space or slab foundation, please specify when ordering

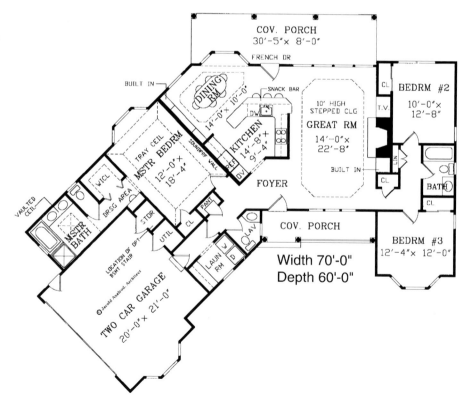

Beautiful Southern Style

Features

- 2,503 total square feet of living area
- 10' ceilings throughout the first floor
- A secondary entrance into the kitchen is convenient and casual
- First floor master bedroom has its own bath and walk-in closet
- The living room features a fireplace flanked by doors leading to the rear porch
- 4 bedrooms, 3 1/2 baths, 2-car drive under garage
- Walk-out basement foundation

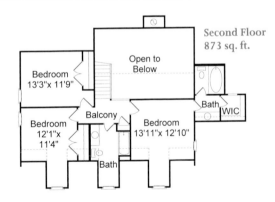

Second Floor
873 sq. ft.

Bedroom
13'3"x 11'9"

Open to
Below

Bath WIC

Bedroom
12'1"x
11'4"

Balcony

Bedroom
13'11"x 12'10"

Bath

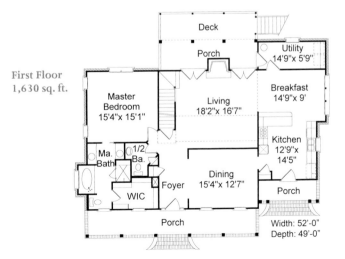

First Floor
1,630 sq. ft.

Deck

Porch

Utility
14'9"x 5'9"

Master
Bedroom
15'4"x 15'1"

Living
18'2"x 16'7"

Breakfast
14'9"x 9'

Kitchen
12'9"x
14'5"

Ma.
Bath

1/2
Ba.

Foyer

WIC

Dining
15'4"x 12'7"

Porch

Porch

Width: 52'-0"
Depth: 49'-0"

Covered Porch Adds Appeal

Features

- 1,480 total square feet of living area
- Energy efficient home with 2" x 6" exterior walls
- Cathedral ceilings in the family and dining rooms
- Master bedroom has a walk-in closet and access to bath
- 2 bedrooms, 2 baths
- Basement foundation

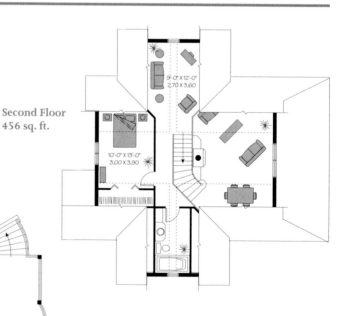

Second Floor
456 sq. ft.

9'-0" X 12'-0"
2,70 X 3,60

10'-0" X 13'-0"
3,00 X 3,90

14'-8" X 12'-0"
4,40 X 3,60

40'-0"
12,0 m

14'-0" X 22'-8"
4,20 X 6,80

14'-8" X 12'-0"
4,40 X 3,60

First Floor
1,024 sq. ft.

32'-0"
9,6 m

Multi-Roof Levels Create Attractive Colonial Home

Features

- 1,364 total square feet of living area
- A large porch and entry door with sidelights lead into a generous living room
- Well-planned U-shaped kitchen features a laundry closet, built-in pantry and open peninsula
- Master bedroom has its own bath with 4' shower
- Convenient to the kitchen is an oversized two-car garage with service door to rear
- 3 bedrooms, 2 baths, 2-car garage
- Basement foundation, drawings also include crawl space and slab foundations

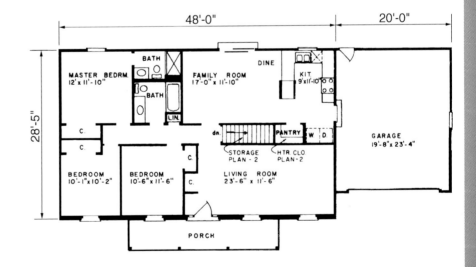

Two-Story Offers Attractive Exterior

Features

- 2,262 total square feet of living area

- Charming exterior features include large front porch, two patios, front balcony and double bay windows

- Den provides an impressive entry to a sunken family room

- Conveniently located first floor laundry

- Large master bedroom has a walk-in closet, dressing area and bath

- 3 bedrooms, 2 1/2 baths, 2-car rear entry garage

- Crawl space foundation, drawings also include basement and slab foundations

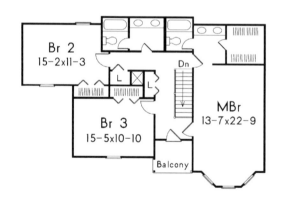

Second Floor
1,135 sq. ft.

Br 2
15-2x11-3

Dn

Br 3
15-5x10-10

MBr
13-7x22-9

Balcony

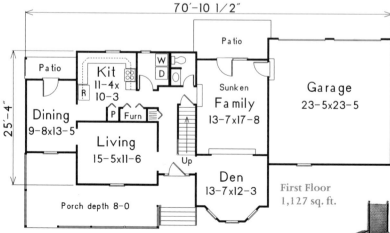

70'-10 1/2"

25'-4"

Patio

Patio

Kit
11-4x
10-3

W
D

Dining
9-8x13-5

Furn

Living
15-5x11-6

Up

Sunken
Family
13-7x17-8

Garage
23-5x23-5

Den
13-7x12-3

Porch depth 8-0

First Floor
1,127 sq. ft.

Rear View

Open Living

Features

- 1,366 total square feet of living area
- Efficient kitchen with sink and dishwasher in island
- Sloped ceiling adds interest to the master bedroom and family room
- Bay windows in breakfast nook look out to patio
- 3 bedrooms, 2 baths, 2-car garage
- Slab foundation

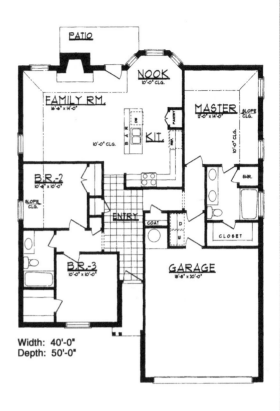

Width: 40'-0"
Depth: 50'-0"

Plan #578-045D-0003

Price Code C

Filled With Great Features

Features

- 1,958 total square feet of living area
- Wrap-around kitchen opens to a bright and cheerful breakfast area
- Master bedroom includes large walk-in closet, double-bowl vanity, garden tub and separate shower
- Foyer has an attractive plant shelf and opens into the living room
- 3 bedrooms, 2 baths, 2-car garage
- Basement foundation

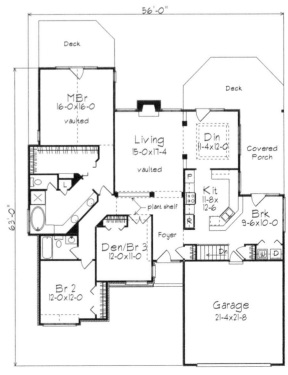

Warm And Inviting

Features

- 1,955 total square feet of living area
- Porch adds outdoor area to this design
- Dining and great rooms are visible from foyer through a series of elegant archways
- Kitchen overlooks great room and breakfast room
- 3 bedrooms, 2 baths, 2-car side entry garage
- Crawl space foundation, drawings also include slab foundation

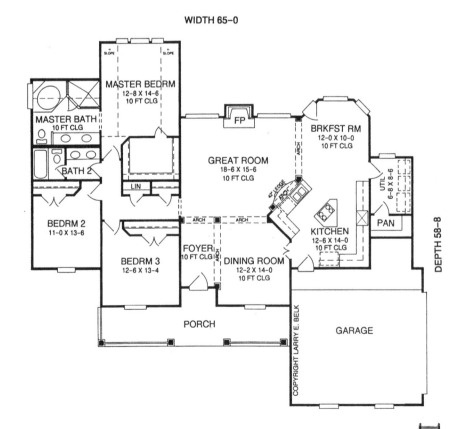

WIDTH 65-0

MASTER BEDRM
12-8 X 14-6
10 FT CLG

MASTER BATH
10 FT CLG

BATH 2

BEDRM 2
11-0 X 13-6

BEDRM 3
12-6 X 13-4

FOYER
10 FT CLG

LIN

FP

GREAT ROOM
18-6 X 15-6
10 FT CLG

BRKFST RM
12-0 X 10-0
10 FT CLG

UTIL
6-8 X 8-6

KITCHEN
12-6 X 14-0
10 FT CLG

PAN

DINING ROOM
12-2 X 14-0
10 FT CLG

PORCH

GARAGE

DEPTH 58-8

COPYRIGHT LARRY E. BELK

Plan #578-013D-0004

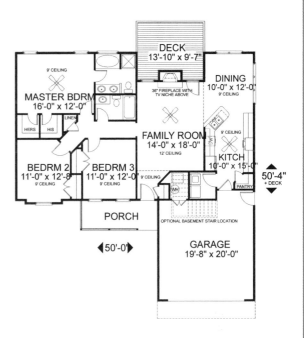

Charming Stone Accent

Features

- 1,381 total square feet of living area
- Two walk-in closets in the master bedroom allow plenty of storage possibilities
- Cozy kitchen has space for dining and plenty of cabinet storage
- Sunny dining room has windows on two walls
- 3 bedrooms, 2 baths, 2-car garage
- Slab foundation

Plan #578-069D-0005

Price Code A

Stylish Ranch

Features

- 1,267 total square feet of living area
- 10' vaulted ceiling in the great room
- Open floor plan creates a spacious feeling
- Master suite is separated from the other bedrooms for privacy
- 3 bedrooms, 2 baths, 2-car garage
- Slab or crawl space foundation, please specify when ordering

Distinctive Front Facade With Generous Porch

Features

- 2,024 total square feet of living area
- King-size master bedroom includes a sitting area
- Living room features a corner fireplace, access to the covered rear porch, 18' ceiling and a balcony
- Closet for handling recyclables
- Future bonus room has an additional 475 square feet of living area
- 3 bedrooms, 2 1/2 baths, 2-car side entry garage
- Crawl space foundation, drawings also include slab and basement foundations

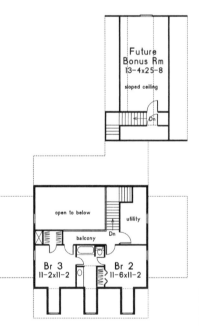

Second Floor
564 sq. ft.

Future Bonus Rm
13-4x25-8
sloped ceiling
Dn

open to below
utility
balcony
Dn
Br 3
11-2x11-2
Br 2
11-6x11-2

First Floor
1,460 sq. ft.

Garage
25-8x22-4

Deck

Storage

Porch

Living
19-6x15-6

Kit
10-8x
11-6

MBr
12-8x11-2

Dining
11-0x11-0

Eating
10-6x9-6

8-0 Porch Depth

82'-0"

54'-0"

Pleasant Covered Front Porch

Features

- 1,416 total square feet of living area
- Excellent floor plan eases traffic
- Master bedroom features private bath
- Foyer opens to both formal living room and informal great room
- Great room has access to the outdoors through sliding doors
- 3 bedrooms, 2 baths, 2-car garage
- Crawl space foundation, drawings also include basement foundation

---

Plan #578-034D-0007

Price Code C

Corner Fireplace Adds Warmth

Features

- 1,842 total square feet of living area
- Vaulted ceilings in the great room, casual and formal dining rooms make home appear much larger
- Covered entry creates a charming facade
- Compact and efficient kitchen
- 3 bedrooms, 2 baths, 2-car garage
- Basement foundation

Width: 56'-4"
Depth: 62'-0"

To order call toll-free 1-800-DREAM HOME **or visit** www.houseplansandmore.com

Large Porches Bring In The Outdoors

Features

- 3,153 total square feet of living area
- Energy efficient home with 2" x 6" exterior walls
- Master bedroom has full amenities
- Covered breezeway and front and rear porches
- Full-sized workshop and storage with garage below is a unique combination
- 4 bedrooms, 2 full baths, 2 half baths, 2-car drive under garage
- Basement foundation, drawings also include crawl space and slab foundations

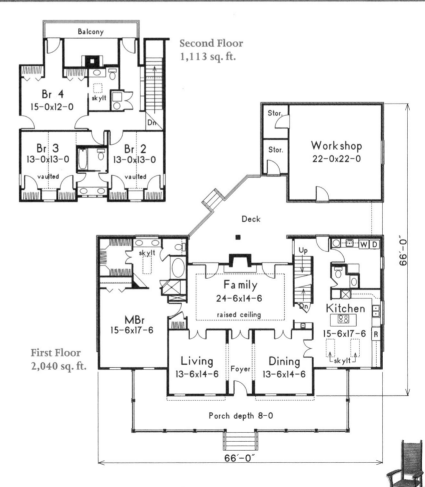

To order call toll-free **1-800-DREAM HOME** or visit www.houseplansandmore.com

Plan #578-001D-0060

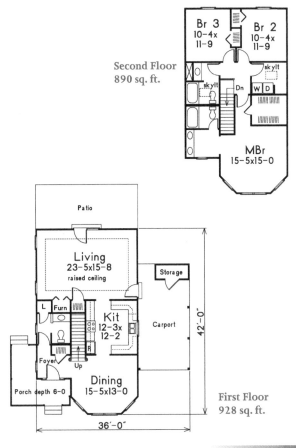

Second Floor
890 sq. ft.

Br 3
10-4x
11-9

Br 2
10-4x
11-9

skylt

skylt

W D

Dn

MBr
15-5x15-0

Patio

Living
23-5x15-8
raised ceiling

Storage

Kit
12-3x
12-2

Carport

42'-0"

Furn
L

Foyer

Up
R

Dining
15-5x13-0

Porch depth 6-0

36'-0"

First Floor
928 sq. ft.

Large Bay Graces Dining Area

Features

- 1,818 total square feet of living area
- Spacious living and dining rooms
- Master bedroom has a walk-in closet, dressing area and bath
- Convenient carport and storage area
- 3 bedrooms, 2 1/2 baths, 1-car carport
- Crawl space foundation, drawings also include basement and slab foundations

Plan #578-007D-0029

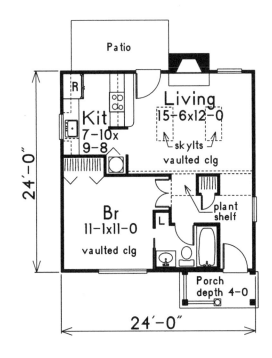

Patio

R

Kit
7-10x
9-8

Living
15-6x12-0

skylts

vaulted clg

24'-0"

Br
11-1x11-0

vaulted clg

plant shelf

L

Porch
depth 4-0

24'-0"

A Cottage With Class

Features

- 576 total square feet of living area
- Perfect country retreat features vaulted living room and entry with skylights and plant shelf above
- A double-door entry leads to the vaulted bedroom with bath access
- Kitchen offers generous storage and pass-through breakfast bar
- 1 bedroom, 1 bath
- Crawl space foundation

To order call toll-free 1-800-DREAM HOME or visit www.houseplansandmore.com

Plan #578-023D-0001

Price Code E

Outdoor Living Created By Decks And Porches

Features

- 3,149 total square feet of living area
- 10' ceilings on the first floor and 9' ceilings on the second floor
- All bedrooms include walk-in closets
- Formal living and dining rooms flank two-story foyer
- 4 bedrooms, 3 1/2 baths, 2-car detached garage
- Slab foundation, drawings also include crawl space foundation

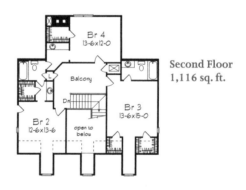

Second Floor
1,116 sq. ft.

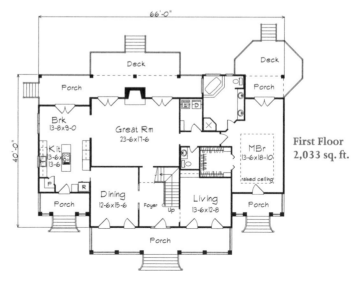

First Floor
2,033 sq. ft.

Plan #578-045D-0002

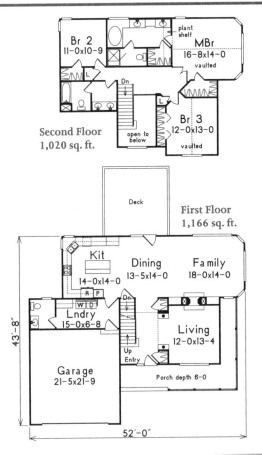

Second Floor
1,020 sq. ft.

First Floor
1,166 sq. ft.

Centralized Living

Features

- 2,186 total square feet of living area
- A see-through fireplace is the focal point in the family and living areas
- Columns grace the entrance into the living room
- Large laundry room has an adjoining half bath
- Ideal second floor bath includes a separate vanity with double sinks
- 3 bedrooms, 2 1/2 baths, 2-car garage
- Basement foundation

Plan #578-060D-0029

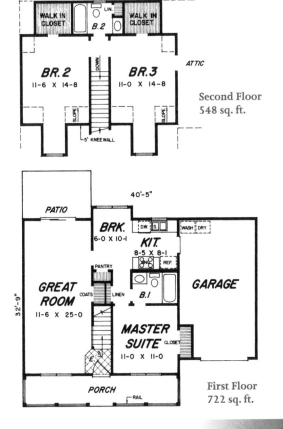

Second Floor
548 sq. ft.

First Floor
722 sq. ft.

Lovely Front Dormers

Features

- 1,270 total square feet of living area
- Convenient master suite on the first floor
- Two bedrooms on the second floor have large walk-in closets
- Sunny breakfast room has easy access to the great room and kitchen
- 3 bedrooms, 2 baths, 1-car garage
- Slab or crawl space foundation, please specify when ordering

Efficient Floor Plan

Features

- 1,609 total square feet of living area
- Sunny bay window in breakfast room
- U-shaped kitchen has a conveniently located pantry
- Spacious utility room creates easy access from the garage to the rest of the home
- Both bedrooms on the second floor feature dormers
- Family room includes plenty of space for entertaining
- 3 bedrooms, 2 1/2 baths, 2-car garage
- Slab foundation

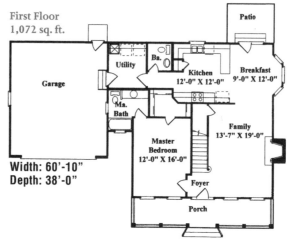

Second Floor
537 sq. ft.

Bath

Bedroom #2
12'-1" X 11'-0"

Bedroom #3
13'-6" X 11'-10"

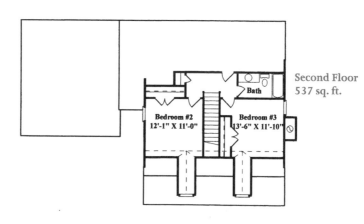

First Floor
1,072 sq. ft.

Patio

Garage

Utility

Ba.

Kitchen
12'-0" X 12'-0"

Breakfast
9'-0" X 12'-0"

Ma. Bath

Family
13'-7" X 19'-0"

Master Bedroom
12'-0" X 16'-0"

Foyer

Porch

Width: 60'-10"
Depth: 38'-0"

Plan #578-053D-0043

Sundeck Creates Outdoor Living

Features

- 1,732 total square feet of living area
- Great room has vaulted ceiling and fireplace overlooks large sundeck
- Dramatic dining room boasts extensive windows and angled walls
- Vaulted master bedroom includes a private bath with laundry area and accesses the sundeck
- Second entrance leads to the screen porch and dining area
- 3 bedrooms, 2 1/2 baths, 2-car drive under garage
- Basement foundation

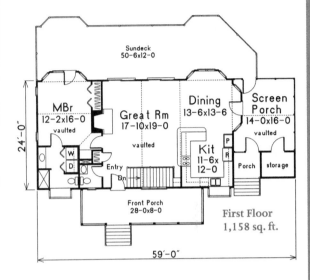

Lower Level
574 sq. ft.

Garage
19-6x23-4

Br 2
11-8x11-6

Br 3
12-6x11-6

Up

Stor

Sundeck
50-6x12-0

MBr
12-2x16-0
vaulted

Great Rm
17-10x19-0
vaulted

Dining
13-6x13-6

Screen Porch
14-0x16-0
vaulted

Kit
11-6x12-0

Entry

Porch

storage

Front Porch
28-0x8-0

24'-0"

59'-0"

First Floor
1,158 sq. ft.

Plan #578-065D-0020

Exciting Features Throughout

Features

- 1,315 total square feet of living area
- First floor laundry room and kitchen are convenient work spaces
- Windows on both sides of the fireplace make the great room very pleasant for relaxing and enjoying views outdoors
- Open stairs to the lower level make it simple to finish the basement
- 3 bedrooms, 2 baths, 2-car side entry garage
- Walk-out basement foundation

Deck

Master Bedroom
12'-4" x 13'-0"

Great Room
18'-8" x 17'-4"

Bedroom
11'-4" x 10'-8"

Bath

Dining

Bath

Kitchen
13'-4" x 9'-11"

Foyer

Bedroom
12'-4" x 10'-10"

Laun.

Porch

54'-8"

Garage
20'-0" x 26'-2"

50'-0"

Bath

Optional Library

Charming Country Cottage

Features

- 864 total square feet of living area
- Large laundry area accesses the outdoors as well as the kitchen
- Front covered porch creates an ideal outdoor living area
- Snack bar in kitchen creates a quick and easy dining area
- 2 bedrooms, 1 bath
- Crawl space or slab foundation, please specify when ordering

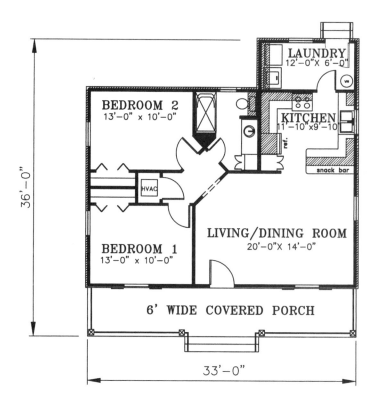

Plan #578-070D-0005

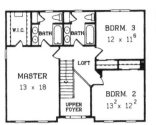

Symmetrically Charming Home

Features

- 1,835 total square feet of living area
- Screen porch accesses the patio and breakfast room
- All bedrooms on the second floor for privacy
- Built-in bookshelves flank the cozy fireplace
- 3 bedrooms, 2 1/2 baths, 2-car garage
- Basement foundation

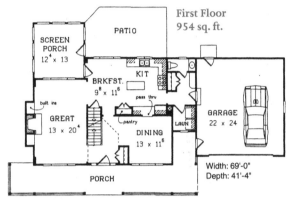

Second Floor
881 sq. ft.

First Floor
954 sq. ft.

Width: 69'-0"
Depth: 41'-4"

Plan #578-073D-0024

Price Code B

Wall Of Windows

Features

- 1,591 total square feet of living area
- Expansive beams span the length of the great room and dining area adding rustic appeal
- Private master bedroom has a walk-in closet and bath
- Central first floor laundry and full bath
- 3 bedrooms, 2 baths
- Crawl space foundation

Second Floor
199 sq. ft.

First Floor
1,392 sq. ft.

To order call toll-free 1-800-DREAM HOME **or visit** www.houseplansandmore.com

All The Features

Features

- 2,643 total square feet of living area
- Living and dining rooms combine to create a lovely area for entertaining
- Kitchen has snack bar which overlooks an octagon-shaped dining area
- Family room is centrally located with entertainment center
- Private study at rear of home
- 4 bedrooms, 2 1/2 baths, 2-car side entry garage
- Basement foundation

Second Floor
768 sq. ft.

Width: 72'-8"
Depth: 50'-10"

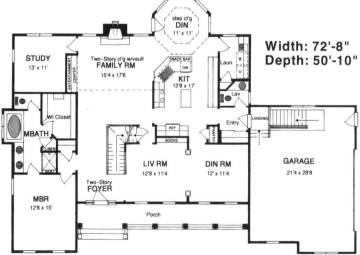

First Floor
1,875 sq. ft.

Plan #578-060D-0030

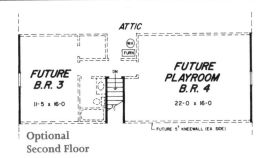

Optional
Second Floor

Decorative Accents On Porch

Features

- 1,455 total square feet of living area
- Spacious mud room has a large pantry, space for a freezer, sink/counter area and bath with shower
- Bedroom #2 can easily be converted to a study or office area
- Optional second floor bedroom and playroom have an additional 744 square feet of living area
- 2 bedrooms, 2 baths
- Slab or crawl space foundation, please specify when ordering

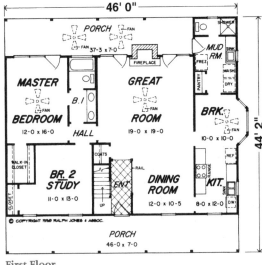

First Floor
1,455 sq. ft.

Plan #578-069D-0009

Price Code A

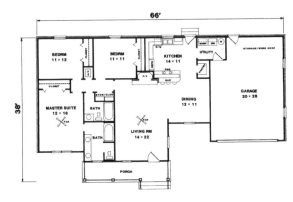

Terrific Layout For Family

Features

- 1,409 total square feet of living area
- Striking fireplace in the living room
- Eating bar off kitchen provides extra seating for dining
- Large master suite has its own bath
- 3 bedrooms, 2 baths, 2-car garage
- Slab or crawl space foundation, please specify when ordering

Inviting Double French Doors

Features

- 2,327 total square feet of living area
- 9' ceilings throughout
- Covered porches on both floors create outdoor living space
- Secondary bedrooms share a full bath
- L-shaped kitchen features an island cooktop and convenient laundry room
- 3 bedrooms, 2 1/2 baths, 2-car side entry garage
- Basement foundation

Second Floor
1,011 sq. ft.

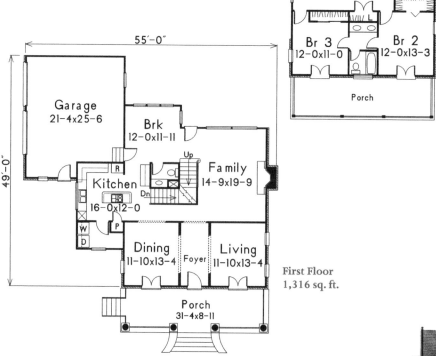

First Floor
1,316 sq. ft.

Plan #578-047D-0002

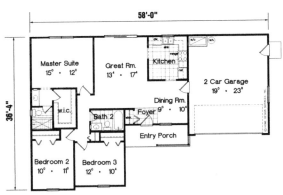

Comfortable Ranch Styling

Features

- 1,167 total square feet of living area
- Master suite includes a private bath
- Handy coat closet in the foyer
- Lots of storage space throughout
- 3 bedrooms, 2 baths, 2-car garage
- Slab foundation

Plan #578-068D-0015

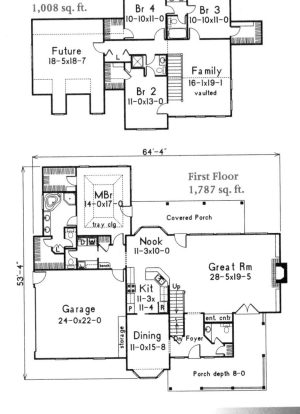

Cozy Country-Style Home

Features

- 2,795 total square feet of living area
- Second floor has a cozy vaulted family room
- Great room with fireplace has a built-in entertainment center
- Bonus room has an additional 387 square feet of living area
- 4 bedrooms, 3 1/2 baths, 2-car side entry garage
- Basement foundation, drawings also include crawl space and slab foundations

To order call toll-free 1-800-DREAM HOME or visit www.houseplansandmore.com

Uncommon Details

Features

- 2,862 total square feet of living area
- Remarkably comfortable great room has a cathedral ceiling, two sets of French doors leading to a covered porch and a fireplace flanked by built-in bookcases
- An enjoyable screen porch is located off the breakfast nook
- Enormous kitchen island/table provides spacious seating for at least four people
- Bonus room above the garage has an additional 450 square feet of living area
- 3 bedrooms, 2 1/2 baths, 3-car side entry garage
- Basement foundation

Second Floor
690 sq. ft.

First Floor
2,172 sq. ft.

Plan #578-030D-0005

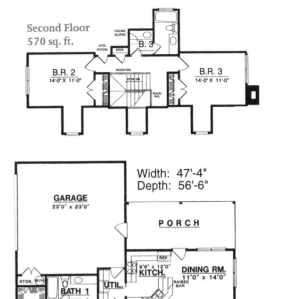

Second Floor 570 sq. ft.

B.R. 2 14'-0" X 11'-0"

B. 3

B.R. 3 14'-0" X 11'-0"

Width: 47'-4"
Depth: 56'-6"

GARAGE 23'0" x 23'0"

PORCH

KITCH. 9'8" x 12'0"

DINING RM. 11'0" X 14'0"

STOR. W/H

BATH 1

UTIL.

WALK IN CLOSET

POWDER ROOM

LIVING RM. 20'6" X 16'0"

MASTER SUITE 17'0" X 12'6"

ENT.

PORCH

First Floor 1,245 sq. ft.

Kitchen Overlooks Living Area

Features

- 1,815 total square feet of living area
- Well-designed kitchen opens to the dining room and features a raised breakfast bar
- First floor master suite has a walk-in closet
- Front and back porches unite this home with the outdoors
- 3 bedrooms, 2 baths, 2-car side entry garage
- Basement, crawl space or slab foundation, please specify when ordering

Plan #578-067D-0004

GARAGE 21'-0"x22'-0" (CARPORT OR NO GARAGE OPTIONAL)

PATIO 20'-0"x12'-0"

WALK-IN CLOSET

MSTR BATH

PWDR

PANTRY

KITCHEN 13'-0"x10'-0"

DINING 11'-0"x10'-0"

BEDROOM #3 13'-0"x11'-10"

HALL

BATH

SITTING AREA

FP

GREAT ROOM 24'-0"x20'-0" (10' CLG)

MASTER BEDROOM 15'-5"x16'-0" (VAULTED CLG)

OPTIONAL PRIVACY DOOR (POCKET)

OPTIONAL ROOM DIVIDER

BEDROOM #2 13'-0"x11'-10"

Width 59'-0"
Depth 61'-0"

COVERED PORCH 25'-0"x8'-0" (10' CLG)

Stunning Triple Dormers

Features

- 1,698 total square feet of living area
- Vaulted master bedroom has a private bath and a walk-in closet
- Decorative columns flank the entrance to the dining room
- Open great room is perfect for gathering family together
- 3 bedrooms, 2 1/2 baths, 2-car side entry garage with storage
- Basement, crawl space or slab foundation, please specify when ordering

To order call toll-free 1-800-DREAM HOME **or visit** www.houseplansandmore.com

Spacious Country Ranch

Features

- 1,806 total square feet of living area
- Two additional bedrooms share a full bath and linen closet
- Kitchen has direct access to the dining room and nook area
- Large great room has vaulted ceiling, centered fireplace and large windows to let in plenty of light
- 3 bedrooms, 2 baths, 2-car garage
- Basement foundation

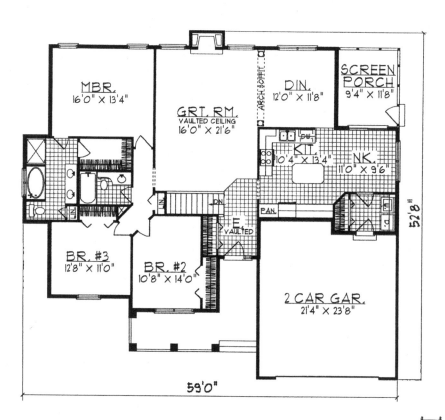

Plan #578-051D-0051

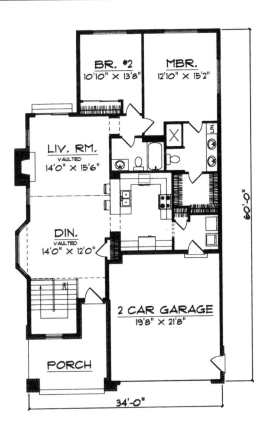

Simple Style For Living

Features

- 1,346 total square feet of living area
- Centrally located kitchen is easily accessible from many parts of the home
- Dining and living areas are combined creating one large living area with bay window and fireplace
- Bedrooms are both separated from main living areas
- 2 bedrooms, 2 baths, 2-car garage
- Basement foundation

Plan #578-062D-0055

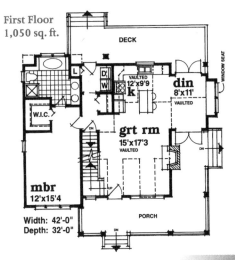

Turn Of The Century Exterior

Features

- 1,583 total square feet of living area
- Energy efficient home with 2" x 6" exterior walls
- Open kitchen includes a preparation island
- Wrap-around railed porch and rear deck expand the living space to include outdoor entertaining
- 3 bedrooms, 2 baths
- Basement or crawl space foundation, please specify when ordering

Wrap-Around Porch Adds Outdoor Living

Features

- 1,814 total square feet of living area
- Vaulted master bedroom features a walk-in closet and private bath
- Exciting two-story entry with views into the dining room
- Kitchen, family and dining rooms combine to make a great entertaining space with lots of windows
- 3 bedrooms, 2 1/2 baths, 2-car garage
- Basement foundation

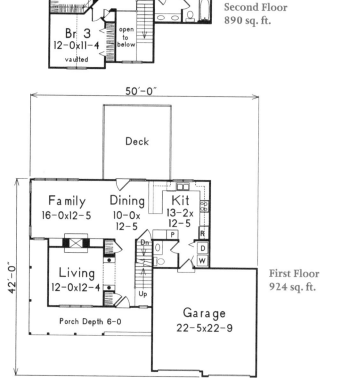

Second Floor
890 sq. ft.

First Floor
924 sq. ft.

Plan #578-024D-0002

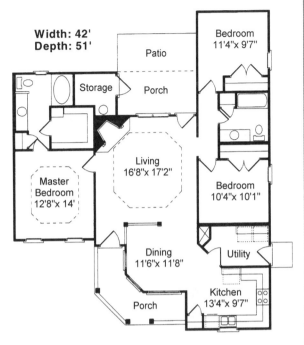

Width: 42'
Depth: 51'

Patio

Storage

Porch

Bedroom 11'4"x 9'7"

Living 16'8"x 17'2"

Master Bedroom 12'8"x 14'

Bedroom 10'4"x 10'1"

Dining 11'6"x 11'8"

Utility

Porch

Kitchen 13'4"x 9'7"

Central Living Room Is Great

Features

- 1,405 total square feet of living area
- Compact design has all the luxuries of a larger home
- Master bedroom has its privacy away from other bedrooms
- Living room has corner fireplace, access to the outdoors and easily reaches the dining area and kitchen
- Large utility room has access to the outdoors
- 3 bedrooms, 2 baths
- Slab foundation

Plan #578-070D-0003

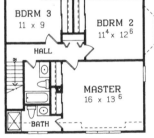

Second Floor 756 sq. ft.

BDRM 3 11 x 9

BDRM 2 11^4 x 12^6

HALL

MASTER 16 x 13^6

BATH

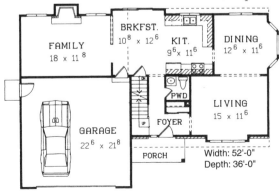

First Floor 978 sq. ft.

BRKFST. 10^8 x 12^6

KIT. 9^6x 11^6

DINING 12^6 x 11^6

FAMILY 18 x 11^8

PWD

LIVING 15 x 11^6

FOYER

GARAGE 22^6 x 21^8

PORCH

Width: 52'-0"
Depth: 36'-0"

Perfectly Designed Two-Story

Features

- 1,734 total square feet of living area
- Bayed dining room is cheerful and convenient to the kitchen
- Large breakfast room is tucked between the kitchen and the family room
- Master bedroom has its own bath and two closets
- 3 bedrooms, 2 1/2 baths, 2-car garage
- Basement foundation

Double-Gabled Ranch Cottage

Features

- 1,580 total square feet of living area
- Dining room has columns which maintain an open feeling
- Sunny breakfast room is located off the kitchen
- 9' ceilings throughout the first floor
- Optional second floor has an additional 336 square feet of living area
- 2 bedrooms, 2 baths, 3-car side entry garage
- Slab foundation

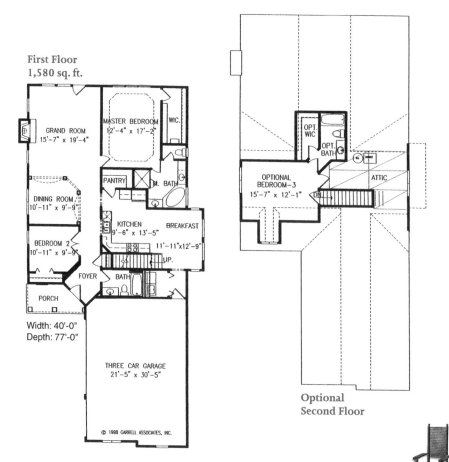

First Floor
1,580 sq. ft.

GRAND ROOM
15'-7" x 19'-4"

MASTER BEDROOM
12'-4" x 17'-2"

WIC.

PANTRY

M. BATH

DINING ROOM
10'-11" x 9'-9"

KITCHEN
9'-6" x 13'-5"

BREAKFAST
11'-11"x12'-9"

BEDROOM 2
10'-11" x 9'-9"

UP.

FOYER

BATH

PORCH

Width: 40'-0"
Depth: 77'-0"

THREE CAR GARAGE
21'-5" x 30'-5"

© 1998 GARRELL ASSOCIATES, INC.

OPT. WIC

OPT. BATH

OPTIONAL BEDROOM-3
15'-7" x 12'-1"

ATTIC

DN.

Optional
Second Floor

Plan #578-034D-0002

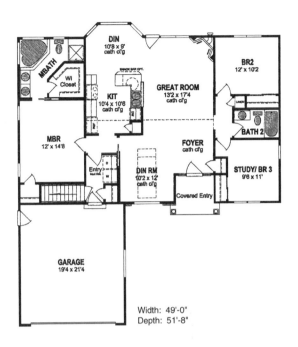

GARAGE
19'4 x 21'4

Width: 49'-0"
Depth: 51'-8"

Luxurious Master Bath

Features

- 1,456 total square feet of living area
- Open floor plan adds spaciousness to this design
- Bayed dining area creates a cheerful setting
- Corner fireplace in the great room is a terrific focal point
- 3 bedrooms, 2 baths, 2-car garage
- Basement foundation

Plan #578-015D-0039

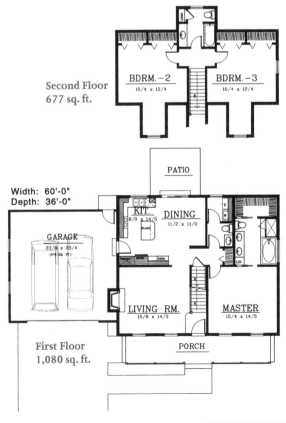

Second Floor
677 sq. ft.

BDRM. - 2
15/4 x 12/4

BDRM. - 3
15/4 x 12/4

Width: 60'-0"
Depth: 36'-0"

PATIO

GARAGE
23/8 x 23/4

KIT
8/0 x 14/5

DINING
11/2 x 11/0

LIVING RM.
15/8 x 14/3

MASTER
15/4 x 14/3

First Floor
1,080 sq. ft.

PORCH

Inviting Country Home

Features

- 1,757 total square feet of living area
- Energy efficient home with 2" x 6" exterior walls
- Private master bedroom has its own bath and walk-in closet
- Cozy living room includes fireplace for warmth
- 3 bedrooms, 2 1/2 baths, 2-car garage
- Crawl space, basement or slab foundation, please specify when ordering

To order call toll-free 1-800-DREAM HOME or visit www.houseplansandmore.com

249

Rustic Design With Modern Features

Features

- 1,000 total square feet of living area
- Large mud room has a separate covered porch entrance
- Full-length covered front porch
- Bedrooms are on opposite sides of the home for privacy
- Vaulted ceiling creates an open and spacious feeling
- 2 bedrooms, 1 bath
- Crawl space foundation

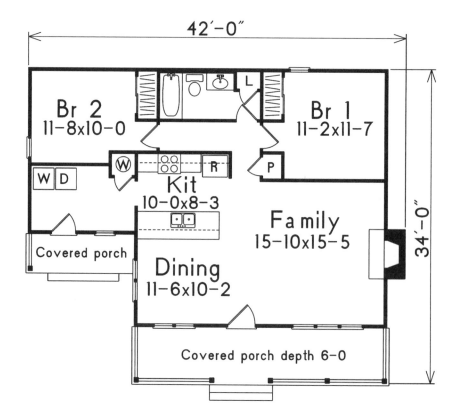

42'-0"

34'-0"

Br 2
11-8x10-0

Br 1
11-2x11-7

L

W D

W

R

P

Kit
10-0x8-3

Family
15-10x15-5

Covered porch

Dining
11-6x10-2

Covered porch depth 6-0

Plan #578-026D-0113

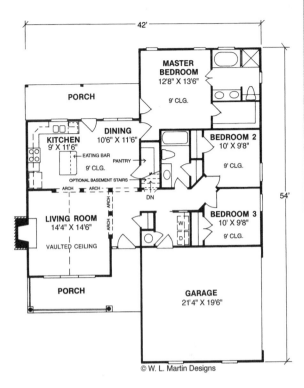

© W. L. Martin Designs

Arched Entry Adds Appeal

Features

- 1,263 total square feet of living area
- 9' ceilings throughout most of home
- Kitchen features a large island eating bar
- The master bedroom is separated for privacy and features a double-door entry into bath and porch access
- 3 bedrooms, 2 baths, 2-car side entry garage
- Slab foundation

Plan #578-036D-0001

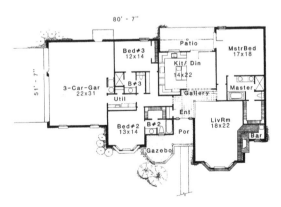

Victorian Details Grace Gables

Features

- 2,267 total square feet of living area
- A unique built-in gazebo in the front creates a lovely place for enjoying the outdoors
- Living room is perfect for entertaining with a corner wet bar
- Master bedroom accesses the patio directly
- 3 bedrooms, 3 baths, 3-car side entry garage
- Slab foundation

Cottage Style Adds Charm

Features

- 1,496 total square feet of living area
- Large utility room with sink and extra counterspace
- Covered patio off breakfast nook extends dining to the outdoors
- Eating counter in kitchen overlooks vaulted family room
- 3 bedrooms, 2 baths, 2-car side entry garage
- Crawl space foundation

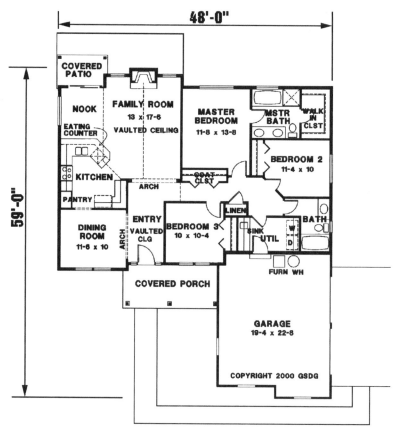

Plan #578-026D-0155

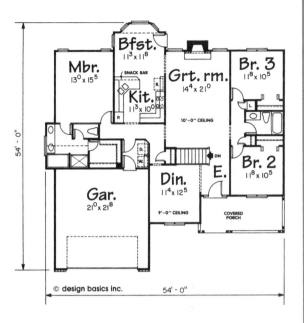

Private Master Bedroom

Features

- 1,691 total square feet of living area
- Bay windowed breakfast room allows for plenty of sunlight
- Large inviting covered porch in the front of the home
- Great room fireplace is surrounded by windows
- 3 bedrooms, 2 baths, 2-car garage
- Basement foundation

Plan #578-031D-0004

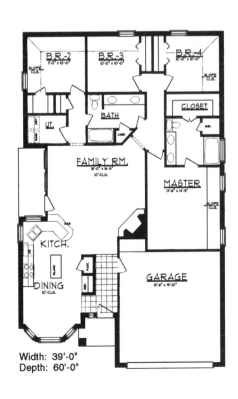

Width: 39'-0"
Depth: 60'-0"

Bedrooms With Sloped Ceilings

Features

- 1,710 total square feet of living area
- Bedrooms have plenty of closet space
- Laundry area is located near the bedrooms for efficiency
- The large family room enjoys a 10' ceiling and is warmed by a corner fireplace
- 4 bedrooms, 2 baths, 2-car garage
- Slab foundation

Plenty Of Closet Space

Features

- 1,868 total square feet of living area
- Open floor plan creates an airy feeling
- Secluded study makes an ideal home office
- Large master bedroom has a luxurious private bath with a walk-in closet
- Formal dining room has convenient access to kitchen
- 3 bedrooms, 2 1/2 baths, 2-car garage
- Basement foundation

Second Floor
848 sq. ft.

MBR
16'6 x 13'6

M.BATH

BATH 2

WI Closet

HALL

BR3
10'8 x 10'

BR2
11'4 x 10'10

First Floor
1,020 sq. ft.

DIN
11'8 x 10'2

Laun

WI Closet

STUDY
10'6 x 9'8

GREAT RM
16'8 x 13'6

Gas fpl

KIT
11'4 x 11'6

GARAGE
21'4 x 21'4

LAV

FOYER

PANTRY

Covered Porch

DIN RM
11'4 x 10'8

Width: 52'-8"
Depth: 34'-0"

Plan #578-045D-0013

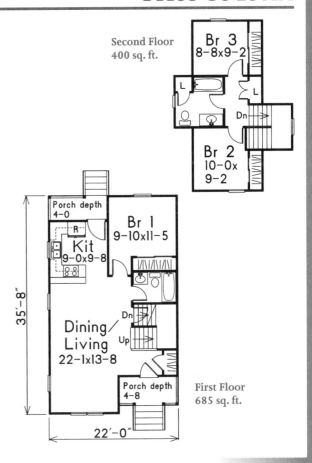

Second Floor
400 sq. ft.

Br 3
8-8x9-2

Br 2
10-0x
9-2

Porch depth
4-0

Br 1
9-10x11-5

Kit
9-0x9-8

35'-8"

Dining/
Living
22-1x13-8

Dn

Up

Porch depth
4-8

First Floor
685 sq. ft.

22'-0"

Home Perfect For Narrow Lot

Features

- 1,085 total square feet of living area
- Rear porch provides handy access through the kitchen
- Convenient hall linen closet is located on the second floor
- Breakfast bar in the kitchen offers additional counterspace
- Living and dining rooms combine for open living
- 3 bedrooms, 2 baths
- Basement foundation

Plan #578-065D-0034

Dining
11'6" x 14'2"

Covered
Porch

Great Room
16'10" x 17'

Master Bedroom
14' x 11'8"

Kitchen
18'2" x 10'10"

Foyer

Bath

46'-4"

Two-Car
Garage
22' x 20'

Laun.
6'9" x 7'

Porch

Bedroom
11' x 10'6"

Bedroom
10'6" x 10'4"

59'-4"

Stone Adds Charm To Exterior

Features

- 1,509 total square feet of living area
- A grand opening between the great room and dining area visually expands the living space
- The kitchen with a snack bar is a delightful place to prepare meals
- Master bedroom has a bath with double vanity and walk-in closet
- 3 bedrooms, 2 baths, 2-car garage
- Basement foundation

To order call toll-free 1-800-DREAM HOME or visit www.houseplansandmore.com

Sweeping Elegant Front Colonnade

Features

- 2,824 total square feet of living area
- 9' ceilings on the first floor
- Second floor bedrooms feature private dressing areas and share a bath
- Large great room includes a fireplace flanked by French doors leading to the rear patio
- Kitchen conveniently serves the formal dining room and breakfast area which features a large bay window
- 4 bedrooms, 3 baths, 2-car side entry garage
- Slab foundation, drawings also include crawl space foundation

Second Floor
704 sq. ft.

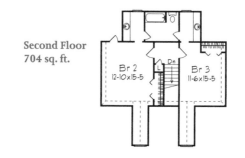

First Floor
2,120 sq. ft.

Vaulted Second Floor Sitting Area

Features

- 2,433 total square feet of living area
- Two second floor bedrooms share a Jack and Jill bath
- Terrific covered porch has access into master bedroom or great room
- Snack bar in kitchen provides additional seating for dining
- 3 bedrooms, 2 1/2 baths, 2-car side entry garage
- Basement, crawl space or slab foundation, please specify when ordering

First Floor
1,590 sq. ft.

Second Floor
843 sq. ft.

Ranch Of Enchantment

Features

- 1,559 total square feet of living area
- A cozy country appeal is provided by a spacious porch, masonry fireplace, roof dormers and a perfect balance of stonework and siding
- Large living room enjoys a fireplace, bayed dining area and separate entry
- A U-shaped kitchen is adjoined by a breakfast room with bay window and large pantry
- 3 bedrooms, 2 1/2 baths, 2-car drive under side entry garage
- Basement foundation

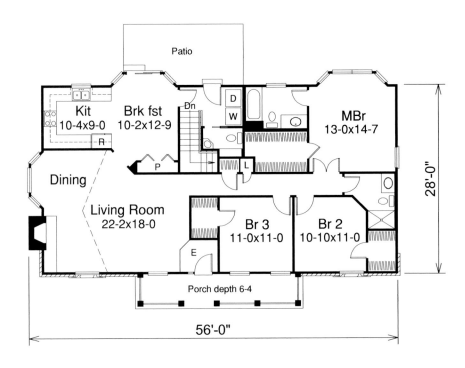

Outdoor Living Area Created By Veranda

Features

- 2,213 total square feet of living area
- Master bedroom features a full bath with separate vanities, large walk-in closet and access to the covered porch
- Living room is enhanced by a fireplace, bay window and columns framing the gallery
- 9' ceilings throughout home add to open feeling
- 4 bedrooms, 2 1/2 baths, 2-car side entry garage
- Slab foundation

First Floor
1,351 sq. ft.

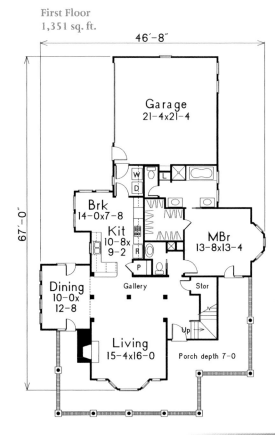

Second Floor
862 sq. ft.

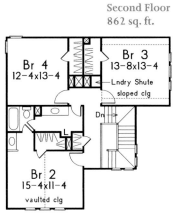

Circle-Top Windows Grace The Facade Of This Home

Features

- 1,672 total square feet of living area
- Vaulted master bedroom features a walk-in closet and adjoining bath with separate tub and shower
- Energy efficient home with 2" x 6" exterior walls
- Covered front and rear porches
- 12' ceilings in the living room, kitchen and bedroom #2
- Kitchen is complete with a pantry, angled bar and adjacent eating area
- Sloped ceiling in the dining room
- 3 bedrooms, 2 baths, 2-car side entry garage
- Crawl space foundation, drawings also include basement and slab foundations

Side Elevation

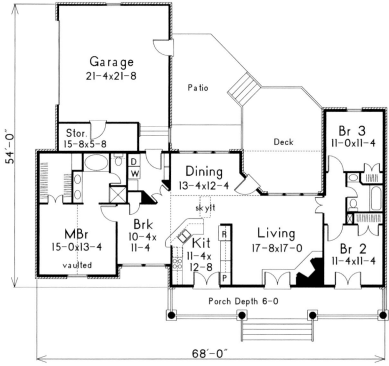

Charming For A Narrow Lot

Features

- 2,356 total square feet of living area
- Transoms above front windows create a custom feel to this design
- Spacious master bath has double vanities, toilet closet, and an oversized whirlpool tub
- Covered rear porch off sunny breakfast area is ideal for grilling or relaxing
- 4 bedrooms, 2 1/2 baths, 2-car side entry garage
- Slab foundation

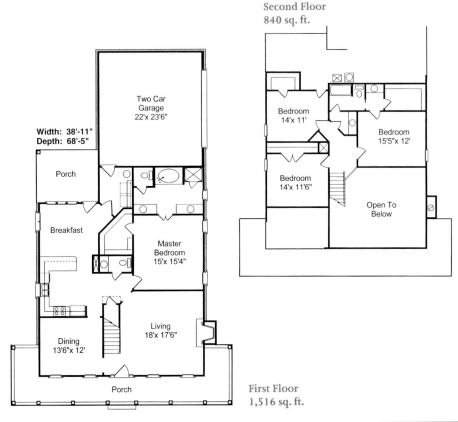

Second Floor
840 sq. ft.

Width: 38'-11"
Depth: 68'-5"

Two Car Garage
22'x 23'6"

Porch

Breakfast

Master Bedroom
15'x 15'4"

Dining
13'6"x 12'

Living
18'x 17'6"

Porch

Bedroom
14'x 11'

Bedroom
15'5"x 12'

Bedroom
14'x 11'6"

Open To Below

First Floor
1,516 sq. ft.

Country Flavor With Atrium

Features

- 2,384 total square feet of living area
- Bracketed box windows create an exterior with country charm
- Massive-sized great room features a majestic atrium, fireplace, box window wall, dining balcony and a vaulted ceiling
- An atrium balcony with large bay window off the sundeck is enjoyed by the spacious breakfast room
- 1,038 square feet of optional living area below with family room, wet bar, bedroom #4 and bath
- 3 bedrooms, 2 1/2 baths, 2-car side entry garage
- Walk-out basement foundation

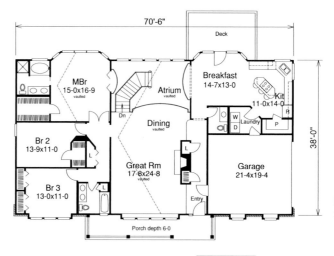

70'-6"

Deck

MBr
15-0x16-9
vaulted

Atrium
vaulted

Breakfast
14-7x13-0

Kit
11-0x14-0

Dining
vaulted

Dn

W D
Laundry
P

Br 2
13-9x11-0

Great Rm
17-8x24-8
vaulted

Garage
21-4x19-4

38'-0"

Br 3
13-0x11-0

Entry

Porch depth 6-0

First Floor
2,384 sq. ft.

Patio

Up

Atrium
20-0x12-6

Guest Rm
16-0x17-0

Basement

Family Rm
20-0x24-4

Optional
Lower Level

To order call toll-free 1-800-DREAM HOME or visit www.houseplansandmore.com

Triple Dormers Create Terrific Curb Appeal

Features

- 1,992 total square feet of living area
- Interesting angled walls add drama to many of the living areas including the family room, master bedroom and breakfast area
- Covered porch includes a spa and the outdoor kitchen with sink, refrigerator and cooktop
- Enter the majestic master bath to find a dramatic corner oversized tub
- 4 bedrooms, 3 baths, 2-car side entry garage
- Basement, crawl space or slab foundation, please specify when ordering

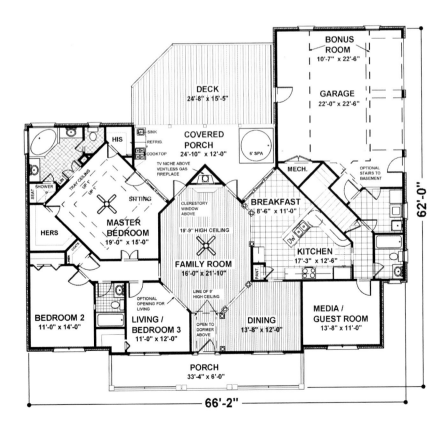

Sensational Home Designed For Views

Features

- 1,621 total square feet of living area
- The front exterior includes an attractive gable-end arched window and extra-deep porch
- A grand-scale great room enjoys a coffered ceiling, fireplace, access to the wrap-around deck and is brightly lit with numerous French doors and windows
- The master bedroom suite has a sitting area, double walk-in closets and a luxury bath
- 223 square feet of optional finished space on the lower level
- 3 bedrooms, 2 baths, 2-car drive under side entry garage
- Basement foundation

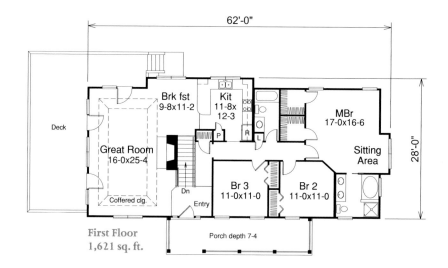

62'-0"

28'-0"

Deck

Brk fst
9-8x11-2

Kit
11-8x
12-3

MBr
17-0x16-6

Great Room
16-0x25-4

Sitting
Area

Coffered clg.

Dn

Entry

Br 3
11-0x11-0

Br 2
11-0x11-0

First Floor
1,621 sq. ft.

Porch depth 7-4

Lower Level With
Optional Laundry Area

W D

Laundry
14-6x9-4

Up

L

Garage
26-2x24-8

To order call toll-free 1-800-DREAM HOME or visit www.houseplansandmore.com

Grand Covered Entry

Features

- 3,369 total square feet of living area
- Large playroom overlooks to great room below and makes a great casual family area
- Extra storage is located in the garage
- Well-planned hearth room and kitchen are open and airy
- Foyer flows into unique diagonal gallery area creating a dramatic entrance into the great room
- 3 bedrooms, 2 1/2 baths, 2-car side entry garage
- Slab foundation

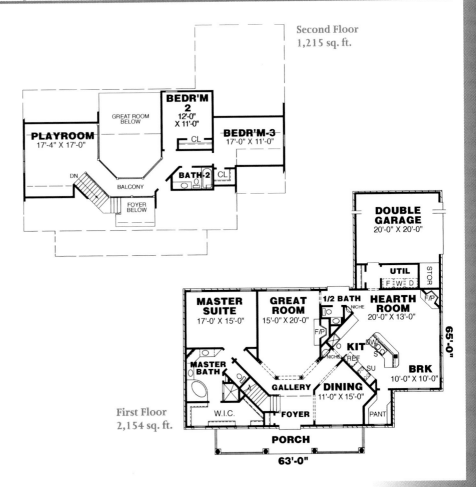

Second Floor
1,215 sq. ft.

PLAYROOM
17'-4" X 17'-0"

GREAT ROOM
BELOW

BEDR'M 2
12'-0" X 11'-0"

BEDR'M-3
17'-0" X 11'-0"

CL

CL

DN

BALCONY

BATH-2

FOYER
BELOW

DOUBLE GARAGE
20'-0" X 20'-0"

UTIL
F W D

STOR

MASTER SUITE
17'-0" X 15'-0"

GREAT ROOM
15'-0" X 20'-0"

1/2 BATH

HEARTH ROOM
20'-0" X 13'-0"

F/P

MASTER BATH

KIT

NICHE

BRK
10'-0" X 10'-0"

GALLERY

DINING
11'-0" X 15'-0"

W.I.C.

FOYER

PANT

First Floor
2,154 sq. ft.

PORCH

63'-0"

65'-0"

Covered Front Porch Is A Terrific Focal Point

Features

- 1,934 total square feet of living area
- Private master suite has access onto covered porch and a private bath with two walk-in closets
- Extra storage in the garage
- Centralized laundry area
- 3 bedrooms, 2 baths, 2-car rear entry garage
- Crawl space or slab foundation, please specify when ordering

Graceful And Functional Front Porch

Features

- 2,255 total square feet of living area
- Master bedroom with adjoining bath has an enormous walk-in closet
- Energy efficient home with 2" x 6" exterior walls
- Deluxe kitchen features a planning desk and a convenient eating area
- Balcony library overlooks living area
- Formal dining area with easy access to the kitchen
- 3 bedrooms, 2 baths, 2-car side entry garage
- Crawl space foundation, drawings also include slab and basement foundations

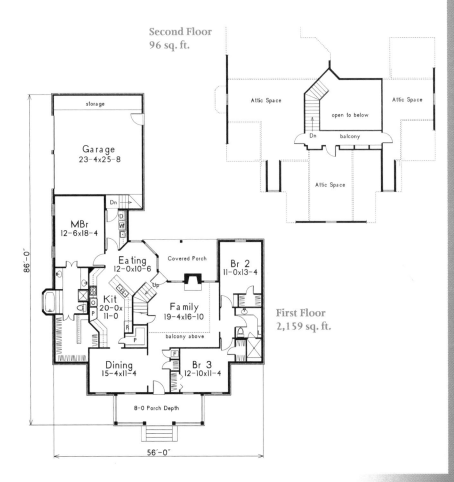

Second Floor
96 sq. ft.

First Floor
2,159 sq. ft.

Angled Porch Greets Guests

Features

- 2,059 total square feet of living area
- Large desk and pantry add to the breakfast room
- The laundry room is located on the second floor near the bedrooms
- Vaulted ceiling in the master bedroom
- Mud room is conveniently located near the garage
- 3 bedrooms, 2 1/2 baths, 2-car garage
- Basement foundation

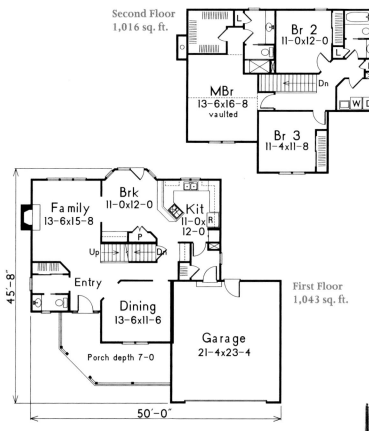

Second Floor 1,016 sq. ft.

First Floor 1,043 sq. ft.

Terrific Facade

Features

- 2,135 total square feet of living area
- 10' ceilings throughout the first floor and 9' ceilings on the second floor
- Wonderful angled entry leads through columns into a cozy social room
- Spacious kitchen has center island with a place for dining as well as food preparation
- Bonus room on the second floor has an additional 247 square feet of living area
- 3 bedrooms, 2 1/2 baths, 2-car rear entry garage
- Slab foundation

First Floor
1,109 sq. ft.

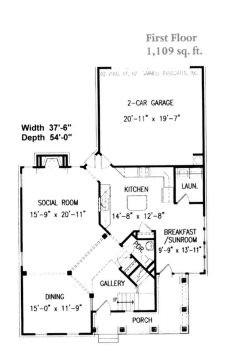

Width 37'-6"
Depth 54'-0"

Second Floor
1,026 sq. ft.

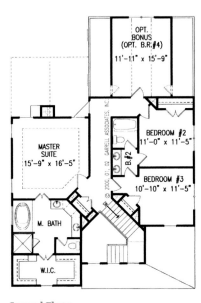

Lower Level Designed Perfectly For An In-Law Suite

Features

- 4,380 total square feet of living area

- 11' ceilings on the first floor and 9' ceilings on the second floor

- Intricate porch details display one-of-a-kind craftsmanship

- Impressive foyer has a curved staircase creating a grand entry

- One second floor bedroom accesses a private balcony for easy outdoor relaxation

- Optional lower level has an additional 1,275 square feet of living area

- 4 bedrooms, 3 1/2 baths, 3-car drive under garage

- Walk-out basement foundation

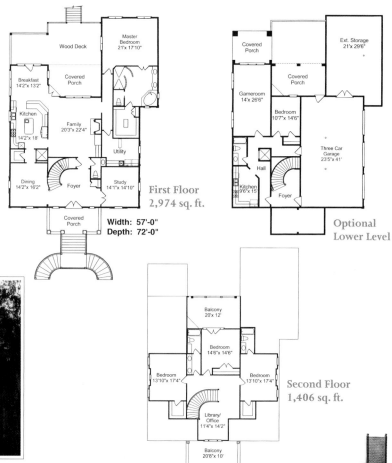

First Floor
2,974 sq. ft.

Width: 57'-0"
Depth: 72'-0"

Optional Lower Level

Second Floor
1,406 sq. ft.

Rear View

Sweeping Roof Lines Make A Sizable Impression

Features

- 1,351 total square feet of living area
- Roof lines and vaulted ceilings make this home appear larger
- Central fireplace provides a focal point for dining and living areas
- Master bedroom features a roomy window seat and a walk-in closet
- Loft can easily be converted to a third bedroom
- 2 bedrooms, 2 1/2 baths, 2-car garage
- Basement foundation

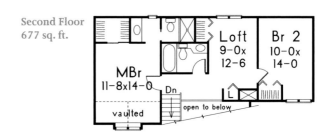

Second Floor
677 sq. ft.

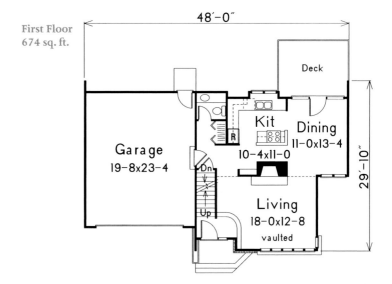

First Floor
674 sq. ft.

Charming Country Farmhouse Has Everything To Offer

Features

- 2,571 total square feet of living area
- 9' ceilings throughout the first floor
- Room off foyer adds versatility and can serve as a home office, guest room or fifth bedroom
- Elegant French doors lead from the kitchen into the formal dining area
- 4 bedrooms, 2 1/2 baths, 2-car side entry garage
- Basement, crawl space or slab foundation, please specify when ordering

Second Floor
913 sq. ft.

First Floor
1,658 sq. ft.

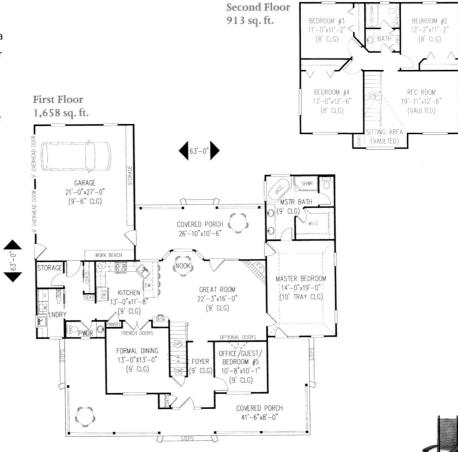

Cozy Covered Front Porch

Features

- 1,583 total square feet of living area
- 9' ceilings throughout this home
- Additional bedrooms are located away from the master suite for privacy
- Optional second floor has an additional 544 square feet of living area
- 3 bedrooms, 2 baths, 2-car garage
- Walk-out basement, slab or crawl space foundation, please specify when ordering

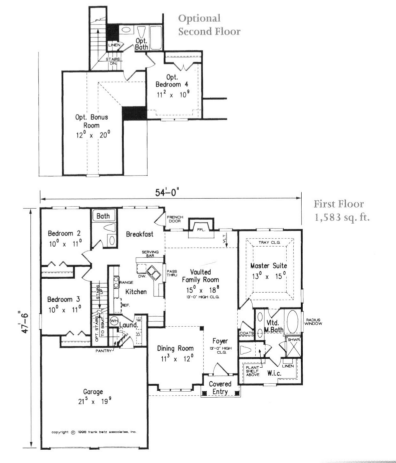

Optional Second Floor

First Floor
1,583 sq. ft.

Log Home Feel To This Design

Features

- 3,098 total square feet of living area

- Screened breezeway and porch add living areas in an outdoor setting

- Large second floor loft is brightened by a trio of skylights and overlooks to the great room below

- Kitchen, dining and great rooms combine creating an area for entertaining and gathering

- 4 bedrooms, 3 baths, 2-car carport

- Crawl space foundation

Second Floor
1,228 sq. ft.

First Floor
1,870 sq. ft.

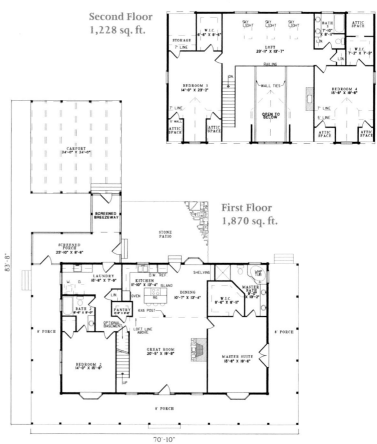

Spacious Country Home

Features

- 2,123 total square feet of living area
- L-shaped porch extends the entire length of this home creating lots of extra space for outdoor living
- Master bedroom is secluded for privacy and has two closets, double vanity in bath and a double-door entry onto covered porch
- Efficiently designed kitchen
- 3 bedrooms, 2 1/2 baths
- Crawl space or slab foundation, please specify when ordering

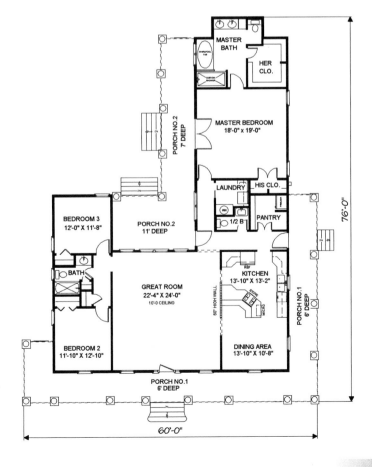

Second Floor Terrace

Features

- 2,300 total square feet of living area
- Cozy fireplace in the master suite
- 9' ceilings on the first floor
- Energy efficient home with 2" x 6" exterior walls
- 3 bedrooms, 2 1/2 baths, 2-car side entry garage
- Basement foundation

Second Floor
1,233 sq. ft.

First Floor
1,067 sq. ft.

Sunny Breakfast Room

Features

- 2,261 total square feet of living area
- Efficiently designed kitchen with work island and snack bar
- Master bath has double vanities, whirlpool tub and two walk-in closets
- Spacious laundry room
- Optional second floor has an additional 367 square feet of living area
- 4 bedrooms, 3 1/2 baths, 2-car side entry garage
- Slab or crawl space foundation, please specify when ordering

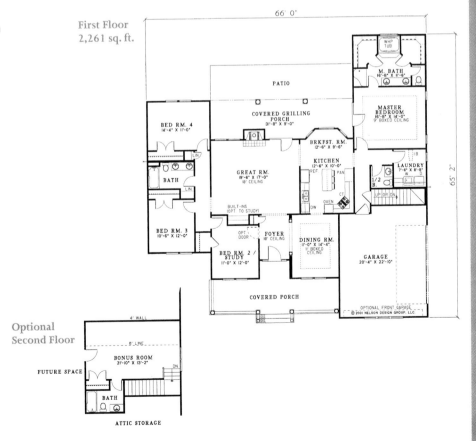

First Floor
2,261 sq. ft.

Optional Second Floor

Nice-Sized Porch Is A Stylish Shelter

Features

- 2,120 total square feet of living area
- First floor vaulted master bedroom has a spacious and open feel
- Built-in shelves adorn the dining room
- Office has a double-door entry helping to maintain privacy
- 3 bedrooms, 2 1/2 baths, 3-car garage
- Crawl space foundation

Second Floor
517 sq. ft.

First Floor
1,603 sq. ft.

Country Style With Spacious Rooms

Features

- 1,197 total square feet of living area
- U-shaped kitchen includes ample workspace, breakfast bar, laundry area and direct access to the outdoors
- Large living room has a convenient coat closet
- Bedroom #1 features a large walk-in closet
- 3 bedrooms, 1 bath
- Crawl space foundation, drawings also include basement and slab foundations

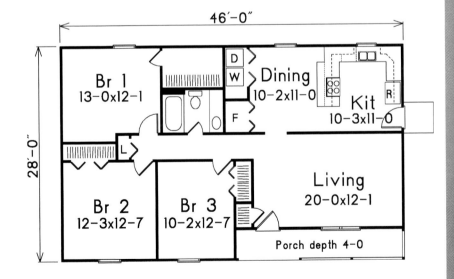

46'-0"

28'-0"

Br 1
13-0x12-1

D
W

Dining
10-2x11-0

Kit
10-3x11-0

F

R

L

Br 2
12-3x12-7

Br 3
10-2x12-7

Living
20-0x12-1

Porch depth 4-0

Private Master Bedroom

Features

- 2,684 total square feet of living area
- Formal dining room off kitchen
- Enormous master bedroom has a private bath and walk-in closet
- The second floor has an additional 926 square feet of living area in three future rooms
- 3 bedrooms, 2 1/2 baths, 2-car side entry garage
- Slab foundation, drawings also include crawl space foundation

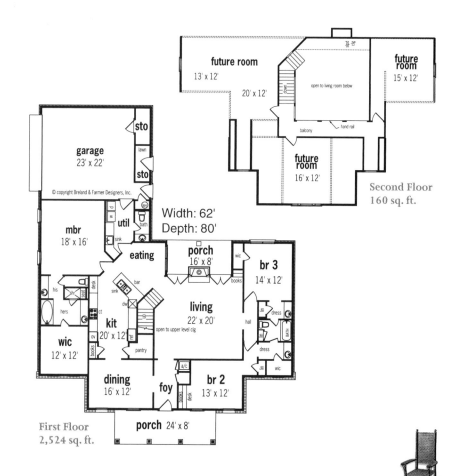

Width: 62'
Depth: 80'

Second Floor
160 sq. ft.

First Floor
2,524 sq. ft.

Unique Country Craftsman Style

Features

- 2,420 total square feet of living area
- A grand master suite has a double-door entry, spacious bath with spa tub and a large walk-in closet
- Den/bedroom #4 has easy access to a full bath and is secluded from other bedrooms
- Central living areas combine for maximum living space
- Second floor bonus room is included in the square footage
- 3 bedrooms, 2 1/2 baths, 2-car garage
- Crawl space foundation

Second Floor
1,168 sq. ft.

First Floor
1,252 sq. ft.

Dramatic Appeal, Inside And Out

Features

- 2,468 total square feet of living area
- Open floor plan has a family room with columns, fireplace, triple French doors and a 12' ceiling
- Master bath features double walk-in closets and vanities
- Bonus room above garage has a private stairway and is included in the total square footage
- Bedrooms are separate from main living space for privacy
- 3 bedrooms, 2 1/2 baths, 2-car side entry garage
- Slab foundation

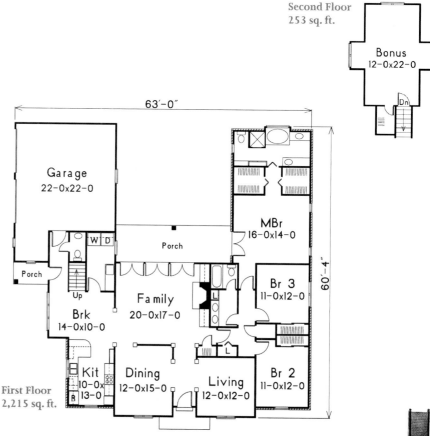

Second Floor
253 sq. ft.

Bonus
12-0x22-0

Dn

63'-0"

Garage
22-0x22-0

Porch

MBr
16-0x14-0

60'-4"

Porch

W D

Porch

Up

Br 3
11-0x12-0

Brk
14-0x10-0

Family
20-0x17-0

Kit
10-0x
13-0

Dining
12-0x15-0

Living
12-0x12-0

Br 2
11-0x12-0

First Floor
2,215 sq. ft.

Open Dining And Living Areas

Features

- 1,275 total square feet of living area
- The kitchen expands into the dining area with the help of a center island
- Decorative columns keep the living area open to other areas
- Covered front porch adds charm to the entry
- 3 bedrooms, 2 baths, 2-car garage
- Crawl space foundation

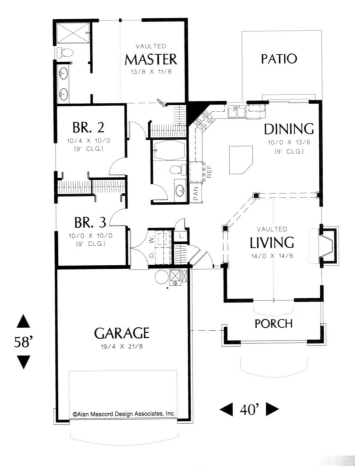

VAULTED
MASTER
13/8 X 11/8

PATIO

BR. 2
10/4 X 10/0
(9' CLG.)

DINING
10/0 X 13/6
(9' CLG.)

PAN.
REF.

BR. 3
10/0 X 10/0
(9' CLG.)

D. W.

VAULTED
LIVING
14/0 X 14/6

58'

GARAGE
19/4 X 21/8

PORCH

©Alan Mascord Design Associates, Inc.

40'

Simple Roof Line Makes Home Economical To Build

Features

- 1,792 total square feet of living area
- Master bedroom has a private bath and large walk-in closet
- A central stone fireplace and windows on two walls are focal points in the living room
- Decorative beams and sloped ceilings add interest to the kitchen, living and dining rooms
- 3 bedrooms, 2 baths, 2-car drive under garage
- Basement foundation

Rear View

Exterior Accents Add Charm To This Compact Cottage

Features

- 1,359 total square feet of living area
- Covered porch, stone chimney and abundant windows lend an outdoor appeal
- Spacious and bright kitchen has pass-through to formal dining room
- Large walk-in closets in all bed-rooms
- Extensive deck expands dining and entertaining areas
- 3 bedrooms, 2 1/2 baths, 2-car garage
- Basement foundation

Second Floor
691 sq. ft.

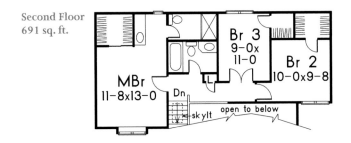

MBr
11-8x13-0

Br 3
9-0x
11-0

Br 2
10-0x9-8

Dn

skylt   open to below

First Floor
668 sq. ft.

48'-0"

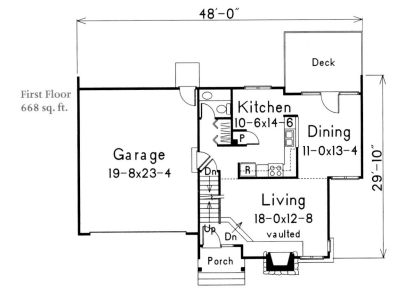

Deck

Kitchen
10-6x14-6

Dining
11-0x13-4

Garage
19-8x23-4

P

Dn

R

Living
18-0x12-8
vaulted

Up   Dn

Porch

29'-10"

Two-Sided Fireplace Makes An Impression

Features

- 1,754 total square feet of living area
- Energy efficient home with 2" x 6" exterior walls
- Utilities are conveniently located in the first floor powder room
- U-shaped island in kitchen has a stovetop as well as additional dining space
- Bonus room on the second floor has an additional 421 square feet of living area
- 3 bedrooms, 2 1/2 baths, 2-car garage
- Basement foundation

Second Floor
880 sq. ft.

First Floor
874 sq. ft.

Sophisticated Southern Style

Features

- 2,561 total square feet of living area
- Sunny vaulted breakfast nook
- Dormers are a charming touch in the second floor bedrooms
- Columns throughout the first floor help separate rooms while creating a feeling of openness
- Bonus room on the second floor has an additional 232 square feet of living area
- 4 bedrooms, 2 1/2 baths, 2-car side entry garage
- Crawl space foundation

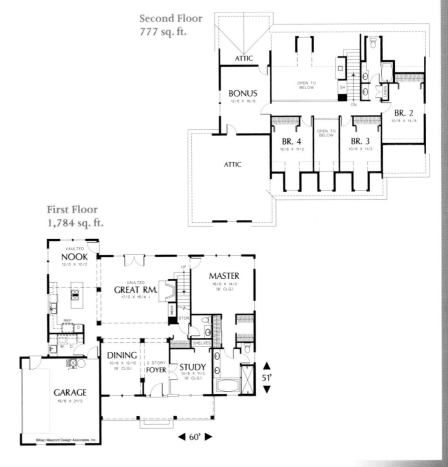

Second Floor
777 sq. ft.

ATTIC

BONUS
12/8 X 16/6

OPEN TO BELOW

BR. 2
10/8 X 14/8

ATTIC

BR. 4
10/6 X 11/2

OPEN TO BELOW

BR. 3
10/6 X 11/2

First Floor
1,784 sq. ft.

VAULTED
NOOK
12/0 X 10/2

VAULTED
GREAT RM.
17/0 X 16/4

MASTER
16/0 X 14/2
(9' CLG.)

UP

REF.

W. D.

DINING
10/6 X 12/10
(9' CLG.)

2 STORY
FOYER

STUDY
10/8 X 11/2
(9' CLG.)

SHELVES

GARAGE
19/6 X 21/0

©Alan Mascord Design Associates, Inc.

51'

◄ 60' ►

Plan #578-040D-0015

Price Code B

Covered Porch Adds Charm To Entrance

Features

- 1,655 total square feet of living area
- Master bedroom features a 9' ceiling, walk-in closet and bath with dressing area
- Oversized family room includes a 10' ceiling and masonry see-through fireplace
- Island kitchen has convenient access to the laundry room
- Handy covered walkway from the garage leads to the kitchen and dining area
- 3 bedrooms, 2 baths, 2-car garage
- Crawl space foundation

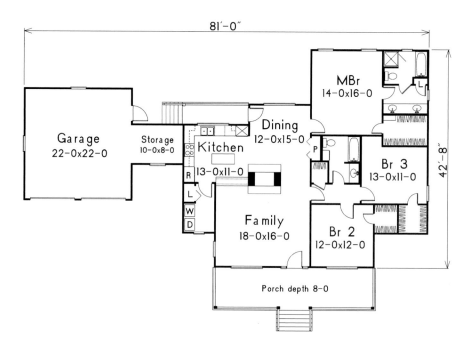

Perfect Country Haven

Features

- 1,232 total square feet of living area
- Ideal porch for quiet quality evenings
- Great room opens to dining room for those large dinner gatherings
- Functional L-shaped kitchen includes broom cabinet
- Master bedroom contains a large walk-in closet and compartmented bath
- 3 bedrooms, 1 bath, optional 2-car garage
- Basement foundation, drawings also include crawl space and slab foundations

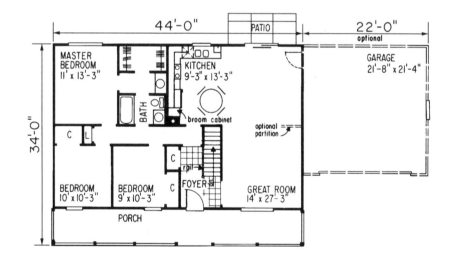

Extra-Large Porches

Features

- 1,716 total square feet of living area
- Great room boasts a fireplace and access to the kitchen/breakfast area through a large arched opening
- Master bedroom includes a huge walk-in closet and French doors that lead onto an L-shaped porch
- Bedrooms #2 and #3 share a bath and linen closet
- 3 bedrooms, 2 baths, 2-car detached garage
- Crawl space or slab foundation, please specify when ordering

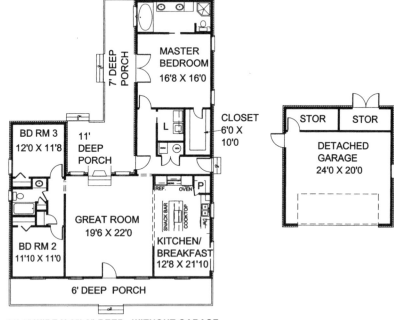

44'-0" WIDE X 65'-0" DEEP - WITHOUT GARAGE

Narrow Lot Home With Rear Entry Garage

Features

- 2,707 total square feet of living area
- A double-door entry leads into a handsome study
- Kitchen and breakfast room flow into the great room creating a terrific gathering place
- The second floor includes a game room/bonus room which is included in the total square footage
- 4 bedrooms, 3 baths, 2-car rear entry garage
- Crawl space or slab foundation, please specify when ordering

First Floor
1,713 sq. ft.

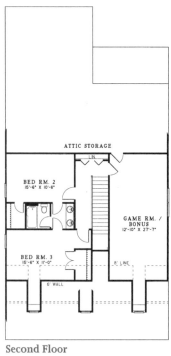

Second Floor
994 sq. ft.

Vaulted Rooms Throughout

Features

- 1,373 total square feet of living area
- 9' ceilings throughout this home
- The sunny breakfast room is very accessible to the kitchen
- Kitchen has a pass-through to the vaulted family room
- 3 bedrooms, 2 baths, 2-car garage
- Crawl space or walk-out basement foundation, please specify when ordering

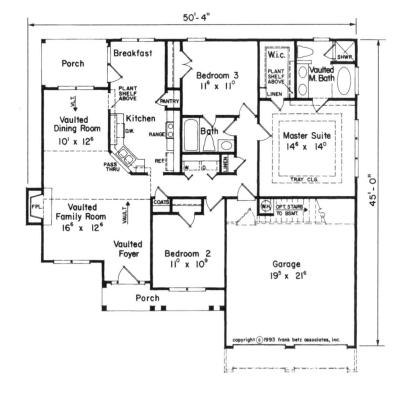

Plan #578-044D-0004

Price Code A

Covered Deck Off Breakfast Room

Features

- 1,231 total square feet of living area
- Covered front porch
- Master bedroom has separate sink area
- Large island in kitchen for eat-in dining or a preparation area
- 3 bedrooms, 1 bath, 2-car garage
- Basement foundation

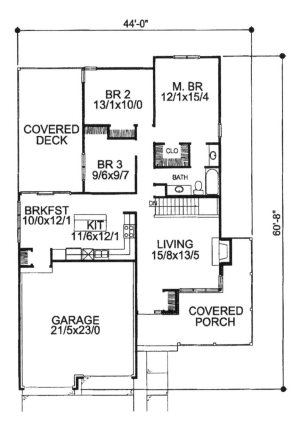

To order call toll-free 1-800-DREAM HOME or visit www.houseplansandmore.com

293

Charming Two-Story With Dormers And Porch

Features

- 1,711 total square feet of living area
- U-shaped kitchen joins the break-fast and family rooms for an open living atmosphere
- Master bedroom has a secluded covered porch and private bath
- Balcony overlooks the family room that features a fireplace and ac-cesses the deck
- 3 bedrooms, 2 1/2 baths, 2-car garage
- Basement foundation

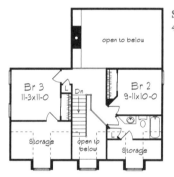

Second Floor
483 sq. ft.

Br 3
11-3x11-0

Br 2
9-11x10-0

open to below

Dn

Storage

open to below

Storage

First Floor
1,288 sq. ft.

63'-0"

43'-0"

Covered Porch

MBr
13-8x13-8

Family
20-4x13-0
vaulted

Deck

Kit
8-3x11-3

Brk
10-6x10-0

Dining
12-4x12-8

Garage
21-4x21-4

Porch

Dn

up

Plenty Of Space For Family Living

Features

- 1,632 total square feet of living area
- Compact and efficient kitchen
- Plenty of closet space throughout
- Charming covered front porch
- 4 bedrooms, 2 1/2 baths, 2-car garage
- Basement, crawl space or slab foundation, please specify when ordering

Second Floor
930 sq. ft.

First Floor
702 sq. ft.

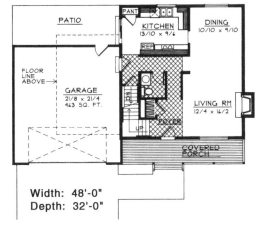

Width: 48'-0"
Depth: 32'-0"

Flexible Two-Story Home

Features

- 2,458 total square feet of living area

- Study in the front of the home makes an ideal home office

- Second floor has four bedrooms centered around a bonus room that could easily convert to a family room or fifth bedroom

- Private second floor master bedroom is situated above garage

- Bonus room on the second floor is included in the square footage

- 4 bedrooms, 2 1/2 baths, 2-car garage

- Basement foundation

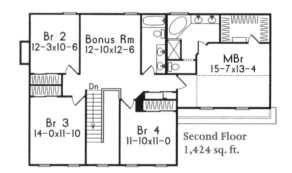

Br 2
12-3x10-6

Bonus Rm
12-10x12-6

MBr
15-7x13-4

Br 3
14-0x11-10

Br 4
11-10x11-0

Second Floor
1,424 sq. ft.

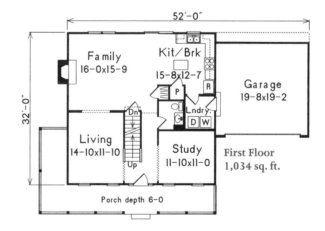

52'-0"

Family
16-0x15-9

Kit/Brk
15-8x12-7

Garage
19-8x19-2

32'-0"

Living
14-10x11-10

Study
11-10x11-0

Lndry.

First Floor
1,034 sq. ft.

Porch depth 6-0

Plan #578-001D-0040

Price Code AAA

Perfect Home For A Small Family

Features

- 864 total square feet of living area
- L-shaped kitchen with convenient pantry is adjacent to dining area
- Easy access to laundry area, linen closet and storage closet
- Both bedrooms include ample closet space
- 2 bedrooms, 1 bath
- Crawl space foundation, drawings also include basement and slab foundations

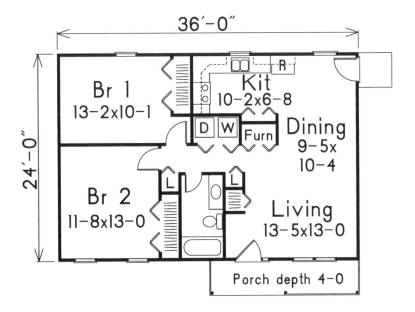

Simply Enchanting

Features

- 1,628 total square feet of living area
- Large circle transom over the front door gives this house a classic look
- 9' ceilings on the first floor
- Salon bath has a tub, separate shower, a double vanity and a large walk-in closet
- Well-lit breakfast area has view to the backyard with large patio area
- Future play room on the second floor has an additional 354 square feet of living area
- 3 bedrooms, 2 1/2 baths, 2-car garage
- Slab foundation

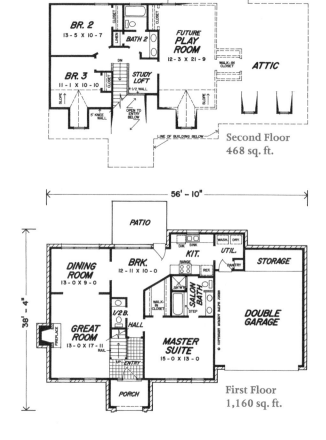

Second Floor
468 sq. ft.

First Floor
1,160 sq. ft.

Charming Style With Traditional Accents

Features

- 2,360 total square feet of living area
- Ample-sized living and dining rooms directly off foyer
- Family room is enhanced with built-in bookshelves and a cozy fireplace
- Master bedroom is complemented with a spacious walk-in closet and private bath with skylight
- 4 bedrooms, 2 1/2 baths, 2-car garage
- Partial basement/crawl space foundation, drawings also include crawl space and slab foundations

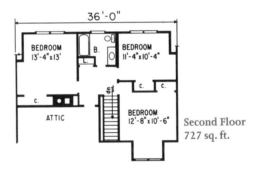

36'-0"

BEDROOM 13'-4"x13'

BEDROOM 11'-4"x10'-4"

B.

c.

c.

c.

BEDROOM 12'-8" x 10'-6"

ATTIC

Second Floor 727 sq. ft.

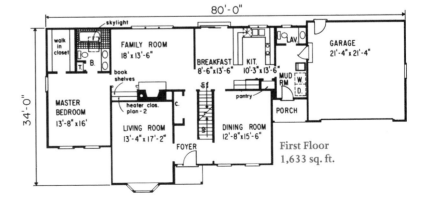

80'-0"

skylight

walk in closet

B.

FAMILY ROOM 18'x13'-6"

book shelves

BREAKFAST 8'-6"x13'-6"

KIT. 10'-3"x13'-6"

LAV.

GARAGE 21'-4" x 21'-4"

MUD RM

W.

D.

34'-0"

MASTER BEDROOM 13'-8"x16'

heater clos. plan - 2

c.

pantry

PORCH

LIVING ROOM 13'-4"x17'-2"

DINING ROOM 12'-8"x15'-6"

FOYER

First Floor 1,633 sq. ft.

Vaulted Ceilings Add Spaciousness

Features

- 1,408 total square feet of living area
- A bright country kitchen boasts an abundance of counterspace and cupboards
- The front entry is sheltered by a broad veranda
- A spa tub is brightened by a box-bay window in the master bath
- 3 bedrooms, 2 baths, 2-car side entry garage
- Basement or crawl space foundation, please specify when ordering

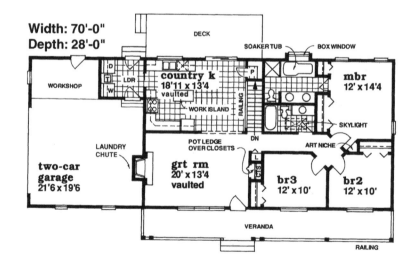

Width: 70'-0"
Depth: 28'-0"

DECK

SOAKER TUB   BOX WINDOW

WORKSHOP

D
T
W

LDR

country k
18'11 x 13'4
vaulted

WORK ISLAND

RAILING

P

mbr
12' x 14'4

SKYLIGHT

LAUNDRY CHUTE

POT LEDGE OVER CLOSETS

DN

ART NICHE

two-car garage
21'6 x 19'6

grt rm
20' x 13'4
vaulted

br3
12' x 10'

br2
12' x 10'

VERANDA

RAILING

Separate Living And Family Rooms

Features

- 1,827 total square feet of living area
- Two large bedrooms are located on the second floor for extra privacy, plus two bedrooms on the first floor
- L-shaped kitchen is adjacent to the family room
- Ample closet space in all bedrooms
- 4 bedrooms, 2 baths, 2-car garage
- Crawl space foundation, drawings also include basement and slab foundations

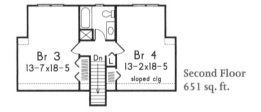

Br 3
13-7x18-5

Br 4
13-2x18-5
sloped clg

Second Floor
651 sq. ft.

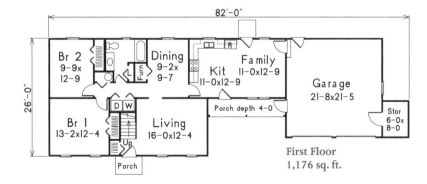

82'-0"

26'-0"

Br 2
9-9x
12-9

Dining
9-2x
9-7

Kit
11-0x12-9

Family
11-0x12-9

Garage
21-8x21-5

Fur

Br 1
13-2x12-4

D W

Living
16-0x12-4

Porch depth 4-0

Stor
6-0x
8-0

Up

Porch

First Floor
1,176 sq. ft.

Stately Front Facade

Features

- 2,327 total square feet of living area
- Bayed nook nestled between the great room and kitchen provides ample area for dining
- Vaulted second floor recreation room is an ideal place for casual family living
- Room off the entry has the ability to become an office, guest bedroom or an area for home schooling if needed
- 4 bedrooms, 2 1/2 baths, 2-car side entry garage with shop/storage
- Basement, crawl space or slab foundation, please specify when ordering

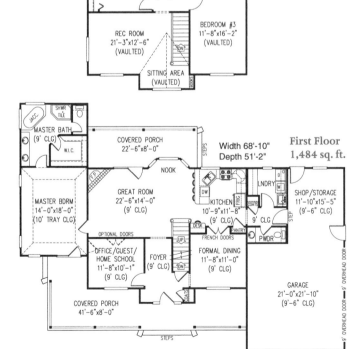

Second Floor
843 sq. ft.

BEDROOM #4
11'-1"x11'-7"
(8' CLG)

BATH

LINEN
STORAGE
TUB/SHWR
LINEN
W.I.C.

REC ROOM
21'-3"x12'-6"
(VAULTED)

BEDROOM #3
11'-8"x16'-2"
(VAULTED)

SITTING AREA
(VAULTED)

First Floor
1,484 sq. ft.

Width 68'-10"
Depth 51'-2"

MASTER BATH
(9' CLG)
JACC
SHWR
TILE
W.I.C.

COVERED PORCH
22'-6"x8'-0"

NOOK

LNDRY

SHOP/STORAGE
11'-10"x15'-5"
(9'-6" CLG)

GREAT ROOM
22'-6"x14'-0"
(9' CLG)

KITCHEN
10'-9"x11'-8"
(9' CLG)

DW
FRG
9' CLG
STEP

MASTER BDRM
14'-0"x18'-0"
(10' TRAY CLG)

OPTIONAL DOORS

DESK
FRENCH DOORS
PANTRY
PWDR

OFFICE/GUEST/
HOME SCHOOL
11'-8"x10'-1"
(9' CLG)

FOYER
(9' CLG)

FORMAL DINING
11'-8"x11'-0"
(9' CLG)

GARAGE
21'-0"x21'-10"
(9'-6" CLG)

COVERED PORCH
41'-6"x8'-0"

9' OVERHEAD DOOR   9' OVERHEAD DOOR

STEPS

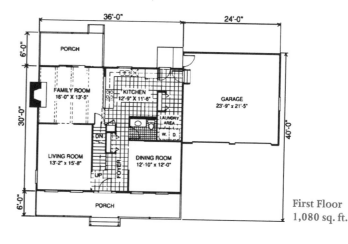

Inviting Home With Country Flavor

Features

- 1,948 total square feet of living area
- Large elongated porch for moonlit evenings
- Stylish family room features beamed ceiling
- Skillfully designed kitchen is convenient to an oversized laundry area
- Second floor bedrooms are all generously sized
- 3 bedrooms, 2 1/2 baths, 2-car garage
- Basement foundation, drawings also include crawl space foundation

Second Floor
868 sq. ft.

First Floor
1,080 sq. ft.

Extravagant Country Inspiration

Features

- 5,800 total square feet of living area
- Covered porch accesses several rooms and features a cozy fireplace for outdoor living
- A spectacular foyer leads directly to a central rotunda with a circular stair
- Luxury amenities on the first floor include a computer room, mud room and butler's pantry
- Bonus room on the second floor has an additional 500 square feet of living area
- 4 bedrooms, 5 1/2 baths, 2-car side entry garage and 2-car detached garage
- Crawl space foundation

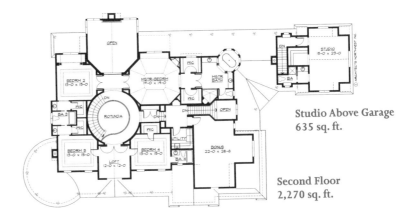

Studio Above Garage
635 sq. ft.

Second Floor
2,270 sq. ft.

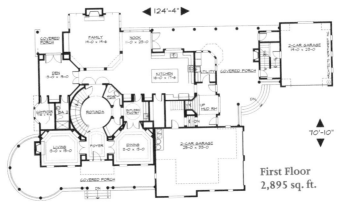

First Floor
2,895 sq. ft.

Impressive Exterior, Spacious Interior

Features

- 2,511 total square feet of living area
- Kitchen, breakfast and living rooms feature tray ceilings
- Various architectural elements combine to create an impressive exterior
- Master bedroom includes large walk-in closet, oversized bay window and private bath with shower and tub
- Large utility room has a convenient workspace
- 4 bedrooms, 2 1/2 baths, 3-car side entry garage
- Basement foundation, drawings also include crawl space and slab foundations

Br 4
11-9x10-10

MBr
16-7x12-11

Br 3
11-9x12-8

Br 2
14-8x10-10

Second Floor
1,174 sq. ft.

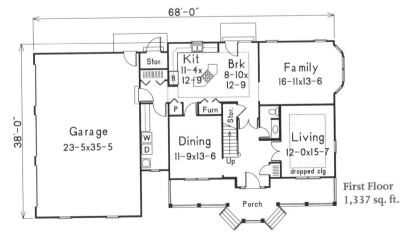

68'-0"

38'-0"

Stor.

Kit
11-4x12-9

Brk
8-10x12-9

Family
16-11x13-6

Garage
23-5x35-5

Dining
11-9x13-6

Living
12-0x15-7
dropped clg

P

Furn

Stor.

W D

Up

Porch

First Floor
1,337 sq. ft.

Beams And Gables Attract Attention

Features

- 1,743 total square feet of living area
- Second floor loft is open to below and has access to its own private deck
- Efficiently designed kitchen has an L-shaped counter perfect for dining
- Large master suite features a private deck and luxurious bath
- 2 bedrooms, 2 1/2 baths
- Crawl space foundation

Second Floor
549 sq. ft.

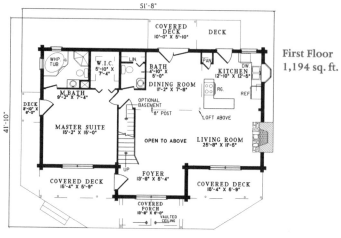

First Floor
1,194 sq. ft.

To order call toll-free 1-800-DREAM HOME or visit www.houseplansandmore.com

Economical Ranch For Easy Living

Features

- 1,314 total square feet of living area
- Energy efficient home with 2" x 6" exterior walls
- Covered porch adds immediate appeal and welcoming charm
- Open floor plan combined with a vaulted ceiling offers spacious living
- Functional kitchen is complete with a pantry and eating bar
- Cozy fireplace in the living room
- Private master bedroom features a large walk-in closet and bath
- 3 bedrooms, 2 baths, 2-car garage
- Basement foundation

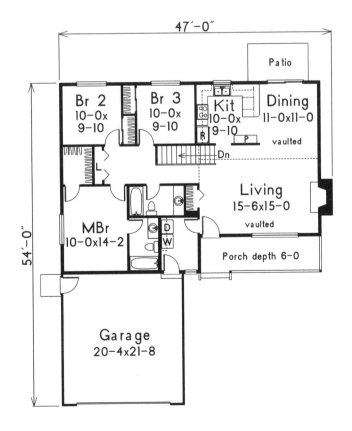

Comfortable Ranch

Features

- 1,495 total square feet of living area
- Dining room has a vaulted ceiling creating a large formal gathering area with access to a screen porch
- Cathedral ceiling in the great room adds spaciousness
- Nice-sized entry with coat closet
- 3 bedrooms, 2 baths, 2-car garage
- Basement foundation

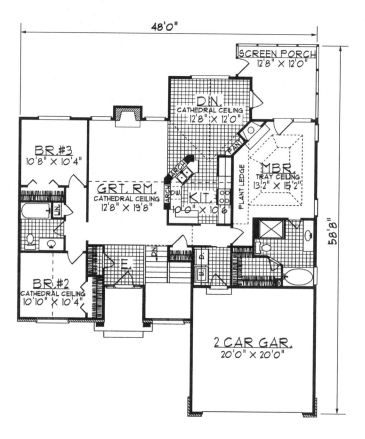

Welcoming Front Porch, A Country Touch

Features

- 2,043 total square feet of living area
- Energy efficient home with 2" x 6" exterior walls
- Two-story central foyer includes two coat closets
- Large combined space is provided by the kitchen, family and breakfast rooms
- Breakfast nook for informal dining looks out to the deck and screened porch
- 3 bedrooms, 2 1/2 baths, 2-car side entry garage
- Basement foundation, drawings also include slab foundation

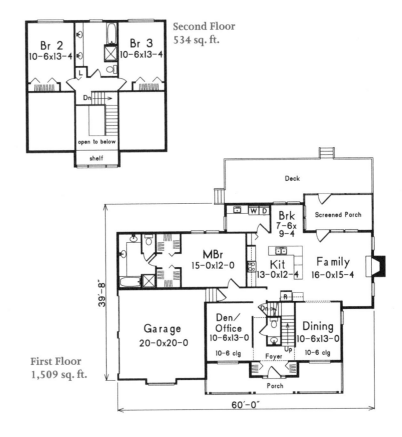

Second Floor
534 sq. ft.

First Floor
1,509 sq. ft.

Sunny Dining Room

Features

- 1,735 total square feet of living area
- Luxurious master bath has a spa tub, shower, double vanity and large walk-in closet
- Peninsula in the kitchen has a sink and dishwasher
- Massive master bedroom has a step-up ceiling and private location
- 3 bedrooms, 2 baths, 2-car garage
- Slab foundation

Width: 50'-0"
Depth: 55'-0"

Living Room Has Balcony Overlook

Interior View

Features

- 2,498 total square feet of living area
- 10' ceilings on the first floor and 9' ceilings on the second floor
- Dining room has a raised ceiling and convenient wet bar
- Master bedroom features an over-sized walk-in closet and bath with garden tub
- 3 bedrooms, 2 1/2 baths, 2-car garage
- Crawl space foundation, drawings also include slab and basement foundations

First Floor
1,530 sq. ft.

40'-0"

62'-0"

Porch

MBr
20-0x16-0

Kit
12-0x
13-0

plant shelf

Dining
15-0x11-0
raised ceiling

Living
18-0x15-0
open to above

Garage
19-8x20-8

Up

Porch

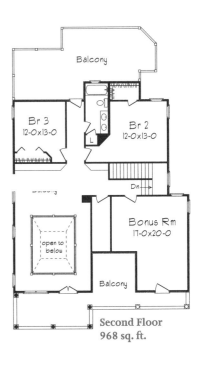

Second Floor
968 sq. ft.

Balcony

Br 3
12-0x13-0

Br 2
12-0x13-0

Bonus Rm
17-0x20-0

open to below

Balcony

Balcony

Dn

Perfect For A Narrow Lot

Features

- 1,042 total square feet of living area
- Dining and living areas combine for added space
- Cozy covered front porch
- Plenty of closet space throughout
- 3 bedrooms, 1 bath
- Basement foundation

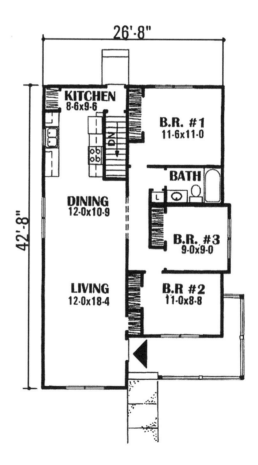

To order call toll-free 1-800-DREAM HOME or visit www.houseplansandmore.com

Gallery Opens Into Grand Living Room

Features

- 2,648 total square feet of living area
- Private study has access to the master bedroom and porch
- Grand-sized living room features a sloped ceiling, fireplace and entry to porches
- Energy efficient home with 2" x 6" exterior walls
- Master bedroom boasts an expansive bath with separate vanities, large walk-in closet and separate tub and shower units
- Large kitchen includes an eating area and breakfast bar
- Large utility room features extra counterspace and a storage closet
- 3 bedrooms, 2 baths, 2-car carport
- Crawl space foundation, drawings also include slab foundation

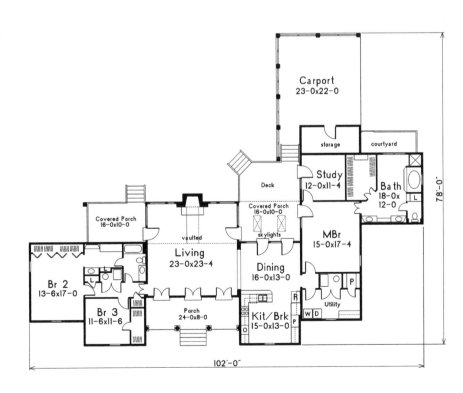

Ranch-Style Home With Many Extras

Features

- 1,295 total square feet of living area
- Wrap-around porch is a lovely place for dining
- A fireplace gives a stunning focal point to the great room that is heightened with a sloped ceiling
- The master suite is full of luxurious touches such as a walk-in closet and a lush private bath
- 2 bedrooms, 2 baths, 2-car garage
- Basement foundation

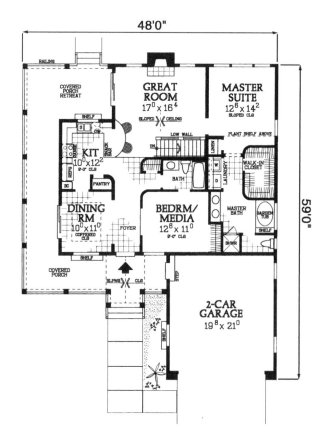

To order call toll-free **1-800-DREAM HOME** or visit www.houseplansandmore.com

Ornate Corner Porch Catches The Eye

Features

- 1,550 total square feet of living area
- Impressive front entrance with a wrap-around covered porch and raised foyer
- Corner fireplace provides a focal point in the vaulted great room
- Loft is easily converted to a third bedroom or activity center
- Large kitchen/family room includes greenhouse windows and access to the deck and utility area
- The secondary bedroom has a large dormer and window seat
- 2 bedrooms, 2 1/2 baths, 2-car garage
- Basement foundation

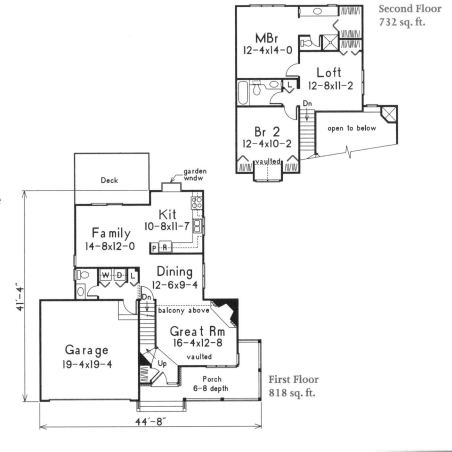

Second Floor
732 sq. ft.

MBr
12-4x14-0

Loft
12-8x11-2

Br 2
12-4x10-2
vaulted

open to below

Dn

Deck

garden wndw

Kit
10-8x11-7

Family
14-8x12-0

P R

Dining
12-6x9-4

W D L

Dn

balcony above

Garage
19-4x19-4

Great Rm
16-4x12-8
vaulted

Up

Porch
6-8 depth

First Floor
818 sq. ft.

41'-4"

44'-8"

Stone Accents Create A Great Feel

Features

- 977 total square feet of living area
- Large storage closet ideal for patio furniture storage or lawn equipment
- Large kitchen with enough room for dining looks into oversized living room
- Front covered porch adds charm
- 3 bedrooms, 2 baths, optional 1-car garage
- Slab or crawl space foundation, please specify when ordering

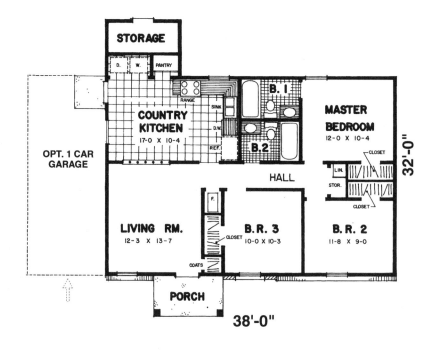

Circle-Top Windows And Columns Decorate Facade

Features

- 2,869 total square feet of living area
- Foyer, flanked by columned living and dining rooms, leads to the vaulted family room with a fireplace and twin sets of French doors
- 10' ceilings on the first floor and 9' ceilings on the second floor
- 4 bedrooms, 3 baths, 2-car rear entry garage
- Slab foundation, drawings also include crawl space foundation

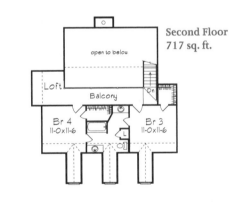

Second Floor
717 sq. ft.

open to below

Loft

Balcony

Br 4
11-0x11-6

Br 3
11-0x11-6

62'-4"

Covered Porch

Garage
21-3x21-4

Family
20-0x19-6
vaulted

MBr
16-0x14-0

up

53'-0"

Living
12-6x13-6

Dining
10-2x13-6

Kitchen
13-10x13-0

Br 2
11-4x13-0

Porch depth 6-0

Brk
13-10x10-0

First Floor
2,152 sq. ft.

Second Floor Bonus Room

Features

- 1,892 total square feet of living area
- Elegant two-story entry
- Great room is airy and open
- Arch accents throughout plan add appeal
- Kitchen has a built-in desk, island and nook
- Second floor bonus room has an additional 223 square feet of living area and is ideal for an office or fourth bedroom
- 3 bedrooms, 2 1/2 baths, 3-car garage
- Crawl space foundation

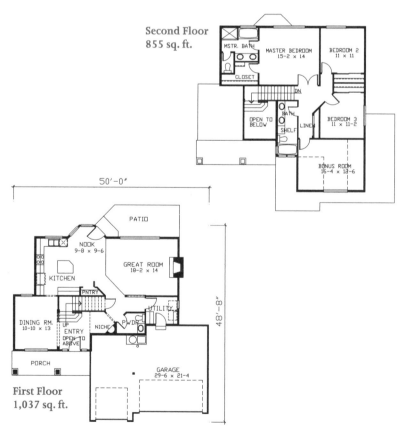

Popular First Floor Master Bedroom

Features

- 1,856 total square feet of living area

- Large secondary bedrooms include plenty of extra storage and share a full bath

- Dining area has direct access to a sundeck and flows into the living area

- The breakfast nook is a cheerful place to spend the morning with plenty of sunshine through many windows

- 3 bedrooms, 2 1/2 baths, 2-car drive under garage

- Basement foundation

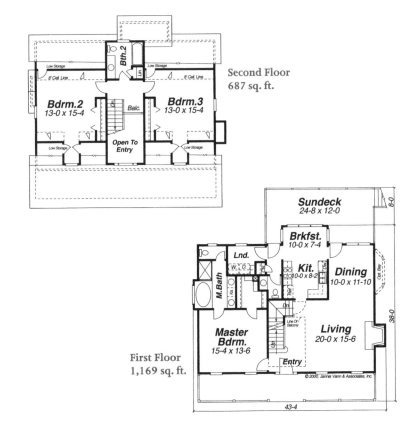

Excellent Design For Comfortable Living

Features

- 2,180 total square feet of living area
- Informal dinette and formal dining area flank the kitchen
- Fireplace is focal point in vaulted family room
- Master bedroom includes bath with walk-in closet, shower and corner garden tub
- 3 bedrooms, 2 1/2 baths, 2-car garage
- Basement foundation

**Second Floor
952 sq. ft.**

MBr
16-0x13-8

Br 3
12-4x10-0

Br 2
12-4x12-7

Dn

open to below

50'-0"

40'-0"

Family
16-2x17-0

vaulted

Dinette
9-0x12-2

Kit
10-0x12-2

Dining
11-3x15-0

L

P R

W D

Dn

Living
12-0x15-6

Garage
21-9x21-8

Foyer

up

Porch
25-0x5-0

**First Floor
1,228 sq. ft.**

Open Living Spaces

Features

- 1,974 total square feet of living area
- Bayed study has a double-door entry
- Large mud room and laundry closet are perfect for family living
- Kitchen island has a sink and space for dining
- 3 bedrooms, 2 1/2 baths, 2-car side entry garage
- Basement foundation

Second Floor
994 sq. ft.

BDRM 3
12 x 11^8

MASTER
14 x 16^4

W.I.C.

whirlpool

M. BATH

BATH

BDRM 2
12 x 14^4

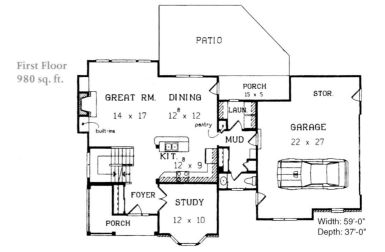

First Floor
980 sq. ft.

PATIO

GREAT RM.
14 x 17

DINING
12^8 x 12

PORCH
15 x 5

STOR.

LAUN.

built-ins

pantry

MUD

GARAGE
22 x 27

KIT.
12^8 x 9

FOYER

STUDY
12 x 10

PORCH

Width: 59'-0"
Depth: 37'-0"

Wood Beams Create A Rustic Country Home

Features

- 2,277 total square feet of living area
- Lots of windows in the great room create an inviting feeling
- First floor den/bedroom #4 would make an ideal home office
- Enormous dining area and kitchen combine to create a large gathering area overlooking into the great room
- 4 bedrooms, 3 baths, 2-car garage
- Crawl space foundation

Second Floor
928 sq. ft.

First Floor
1,349 sq. ft.

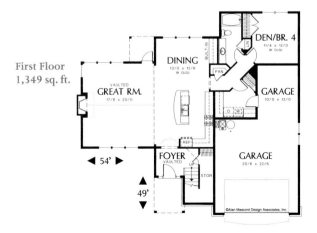

To order call toll-free 1-800-DREAM HOME or visit www.houseplansandmore.com

Loaded With Charm

Features

- 1,618 total square feet of living area
- Secondary bedrooms with walk-in closets are located on the second floor and share a bath
- Utility room is tucked away in the kitchen for convenience but is out of sight
- Dining area is brightened by a large bay window
- 3 bedrooms, 2 1/2 baths
- Slab or crawl space foundation, please specify when ordering

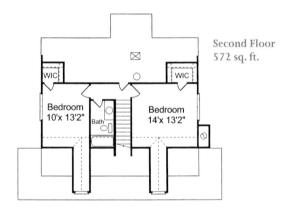

Second Floor
572 sq. ft.

WIC

Bedroom
10'x 13'2"

Bath

Bedroom
14'x 13'2"

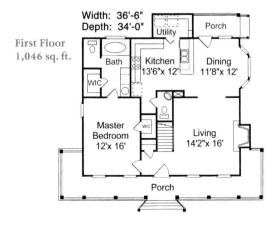

First Floor
1,046 sq. ft.

Width: 36'-6"
Depth: 34'-0"

Utility

Porch

Bath

WIC

Kitchen
13'6"x 12'

Dining
11'8"x 12'

Master
Bedroom
12'x 16'

WIC

Living
14'2"x 16'

Porch

Old-Fashioned Comfort And Privacy

Features

- 1,772 total square feet of living area
- Extended porches in front and rear provide a charming touch
- Large bay windows lend distinction to the dining room and bedroom #3
- Efficient U-shaped kitchen
- Master bedroom includes two walk-in closets
- Full corner fireplace in family room
- 3 bedrooms, 2 baths, 2-car detached garage
- Slab foundation, drawings also include crawl space foundation

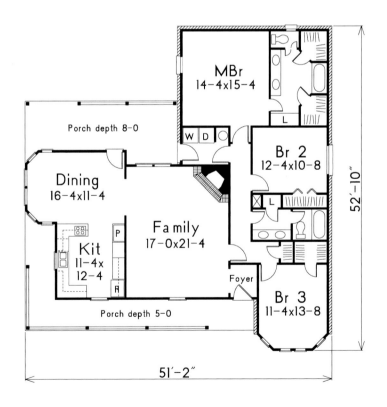

Extra Amenities Enhance Living

Features

- 2,009 total square feet of living area
- Spacious master bedroom has a dramatic sloped ceiling and private bath with double sinks and walk-in closet
- Bedroom #3 has extra storage inside closet
- Versatile screened porch is ideal for entertaining year-round
- Sunny breakfast area is located near the kitchen and screened porch for convenience
- 3 bedrooms, 2 1/2 baths
- Basement foundation

Second Floor
847 sq. ft.

First Floor
1,162 sq. ft.

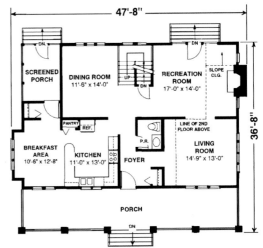

Charming Gazebo Attracts The Eye

Features

- 3,688 total square feet of living area
- A bayed two-story living room connects directly to the gazebo for added living space outdoors
- A coffered ceiling, octagon-shaped sitting area and a fireplace add drama and luxury to the master suite
- Second floor utility room is convenient and time saving
- Bonus room on the second floor has an additional 342 square feet of living area
- 4 bedrooms, 3 1/2 baths, 3-car garage
- Crawl space foundation

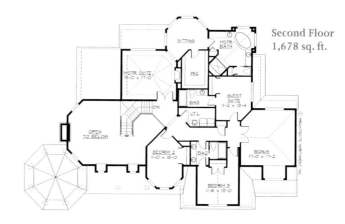

Second Floor
1,678 sq. ft.

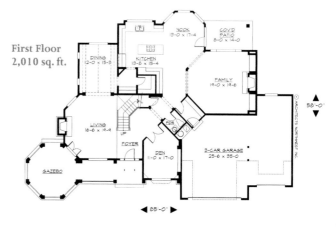

First Floor
2,010 sq. ft.

A True Victorian Treasure

Features

- 2,850 total square feet of living area
- An enormous wrap-around porch surrounds the home on one side creating a lot of outdoor living area
- A double-door entry leads to the master bedroom which features a private bath with spa tub
- Extra space in the garage allows for storage or work area
- Bonus room is included in the second floor square footage
- 3 bedrooms, 3 baths, 2-car side entry garage
- Crawl space foundation

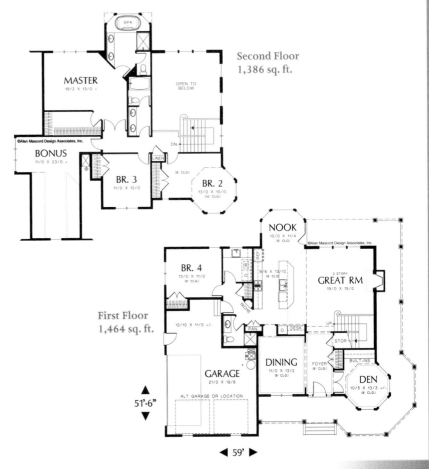

Second Floor
1,386 sq. ft.

First Floor
1,464 sq. ft.

Timeless Country Style

Features

- 1,553 total square feet of living area
- Two-story living area creates an open and airy feel to the interior especially with two dormers above
- First floor master bedroom is private and includes its own bath and walk-in closet
- Two secondary bedrooms share a full bath with double vanity
- 3 bedrooms, 2 1/2 baths, 2-car drive under garage
- Walk-out basement foundation

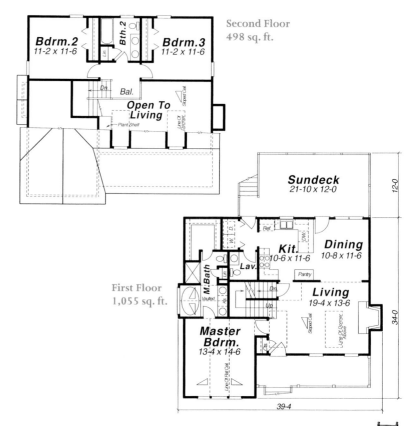

Second Floor
498 sq. ft.

Bdrm.2
11-2 x 11-6

Bth.2

Bdrm.3
11-2 x 11-6

Dn.   Bal.

Open To Living

Plant Shelf

Sundeck
21-10 x 12-0

12-0

First Floor
1,055 sq. ft.

Kit.
10-6 x 11-6

Dining
10-8 x 11-6

Ref.

DW

Lav.

W D

Pantry

M.Bath

Vaulted

Living
19-4 x 13-6

Dn.

Up

34-0

Master Bdrm.
13-4 x 14-6

39-4

An Open Feel With Vaulted Ceilings

Rear View

Features

- 1,470 total square feet of living area
- Vaulted breakfast room is cheerful and sunny
- Private second floor master bedroom has a bath and walk-in closet
- Large utility room has access to the outdoors
- 3 bedrooms, 2 baths
- Basement, crawl space or slab foundation, please specify when ordering

Second Floor
435 sq. ft.

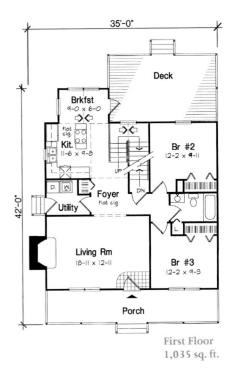

First Floor
1,035 sq. ft.

Serving Bar In Kitchen

Features

- 2,072 total square feet of living area

- Master suite has a large bay sitting area, private vaulted bath and an enormous walk-in closet

- Tray ceilings in the breakfast and dining rooms are charming touches

- Great room has a centered fireplace and a French door leading outdoors

- 3 bedrooms, 2 1/2 baths, 2-car side entry garage

- Walk-out basement, slab or crawl space foundation, please specify when ordering

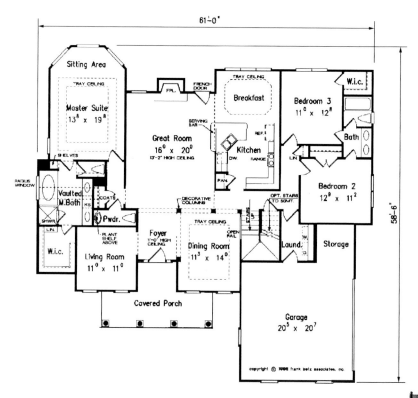

Uncommonly Styled Ranch

Features

- 1,787 total square feet of living area
- Skylights brighten the screen porch which connects to the family room and deck outdoors
- Master bedroom features a comfortable sitting area, large private bath and direct access to the screen porch
- Kitchen has a serving bar which extends dining into the family room
- 3 bedrooms, 2 baths, 2-car side entry garage
- Basement, crawl space or slab foundation, please specify when ordering

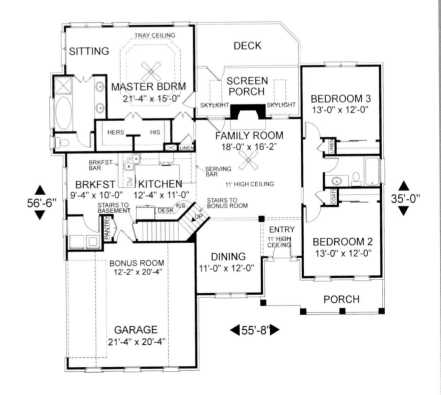

Traditional Southern Design With Modern Floor Plan

Features

- 2,214 total square feet of living area
- Great room has built-in cabinets for an entertainment system, a fireplace and French doors leading to a private rear covered porch
- Dining room has an arched opening from foyer
- Breakfast room has lots of windows for a sunny open feel
- 3 bedrooms, 2 baths, 2-car side entry garage
- Crawl space or slab foundation, please specify when ordering

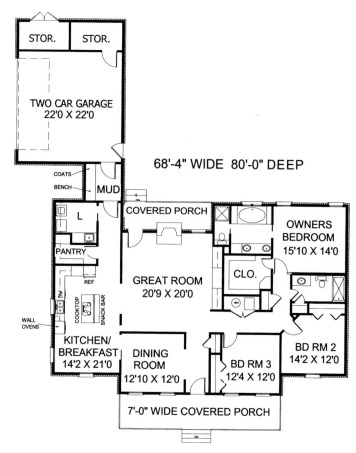

STOR. STOR.

TWO CAR GARAGE
22'0 X 22'0

68'-4" WIDE 80'-0" DEEP

COATS

BENCH

MUD

COVERED PORCH

OWNERS BEDROOM
15'10 X 14'0

L

PANTRY

REF

CLO.

GREAT ROOM
20'9 X 20'0

WALL OVENS

COOKTOP

SNACK BAR

KITCHEN/ BREAKFAST
14'2 X 21'0

DINING ROOM
12'10 X 12'0

BD RM 3
12'4 X 12'0

BD RM 2
14'2 X 12'0

7'-0" WIDE COVERED PORCH

To order call toll-free 1-800-DREAM HOME or visit www.houseplansandmore.com

Circular Stairway Adds To Front Entry

Features

- 2,360 total square feet of living area
- Master bedroom includes a sitting area and large bath
- Sloped family room ceiling provides a view from the second floor balcony
- Kitchen features an island bar and walk-in butler's pantry
- 3 bedrooms, 2 1/2 baths, 2-car side entry garage
- Crawl space foundation, drawings also include slab and basement foundations

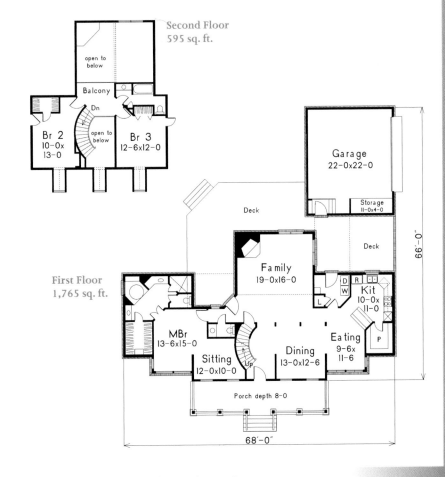

A Media Nook In The Great Room

Features

- 2,729 total square feet of living area
- Formal dining room has lovely views into the beautiful two-story great room
- Second floor loft area makes a perfect home office or children's computer area
- Bonus room on the second floor has an additional 300 square feet of living area
- 3 bedrooms, 2 1/2 baths, 2-car garage
- Basement foundation

Second Floor
951 sq. ft.

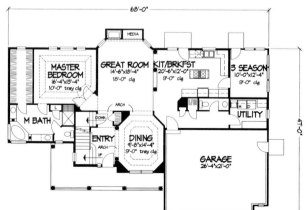

First Floor
1,778 sq. ft.

Double Bay Enhances Front Entry

Features

- 1,992 total square feet of living area
- Distinct living, dining and breakfast areas
- Master bedroom boasts a full-end bay window and a cathedral ceiling
- Storage and laundry area are located adjacent to the garage
- Bonus room over the garage for future office or playroom is included in the square footage
- 3 bedrooms, 2 1/2 baths, 2-car garage
- Crawl space foundation, drawings also include basement foundation

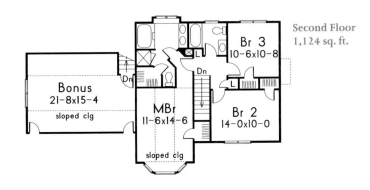

Second Floor
1,124 sq. ft.

Bonus
21-8x15-4
sloped clg

MBr
11-6x14-6
sloped clg

Br 3
10-6x10-8

Br 2
14-0x10-0

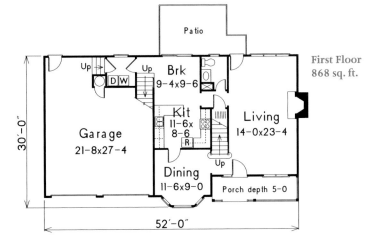

First Floor
868 sq. ft.

Patio

Brk
9-4x9-6

Garage
21-8x27-4

Kit
11-6x
8-6

Living
14-0x23-4

Dining
11-6x9-0

Porch depth 5-0

30'-0"

52'-0"

Wrap-Around Porch Adds Outdoor Style

Features

- 2,198 total square feet of living area
- Great room features a warm fireplace flanked by bookshelves for storage
- Double French doors connect the formal dining room to the kitchen
- An oversized laundry room has extra counterspace
- The second floor bonus room has an additional 385 square feet of living area
- 4 bedrooms, 2 1/2 baths, 2-car side entry garage with shop/storage
- Basement, crawl space or slab foundation, please specify when ordering

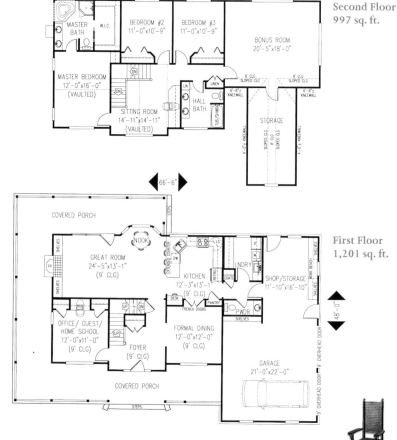

Second Floor
997 sq. ft.

First Floor
1,201 sq. ft.

Charming Home With Great Privacy

Features

- 2,445 total square feet of living area
- Sunken living room has a corner fireplace, vaulted ceiling and is adjacent to the dining room for entertaining large groups
- Large vaulted open foyer with triple skylights provides an especially bright entry
- Loft area overlooks foyer and features a decorative display area
- Bedrooms are located on the second floor for privacy and convenience, with a vaulted ceiling in the master bedroom
- 4 bedrooms, 2 1/2 baths, 3-car garage
- Basement foundation

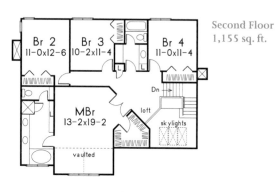

Second Floor
1,155 sq. ft.

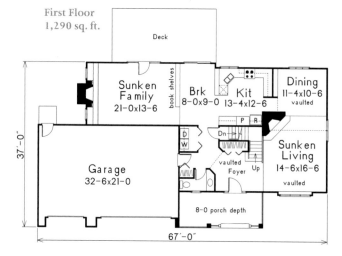

First Floor
1,290 sq. ft.

Covered Front Porch

Features

- 1,966 total square feet of living area
- Private dining room remains the focal point when entering the home
- Kitchen and breakfast room join to create a functional area
- Lots of closet space in the second floor bedrooms
- 3 bedrooms, 2 1/2 baths, 2-car side entry garage
- Basement foundation

Width: 48'-2"
Depth: 67'-5"

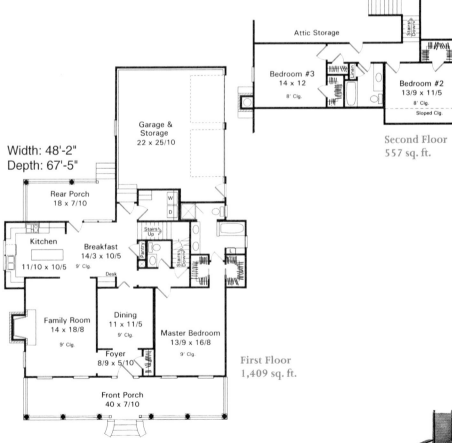

Attic Storage

Bedroom #3
14 x 12
8' Clg.

Bedroom #2
13/9 x 11/5
8' Clg.
Sloped Clg.

Second Floor
557 sq. ft.

Garage & Storage
22 x 25/10

Rear Porch
18 x 7/10

Kitchen
11/10 x 10/5

Breakfast
14/3 x 10/5
9' Clg.

Stairs Up

Desk

Family Room
14 x 18/8
9' Clg.

Dining
11 x 11/5
9' Clg.

Master Bedroom
13/9 x 16/8
9' Clg.

Foyer
8/9 x 5/10

First Floor
1,409 sq. ft.

Front Porch
40 x 7/10

Stone Accents The Front Facade

Features

- 2,089 total square feet of living area
- First floor garden solarium
- 9' ceilings on the first floor
- Energy efficient home with 2" x 6" exterior walls
- Bonus room on the second floor has an additional 313 square feet of living area
- 3 bedrooms, 2 1/2 baths, 2-car side entry garage
- Basement foundation

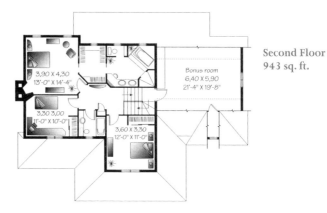

Second Floor
943 sq. ft.

First Floor
1,146 sq. ft.

Sprawling Log Ranch Design

Features

- 1,616 total square feet of living area
- Compact U-shaped kitchen designed with everything within reach
- Two sets of doors lead to an outdoor grilling porch from the cozy great room
- Large laundry room connects the garage to living areas
- 3 bedrooms, 2 baths, 2-car side entry garage
- Crawl space foundation

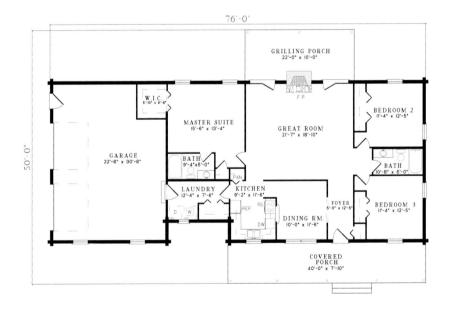

Cathedral Ceiling In Family Room

Features

- 1,288 total square feet of living area
- Energy efficient home with 2" x 6" exterior walls
- Convenient snack bar in kitchen
- Half bath has laundry facilities on first floor
- Both second floor bedrooms easily access a full bath
- 2 bedrooms, 1 1/2 baths, 1-car rear entry garage
- Basement foundation

Second Floor
597 sq. ft.

10'-0" X 11'-0"
3,00 X 3,30

11'-0" X 15'-8"
3,30 X 4,70

12'-0" X 19'-0"
3,60 X 5,70

14'-0" X 20'-0"
4,20 X 6,00

40'-0"
12,0 m

12'-8" X 15'-8"
3,80 X 4,70

First Floor
691 sq. ft.

28'-0"
8,4 m

Stylish Master Bedroom Off By Itself

Features

- 1,565 total square feet of living area
- Highly-detailed exterior adds value
- Large vaulted great room with a full wall of glass opens onto the corner deck
- Loft balcony opens to rooms below and adds to the spacious feeling
- Bay-windowed kitchen with a cozy morning room
- Master bath features a platform tub, separate shower and a large walk-in closet
- 3 bedrooms, 2 1/2 baths, 2-car garage
- Basement foundation

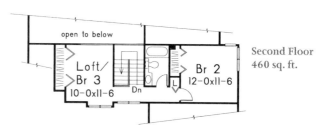

Second Floor
460 sq. ft.

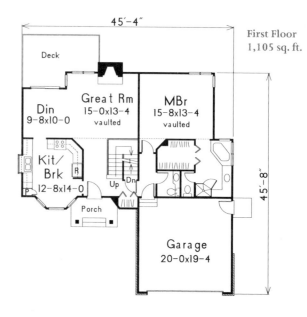

First Floor
1,105 sq. ft.

Plenty Of Bay Windows Fill Home With Sunlight

Kitchen

Features

- 2,890 total square feet of living area
- Formal dining and living rooms in the front of the home create a private place for entertaining
- Kitchen is designed for efficiency including a large island with cooktop and extra counterspace in route to the dining room
- A stunning oversized whirlpool tub is showcased in the private master bath
- Bonus room on the second floor has an additional 240 square feet of living area
- 3 bedrooms, 2 1/2 baths, 3-car side entry garage
- Crawl space foundation

Second Floor
1,260 sq. ft.

First Floor
1,630 sq. ft.

Two-Story Kitchen Attracts Attention

Features

- 3,509 total square feet of living area
- Cozy living room has built-in bookshelves flanking the entry into the great room with wet bar
- Large playroom on the second floor has a built-in seat and cabinets
- Lavish master suite features an unbelievable bath
- 4 bedrooms, 3 1/2 baths, 2-car side entry garage
- Slab foundation

Country Charm With Dormers And Covered Porch

Features

- 1,497 total square feet of living area

- Master suite has private luxurious bath with spacious walk-in closet

- Formal dining room has tray ceiling and views onto front covered porch

- Bonus room on the second floor has an additional 175 square feet of living area

- 3 bedrooms, 2 1/2 baths, 2-car garage

- Crawl space or walk-out basement foundation, please specify when ordering

Second Floor
432 sq. ft.

First Floor
1,065 sq. ft.

Sunny Eating Area

Features

- 1,925 total square feet of living area
- Energy efficient home with 2" x 6" exterior walls
- Balcony off eating area adds character
- Master bedroom has a dressing room, bath, walk-in closet and access to the utility room
- 3 bedrooms, 2 baths, 2-car side entry garage
- Crawl space foundation, drawings also include slab foundation

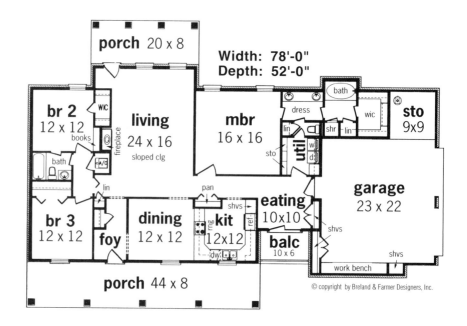

porch 20 x 8

Width: 78'-0"
Depth: 52'-0"

br 2 12 x 12

WIC

living 24 x 16 sloped clg

mbr 16 x 16

dress

bath

wic

sto 9x9

fireplace

books

bath

lin

sto

utll

garage 23 x 22

br 3 12 x 12

foy

dining 12 x 12

kit 12x12

eating 10x10

shvs

balc 10 x 6

work bench

shvs

porch 44 x 8

© copyright by Breland & Farmer Designers, Inc.

Cottage With Modern Amenities

Features

- 1,816 total square feet of living area
- The living room features a two-way fireplace with nearby window seat
- Wrap-around dining room windows create a sunroom appearance
- Master bedroom has an abundant closet and storage space
- Rear dormers, closets and desk areas create an interesting and functional second floor
- 3 bedrooms, 2 1/2 baths, 2-car detached garage
- Slab foundation, drawings also include crawl space foundation

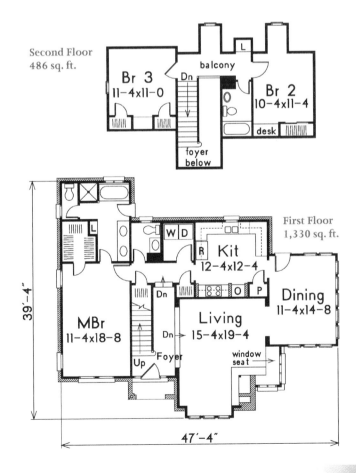

Second Floor
486 sq. ft.

Br 3
11-4x11-0

balcony

Dn

Br 2
10-4x11-4

desk

foyer
below

First Floor
1,330 sq. ft.

W D

R

Kit
12-4x12-4

Dn

O P

Dining
11-4x14-8

MBr
11-4x18-8

Dn

Living
15-4x19-4

Up

Foyer

window seat

39'-4"

47'-4"

Perfect Farmhouse For Family Living

Features

- 2,129 total square feet of living area
- Energy efficient home with 2" x 6" exterior walls
- Home office has a double-door entry and is secluded from other living areas
- Corner fireplace in living area is a nice focal point
- Bonus room above the garage has an additional 407 square feet of living area
- 3 bedrooms, 2 1/2 baths, 2-car side entry garage
- Basement foundation

Second Floor
993 sq. ft.

13'-0" X 14'-4"
3,90 X 4,30

10'-8" X 12'-0"
3,20 X 3,60

12'-0" X 11'-0"
3,60 X 3,30

21'-4" X 16'-0"
6,40 X 4,80

First Floor
1,136 sq. ft.

19'-0" X 13'-4"
5,70 X 4,00

13'-4" X 11'-0"
4,00 X 3,30

13'-4" X 15'-4"
4,00 X 4,60

38'-0"
11,4 m

12'-0" X 13'-4"
3,60 X 4,00

21'-4" X 24'-8"
6,40 X 7,40

56'-0"
16,8 m

To order call toll-free 1-800-DREAM HOME or visit www.houseplansandmore.com

Charming Cedar Shakes

Features

- 1,842 total square feet of living area
- Vaulted family room features a fire-place and an elegant bookcase
- Island countertop in kitchen makes cooking convenient
- Rear facade has an intimate porch area ideal for relaxing
- 3 bedrooms, 2 baths, 2-car garage
- Slab or crawl space foundation, please specify when ordering

Width: 56'-4"
Depth: 68'-6"

Two-Story Foyer Adds Spacious Feeling

Features

- 1,833 total square feet of living area

- Large master bedroom includes a spacious bath with garden tub, separate shower and large walk-in closet

- The spacious kitchen and dining area are brightened by large windows and patio access

- Detached two-car garage with walkway leading to house adds charm to this country home

- 3 bedrooms, 2 1/2 baths, 2-car detached side entry garage

- Crawl space foundation, drawings also include slab foundation

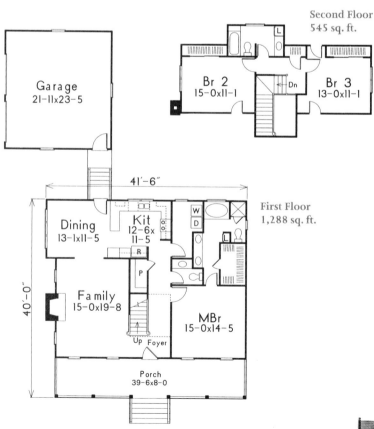

Garage
21-11x23-5

Second Floor
545 sq. ft.

Br 2
15-0x11-1

Br 3
13-0x11-1

Dn

First Floor
1,288 sq. ft.

41'-6"

40'-0"

Dining
13-1x11-5

Kit
12-6x
11-5

W
D

Family
15-0x19-8

R

P

MBr
15-0x14-5

Up   Foyer

Porch
39-6x8-0

Gorgeous Award-Winning Victorian Design

Features

- 5,250 total square feet of living area
- Spacious wrap-around covered porch features an outdoor fireplace and built-in barbecue grill perfect for entertaining
- Each bedroom has its own bath and walk-in closet
- Dramatic circular staircase is high-lighted in rotunda with 27' ceiling
- Master bath showcases an octagon-shaped space featuring a whirlpool tub
- 4 bedrooms, 4 1/2 baths, 4-car side entry garage
- Crawl space foundation

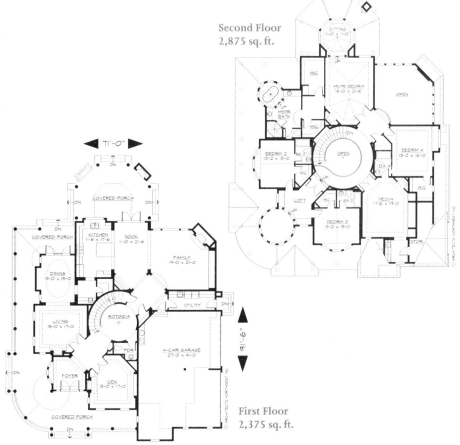

Second Floor
2,875 sq. ft.

First Floor
2,375 sq. ft.

Terrific Accents Enhance Facade

Features

- 1,482 total square feet of living area
- Family room includes 42" high built-in TV cabinet
- Spacious kitchen and dining room also include a built-in desk and a French door leading to the outdoors
- Optional bonus room on the second floor has an additional 141 square feet of living area
- 3 bedrooms, 2 1/2 baths, 2-car garage
- Walk-out basement, crawl space or slab foundation, please specify when ordering

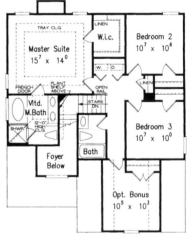

Second Floor
786 sq. ft.

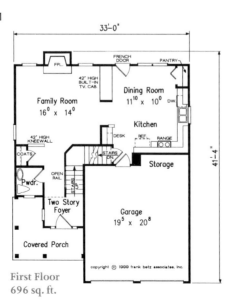

First Floor
696 sq. ft.

Plan #578-001D-0029

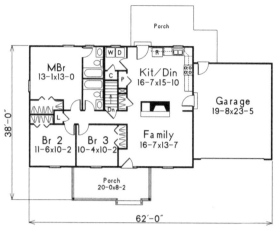

Fireplace Warms Living Area

Features

- 1,260 total square feet of living area
- Spacious kitchen and dining area feature a large pantry, storage area and easy access to the garage and laundry room
- Pleasant covered front porch adds a practical touch
- Master bedroom with a private bath adjoins two other bedrooms, all with plenty of closet space
- 3 bedrooms, 2 baths, 2-car garage
- Basement foundation, drawings also include crawl space and slab foundations

Plan #578-025D-0006

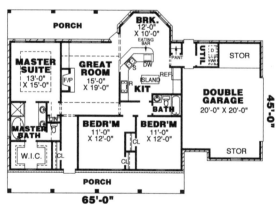

Cozy Home For Family Living

Features

- 1,612 total square feet of living area
- Covered porch in rear of home creates an outdoor living area
- Master suite is separated from other bedrooms for privacy
- Eating bar in kitchen extends into breakfast area for additional seating
- 3 bedrooms, 2 baths, 2-car side entry garage
- Slab foundation

To order call toll-free 1-800-DREAM HOME or visit www.houseplansandmore.com

Traditional Southern-Style Home

Features

- 1,785 total square feet of living area
- 9' ceilings throughout home
- Luxurious master bath includes a whirlpool tub and separate shower
- Cozy breakfast area is convenient to the kitchen
- 3 bedrooms, 3 baths, 2-car detached garage
- Basement, crawl space or slab foundation, please specify when ordering

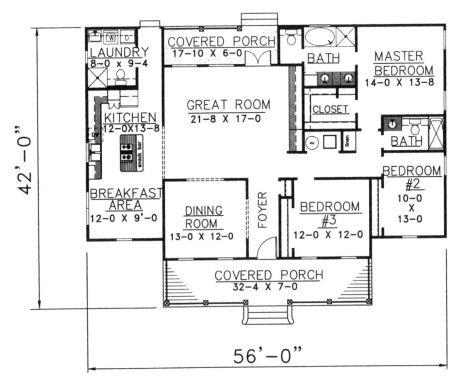

Plan #578-030D-0001

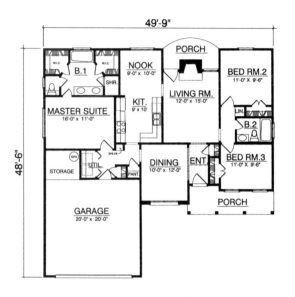

49'-9"

48'-6"

W.I.C. | B.1 | W.I.C.
SHR.
MASTER SUITE
16'-0" x 11'-0"

NOOK
9'-0" x 10'-0"

PORCH

BED RM.2
11'-0" X 9'-6"

KIT.
9' x 10'

LIVING RM.
12'-0" x 15'-0"

LIN.
B.2

SHELVES

UTIL.
STORAGE
PANT

DINING
10'-0" x 12'-0"

ENT

BED RM.3
11'-0" X 9'-6"

GARAGE
20'-0" x 20'-0"

PORCH

Scalloped Front Porch

Features

- 1,374 total square feet of living area
- Garage has extra storage space
- Spacious living room has a fireplace
- Well-designed kitchen enjoys an adjacent breakfast nook
- Secluded master suite maintains privacy
- 3 bedrooms, 2 baths, 2-car garage
- Slab or crawl space foundation, please specify when ordering

Plan #578-047D-0005

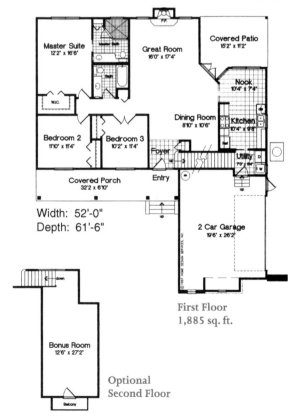

Master Suite
12'2" x 16'6"

Master Bath

Great Room
16'0" x 17'4"

FP.

Covered Patio
15'2" x 11'2"

Bath

Nook
10'4" x 7'4"

W.I.C.

Dining Room
8'10" x 10'6"

Kitchen
10'4" x 9'8"

Bedroom 2
11'10" x 11'4"

Bedroom 3
10'2" x 11'4"

Foyer

Utility
7'9" x 6'4"

Covered Porch
32'2" x 6'10"

Entry

2 Car Garage
19'6" x 26'2"

Width: 52'-0"
Depth: 61'-6"

First Floor
1,885 sq. ft.

Bonus Room
12'6" x 27'2"

Optional
Second Floor

Balcony

Comfortable Rustic Style

Features

- 1,885 total square feet of living area
- Dining and great rooms combine to create one large, versatile area
- Bonus room above the garage has an additional 327 square feet of living area
- 3 bedrooms, 2 baths, 2-car side entry garage
- Basement foundation

Impressive Foyer

Features

- 1,856 total square feet of living area
- Beautiful covered porch creates a Southern accent
- Kitchen has an organized feel with lots of cabinetry
- Large foyer has a grand entrance and leads into the family room through columns and an arched opening
- 3 bedrooms, 2 baths, 2-car side entry garage
- Walk-out basement, crawl space or slab foundation, please specify when ordering

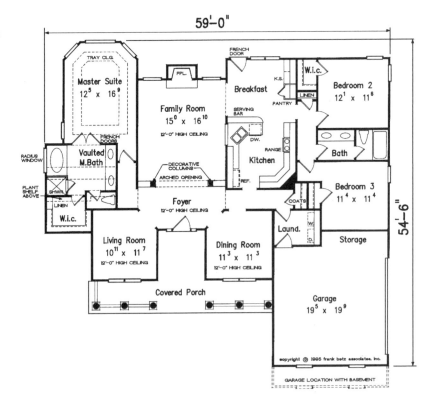

Plan #578-058D-0006

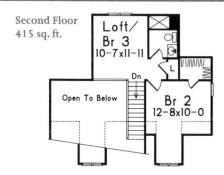

Second Floor
415 sq. ft.

Loft/
Br 3
10-7x11-11

Br 2
12-8x10-0

Open To Below

Dn

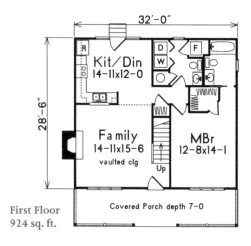

32'-0"

Kit/Din
14-11x12-0

Family
14-11x15-6
vaulted clg

MBr
12-8x14-1

Up

28'-6"

First Floor
924 sq. ft.

Covered Porch depth 7-0

Perfect Getaway Home

Features

- 1,339 total square feet of living area
- Full-length covered porch enhances front facade
- Vaulted ceiling and stone fireplace add drama to the family room
- Walk-in closets in the bedrooms provide ample storage space
- Combined kitchen/dining area adjoins the family room for the perfect entertaining space
- 3 bedrooms, 2 1/2 baths
- Crawl space foundation

Plan #578-060D-0005

STOR.

PATIO
DECK

2 CAR
GARAGE

PORCH

MASTER
SUITE
16-0 X 13-0

SALON
BATH

GREAT ROOM
20-0 X 16-8

BRK.
9-0 X 9-0

B.R. 2
11-0 X 13-2

B.R. 3
10-4 X 11-6

DINING
ROOM
13-0 X 11-6

KIT.
11-0 X
9-10

PORCH

58'-9"

58'-8"

Great Plantation Style Home

Features

- 1,742 total square feet of living area
- Formal entry with columns accesses the dining area and great room
- Kitchen has an eating bar overlooking the bayed breakfast room
- Master bath has a step-up tub with windows on two sides, separate shower and huge walk-in closet
- 3 bedrooms, 2 1/2 baths, 2-car side entry garage with storage
- Slab or crawl space foundation, please specify when ordering

Victorian Exterior With Custom-Feel Interior

Features

- 3,321 total square feet of living area
- Cozy den has two walls of book-shelves making it a quiet retreat
- A useful screen porch is located off the dining room for dining and entertaining outdoors
- Varied ceiling heights throughout bedrooms on the second floor add interest
- 4 bedrooms, 2 1/2 baths, 2-car side entry garage
- Basement foundation

Second Floor
1,701 sq. ft.

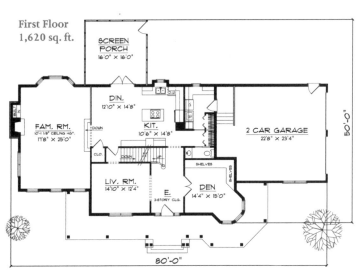

First Floor
1,620 sq. ft.

Plan #578-031D-0011

Width: 70'-6"
Depth: 57'-0"

© David C. Lutz

Convenient And Charming

Features

- 2,164 total square feet of living area
- Country-styled front porch adds charm
- Plenty of counterspace in the kitchen
- Large utility area meets big families' laundry needs
- French doors lead to the covered rear porch
- 4 bedrooms, 2 1/2 baths, 2-car side entry garage
- Slab foundation

Plan #578-068D-0010

Price Code C

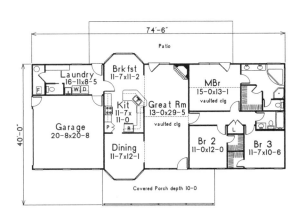

74'-6"

40'-0"

Covered Porch depth 10-0

Secluded Bedrooms

Features

- 1,849 total square feet of living area
- Laundry/mud room features a storage area and half bath
- Master bath has jacuzzi tub, double sinks, shower and walk-in closet
- Kitchen has a wrap-around eating counter and is positioned between the formal dining area and breakfast room for convenience
- 3 bedrooms, 2 1/2 baths, 2-car side entry garage
- Slab foundation, drawings also include crawl space foundation

To order call toll-free 1-800-DREAM HOME **or visit** www.houseplansandmore.com

Fully Columned Front Entrance

Features

- 2,365 total square feet of living area
- 9' ceilings throughout the home
- Expansive central living room is complemented by a corner fireplace
- Breakfast bay overlooks the rear porch
- Master bedroom features a bath with two walk-in closets and vanities, separate tub and shower and handy linen closet
- Peninsula keeps kitchen private
- 4 bedrooms, 2 baths, 2-car carport
- Slab foundation

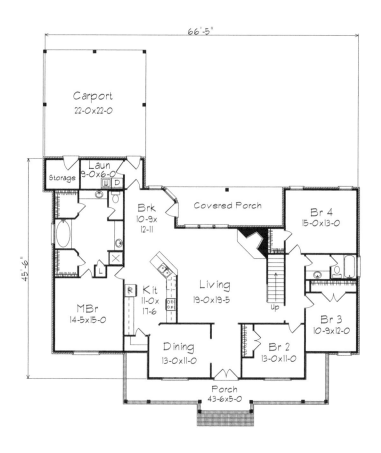

Plan #578-008D-0094

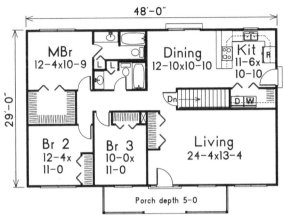

48'-0"

29'-0"

MBr
12-4x10-9

Dining
12-10x10-10

Kit
11-6x
10-10

Br 2
12-4x
11-0

Br 3
10-0x
11-0

Living
24-4x13-4

Porch depth 5-0

Ranch With Country Charm

Features

- 1,364 total square feet of living area
- Master bedroom features a spacious walk-in closet and private bath
- Living room is highlighted with several windows
- Kitchen with snack bar is adjacent to the dining area
- Plenty of storage space throughout
- 3 bedrooms, 2 baths, optional 2-car garage
- Basement foundation, drawings also include crawl space foundation

Plan #578-047D-0008

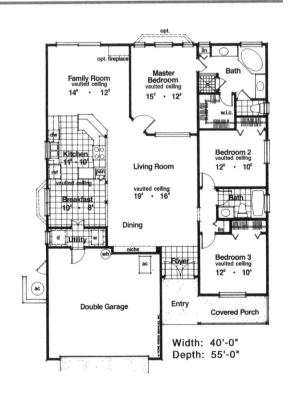

opt.

opt. fireplace

Family Room
vaulted ceiling
14⁰ · 12²

Master
Bedroom
vaulted ceiling
15² · 12⁸

Bath

w.i.c.

Kitchen
11⁴ · 10⁴
vaulted ceiling

Living Room

vaulted ceiling
19⁴ · 16⁴

Bedroom 2
vaulted ceiling
12⁰ · 10⁴

Breakfast
10⁴ · 8⁴

Dining

Bath

Utility

niche

Bedroom 3
vaulted ceiling
12⁰ · 10⁴

Double Garage

ac

Foyer

Entry

Covered Porch

Width: 40'-0"
Depth: 55'-0"

Whirlpool Tub In Master Bath

Features

- 1,571 total square feet of living area
- Bedrooms #2 and #3 share a bath in their own private hall
- Kitchen counter overlooks family room
- Open living area adds appeal with vaulted ceiling and display niche
- 3 bedrooms, 2 baths, 2-car garage
- Slab foundation

Many Decorative Touches Throughout

Features

- 2,788 total square feet of living area
- Breakfast nook is flooded with sunlight from skylights
- Fireplace in great room is framed by media center and shelving
- Large game room is secluded for active children
- 3 bedrooms, 2 1/2 baths, 3-car side entry garage
- Crawl space foundation

Width: 76'-6"
Depth: 72'-0"

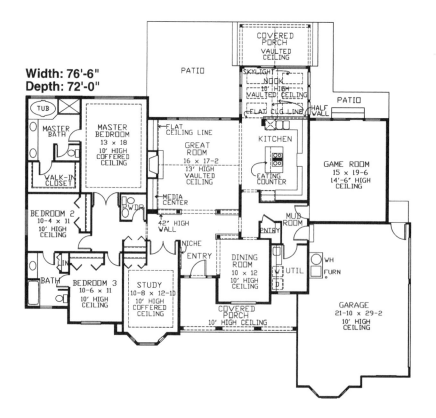

Plan #578-034D-0008

Open Floor Plan

Features

- 1,875 total square feet of living area
- Peninsula separating the kitchen and dining room has a sink, dishwasher and eating area
- Tall ceilings throughout living area create spaciousness
- Columned foyer adds style
- 3 bedrooms, 2 1/2 baths, 2-car garage
- Basement foundation

Plan #578-068D-0005

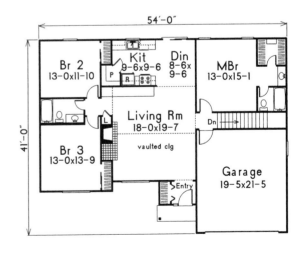

Spacious Living In This Ranch

Features

- 1,433 total square feet of living area
- Vaulted living room includes a fireplace and entertainment center
- Bedrooms #2 and #3 share a full bath
- Master bedroom has a full bath and large walk-in closet
- 3 bedrooms, 2 baths, 2-car garage
- Basement foundation, drawings also include crawl space and slab foundations

To order call toll-free 1-800-DREAM HOME or visit www.houseplansandmore.com

Attractive Stone Accents

Features

- 3,230 total square feet of living area
- Efficiently designed eating counter in kitchen for added dining
- Enormous deck surrounds the rear of this home making it perfect for entertaining
- Interesting two-sided fireplace in the master bedroom
- Open living areas create a feeling of spaciousness
- 3 bedrooms, 2 1/2 baths
- Walk-out basement foundation

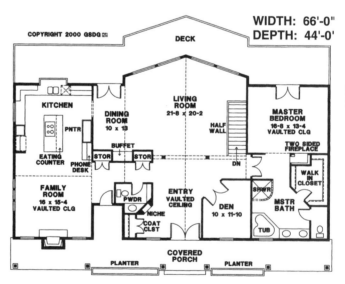

WIDTH: 66'-0"
DEPTH: 44'-0'

COPYRIGHT 2000 GSDG

First Floor
2,169 sq. ft.

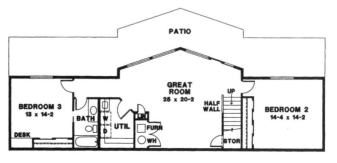

Lower Level
1,061 sq. ft.

Plan #578-008D-0178

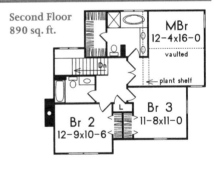

Second Floor
804 sq. ft.

First Floor
1,068 sq. ft.

Country Elegance

Features

- 1,872 total square feet of living area
- Recessed porch has entry door with sidelights and roof dormers
- Foyer with handcrafted stair adjoins living room with fireplace
- Largest of three second floor bedrooms enjoys double closets and private access to hall bath
- 4 bedrooms, 2 baths, 2-car garage
- Basement foundation, drawings also include crawl space and slab foundations

Plan #578-045D-0005

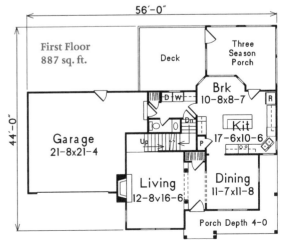

Second Floor
890 sq. ft.

First Floor
887 sq. ft.

Cozy Columned Archway

Features

- 1,777 total square feet of living area
- Large master bedroom has a bath with whirlpool tub, separate shower and spacious walk-in closet
- Large island kitchen features a breakfast bay and access to the three-season porch
- 3 bedrooms, 2 1/2 baths, 2-car garage
- Basement foundation

Stately Ranch With Large Porch

Features

- 1,389 total square feet of living area
- Great open space for entertaining with eating bar in kitchen overlooking the breakfast and great rooms
- Private master suite has a sloped ceiling and secluded bath
- Handy extra storage space in the garage
- 3 bedrooms, 2 baths, 2-car garage
- Slab or crawl space foundation, please specify when ordering

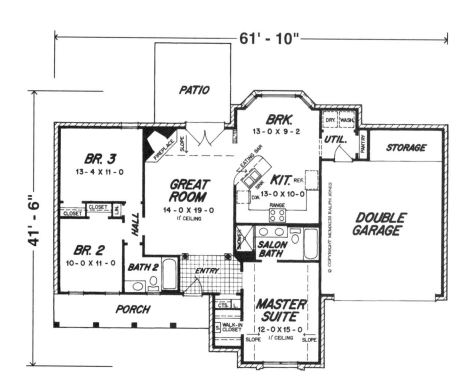

Plan #578-008D-0090

Covered Porch Highlights Home

Features

- 1,364 total square feet of living area
- Bedrooms are separated from the living area for privacy
- Master bedroom has a private bath and large walk-in closet
- Laundry area is conveniently located near the kitchen
- Built-in pantry in the kitchen
- 3 bedrooms, 2 baths, optional 2-car garage
- Basement foundation

Plan #578-062D-0034

Price Code C

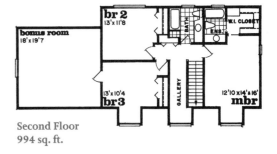

Second Floor
994 sq. ft.

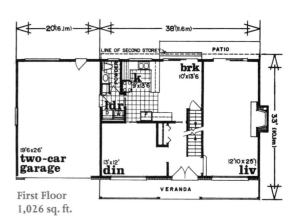

First Floor
1,026 sq. ft.

Triple Dormer Delight

Features

- 2,020 total square feet of living area
- Gallery hall on second floor is the perfect place to spotlight artwork
- Large living room has front and rear views along with a fireplace
- Bonus room on the second floor has an additional 377 square feet of living area
- 3 bedrooms, 2 1/2 baths, 2-car garage
- Basement foundation

To order call toll-free 1-800-DREAM HOME or visit www.houseplansandmore.com

Vaulted Two-Story Foyer Makes A Grand Entry

Features

- 2,599 total square feet of living area

- Office/home school room could easily be converted to a fifth bedroom

- Recreation room on the second floor would make a great casual living area or children's play room

- Large shop/storage has an oversized work bench for hobbies or projects

- Bonus room on the second floor has an additional 385 square feet of living area

- 4 bedrooms, 2 1/2 baths, 2-car garage with shop/storage

- Basement, crawl space or slab foundation, please specify when ordering

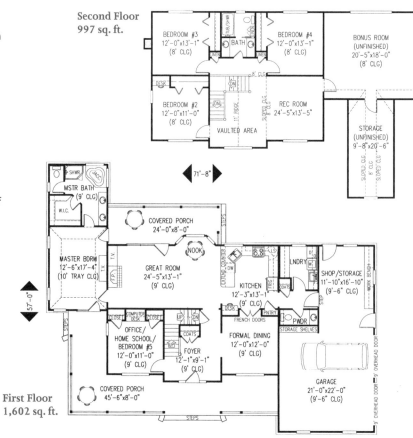

Second Floor 997 sq. ft.

BEDROOM #3 12'-0"x13'-1" (8' CLG)

BATH

BEDROOM #4 12'-0"x13'-1" (8' CLG)

BONUS ROOM (UNFINISHED) 20'-5"x18'-0" (8' CLG)

DESK

BEDROOM #2 12'-0"x11'-0" (8' CLG)

REC ROOM 24'-5"x13'-5"

VAULTED AREA

STORAGE (UNFINISHED) 9'-8"x20'-6"

71'-8"

MSTR BATH (9' CLG)

W.I.C.

COVERED PORCH 24'-0"x8'-0"

NOOK

LNDRY

SHOP/STORAGE 11'-10"x16'-10" (9'-6" CLG)

MASTER BDRM 12'-6"x17'-4" (10' TRAY CLG)

GREAT ROOM 24'-5"x13'-1" (9' CLG)

KITCHEN 12'-3"x13'-1" (9' CLG)

57'-0"

COMPUTER DESK

OFFICE/ HOME SCHOOL/ BEDROOM #5 12'-0"x11'-0" (9' CLG)

FOYER 12'-1"x9'-1"

FORMAL DINING 12'-0"x12'-0" (9' CLG)

PWDR

STORAGE SHELVES

GARAGE 21'-0"x22'-0" (9'-6" CLG)

First Floor 1,602 sq. ft.

COVERED PORCH 45'-6"x8'-0"

STEPS

Plan #578-008D-0026

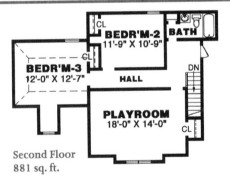

Lovely Inviting Covered Porch

Features

- 1,120 total square feet of living area
- Kitchen/family room creates a useful spacious area
- Rustic, colonial design is perfect for many surroundings
- Oversized living room is ideal for entertaining
- Carport includes a functional storage area
- 3 bedrooms, 2 baths, 1-car carport
- Basement foundation, drawings also include crawl space and slab foundations

Plan #578-025D-0022

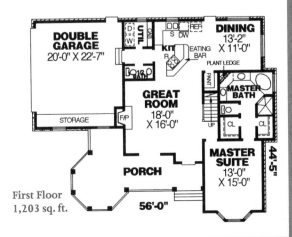

Second Floor
881 sq. ft.

First Floor
1,203 sq. ft.

Enchanting Victorian Gazebo

Features

- 2,084 total square feet of living area
- Charming bay window in the master suite allows sunlight in
- Great room accesses front covered porch
- Large playroom on the second floor is ideal for family living
- 3 bedrooms, 2 1/2 baths, 2-car side entry garage
- Slab, crawl space or basement foundation, please specify when ordering

Pleasant Country Front Porch

Features

- 1,233 total square feet of living area
- A versatile dressing area is featured in the full bath shared by the secondary bedrooms
- Lovely master suite has a private bath and a walk-in closet
- The foyer has a coat closet as well as an additional storage closet
- 3 bedrooms, 2 baths, 2-car garage
- Slab or crawl space foundation, please specify when ordering

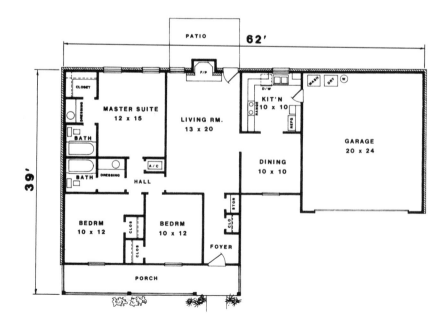

Plan #578-008D-0085

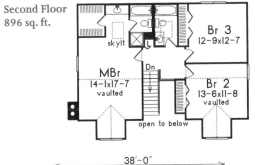

Second Floor
896 sq. ft.

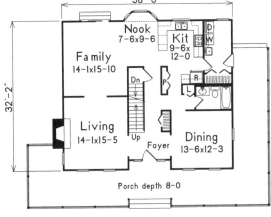

First Floor
1,216 sq. ft.

Dormers Enhance Facade

Features

- 2,112 total square feet of living area
- Kitchen efficiently connects to the formal dining area
- Nook located between the family room and kitchen creates an ideal breakfast area
- Both baths on the second floor feature skylights
- 3 bedrooms, 2 1/2 baths
- Basement foundation, drawings also include crawl space foundation

Plan #578-065D-0028

Price Code B

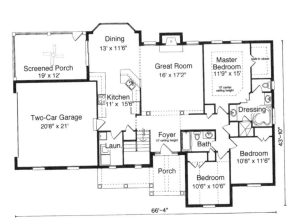

Spacious Feel To This Home

Features

- 1,611 total square feet of living area
- Sliding doors lead to a delightful screened porch
- Master bedroom has a lavish dressing room and large walk-in closet
- The kitchen offers an abundance of cabinets and counterspace with convenient access to the laundry room and garage
- 3 bedrooms, 2 baths, 2-car side entry garage
- Basement foundation

To order call toll-free 1-800-DREAM HOME or visit www.houseplansandmore.com

Christine Canova 03/02

Comfortable Colonial Ranch

Features

- 1,404 total square feet of living area
- Dining area and kitchen connect allowing for convenience and ease
- Well-located laundry area is within steps of bedrooms and baths
- Vaulted grand room creates a feeling of spaciousness for this gathering area
- 3 bedrooms, 2 1/2 baths, 2-car garage
- Slab foundation

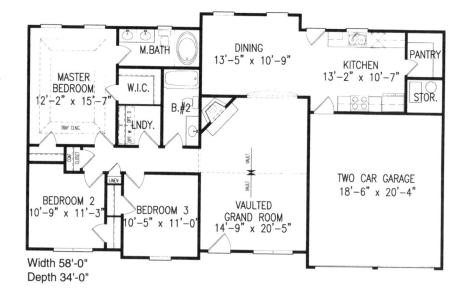

M.BATH

DINING
13'-5" x 10'-9"

KITCHEN
13'-2" x 10'-7"

PANTRY

MASTER BEDROOM
12'-2" x 15'-7"

W.I.C.

B. #2

STOR.

TRAY CLNG.

OPT. D

LNDY.

VAULT

TWO CAR GARAGE
18'-6" x 20'-4"

COAT CLOSET

LINEN

VAULT

BEDROOM 2
10'-9" x 11'-3"

BEDROOM 3
10'-5" x 11'-0"

VAULTED GRAND ROOM
14'-9" x 20'-5"

Width 58'-0"
Depth 34'-0"

To order call toll-free 1-800-DREAM HOME or visit www.houseplansandmore.com

Plan #578-008D-0011

Rustic Facade

Features

- 1,550 total square feet of living area
- Convenient mud room between the garage and kitchen
- Oversized dining area allows plenty of space for entertaining
- Master bedroom has a private bath and ample closet space
- Large patio off the family room brings the outdoors in
- 3 bedrooms, 2 baths, 2-car side entry garage
- Basement foundation, drawings also include crawl space or slab foundations

Plan #578-021D-0015

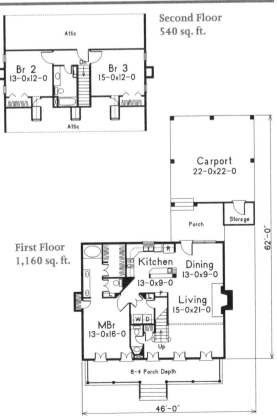

Authentic Southern Home

Features

- 1,700 total square feet of living area
- Fully appointed kitchen with wet bar
- Energy efficient home with 2" x 6" exterior walls
- Linen drop from the second floor bath to the utility room
- 3 bedrooms, 2 1/2 baths, 2-car attached carport
- Crawl space foundation, drawings also include basement and slab foundations

To order call toll-free 1-800-DREAM HOME or visit www.houseplansandmore.com

Plan #578-019D-0014

Price Code D

Striking Great Room

Features

- 2,586 total square feet of living area
- Great room has an impressive tray ceiling and see-through fireplace into the bayed breakfast room
- Master bedroom has a walk-in closet and private bath
- 4 bedrooms, 3 baths, 2-car side entry garage
- Basement foundation, drawings also include crawl space and slab foundations

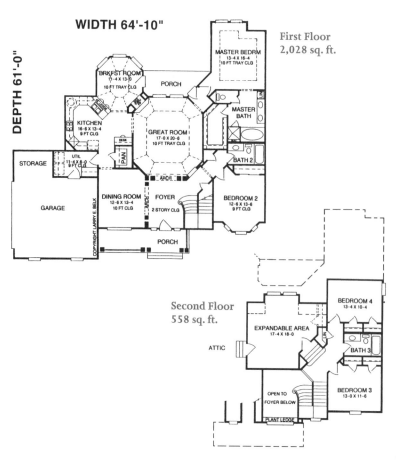

WIDTH 64'-10"

DEPTH 61'-0"

First Floor
2,028 sq. ft.

MASTER BEDRM
13-4 X 16-4
10 FT TRAY CLG

PORCH

BRKFST ROOM
11-4 X 13-0
10 FT TRAY CLG

MASTER BATH

KITCHEN
16-6 X 13-4
9 FT CLG

GREAT ROOM
17-0 X 20-6
10 FT TRAY CLG

BATH 2

STORAGE

UTIL
11-4 X 6-0
9 FT CLG

PAN

GARAGE

DINING ROOM
12-6 X 13-4
10 FT CLG

FOYER
2 STORY CLG

ARCH

BEDROOM 2
12-6 X 13-6
9 FT CLG

PORCH

COPYRIGHT LARRY E. BELK

Second Floor
558 sq. ft.

BEDROOM 4
13-4 X 10-4

EXPANDABLE AREA
17-4 X 18-0

ATTIC

BATH 3

OPEN TO
FOYER BELOW

BEDROOM 3
13-0 X 11-6

PLANT LEDGE

Plan #578-001D-0041

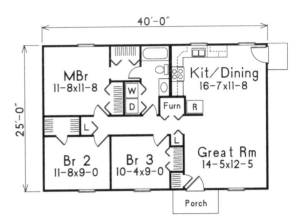

Comfortable Atmosphere

Features

- 1,000 total square feet of living area
- Bath includes convenient closeted laundry area
- Master bedroom includes double closets and private access to bath
- The foyer features a handy coat closet
- L-shaped kitchen provides easy access outdoors
- 3 bedrooms, 1 bath
- Crawl space foundation, drawings also include basement and slab foundations

Plan #578-028D-0017

Southern Elegance

Features

- 2,669 total square feet of living area
- Guest bedroom, located off the great room, has a full bath and would make an excellent office
- Master bath has double walk-in closets, whirlpool tub and shower
- 4 bedrooms, 3 1/2 baths, 2-car side entry garage
- Basement, crawl space or slab foundation, please specify when ordering

Fireplaces Are Unique Focal Points

Features

- 2,481 total square feet of living area
- Varied ceiling heights throughout this home
- Master bedroom features a built-in desk and pocket-door entrance into the large master bath
- Master bath includes a corner vanity and garden tub
- Breakfast area accesses the court-yard
- 3 bedrooms, 2 baths, 3-car side entry garage
- Slab foundation

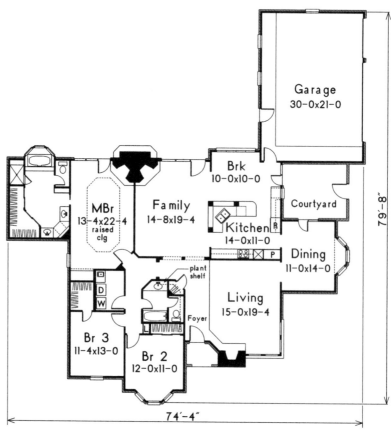

Plan #578-001D-0034

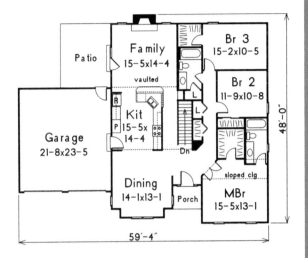

Attractive Front Dormers

Features

- 1,642 total square feet of living area
- Walk-through kitchen boasts a vaulted ceiling and corner sink over-looking the family room
- Vaulted family room features a fireplace and access to the rear patio
- Master bedroom includes a sloped ceiling, walk-in closet and bath
- 3 bedrooms, 2 baths, 2-car garage
- Basement foundation, drawings also include slab and crawl space foundations

---

Plan #578-022D-0006

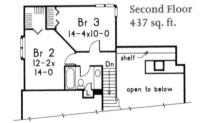

Second Floor
437 sq. ft.

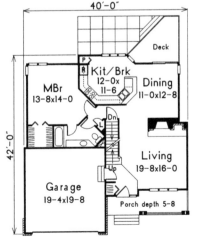

First Floor
1,006 sq. ft.

Gabled Front Porch

Features

- 1,443 total square feet of living area
- Impressive tall-wall fireplace between living and dining rooms
- Open U-shaped kitchen features a cheerful breakfast bay
- Angular side deck accentuates patio and garden
- First floor master bedroom has a walk-in closet and a corner window
- 3 bedrooms, 2 baths, 2-car garage
- Basement foundation

To order call toll-free 1-800-DREAM HOME **or visit** www.houseplansandmore.com

Plan #578-045D-0010

Price Code B

Innovative Design For That Narrow Lot

Features

- 1,558 total square feet of living area
- Illuminated spaces are created by visual access to the outdoor living areas
- Vaulted master bedroom features a private bath with whirlpool tub, separate shower and large walk-in closet
- Convenient laundry area has garage access
- Practical den or third bedroom is ideal for a variety of uses
- U-shaped kitchen is adjacent to a sunny breakfast area
- 2 bedrooms, 2 baths, 2-car rear entry garage
- Basement foundation

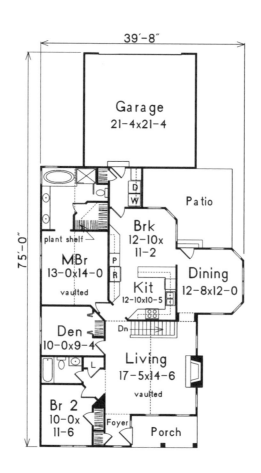

Plan #578-001D-0048

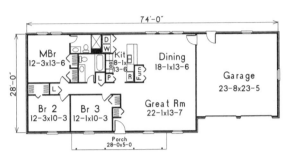

Spacious Interior

Features

- 1,400 total square feet of living area
- Front porch offers warmth and welcome
- Large great room opens into dining room creating an open living atmosphere
- Kitchen features convenient laundry area, pantry and breakfast bar
- 3 bedrooms, 2 baths, 2-car garage
- Crawl space foundation, drawings also include basement and slab foundations

Plan #578-024D-0004

Price Code B

Full-Length Front Porch

Features

- 1,500 total square feet of living area
- Living room features corner fireplace adding warmth
- Master bedroom has all the amenities including a walk-in closet, private bath and porch access
- Sunny bayed breakfast room is cheerful and bright
- 3 bedrooms, 2 baths, 2-car garage
- Slab foundation

To order call toll-free 1-800-DREAM HOME or visit www.houseplansandmore.com

Deluxe Master Bedroom Provides Ultimate Style

Features

- 3,019 total square feet of living area
- Master bedroom features a double-door entry, dramatic vaulted ceiling and spacious master bath with large bay window
- Bonus room on the second floor, which is included in the square footage, is accented by dormer windows and ceiling vaults
- Handy additional storage in secondary bath
- 4 bedrooms, 2 1/2 baths, 3-car side entry garage
- Basement foundation

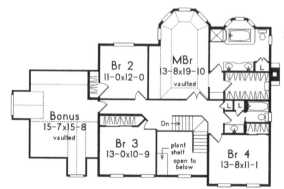

Second Floor
1,659 sq. ft.

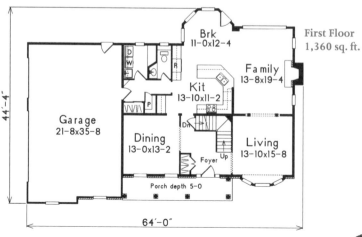

First Floor
1,360 sq. ft.

Plan #578-001D-0080

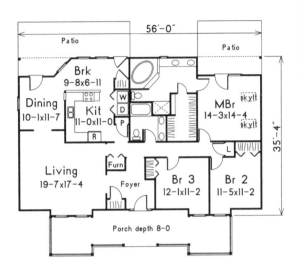

Double Gables Frame Front

Features

- 1,832 total square feet of living area
- Distinctive master bedroom is enhanced by skylights, garden tub, separate shower and walk-in closet
- U-shaped kitchen features a convenient pantry, laundry area and full view to breakfast room
- 3 bedrooms, 2 baths, 2-car detached garage
- Crawl space foundation, drawings also include basement and slab foundations

Plan #578-020D-0006

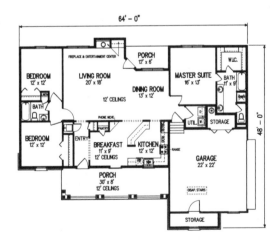

Open Living

Features

- 1,770 total square feet of living area
- Open floor plan makes this home feel spacious
- 12' ceilings in kitchen, living, breakfast and dining areas
- Kitchen is the center of activity with views into all gathering places
- 3 bedrooms, 2 baths, 2-car side entry garage
- Slab foundation, drawings also include crawl space foundation

Gorgeous Grand Victorian

Features

- 3,189 total square feet of living area
- Enormous study on the second floor could easily be a home office or a children's play area
- Octagon-shaped landing in staircase is intriguing to the eye
- Intricate details on the covered front porch give this home a custom feel
- 4 bedrooms, 3 1/2 baths, 2-car side entry garage
- Slab foundation

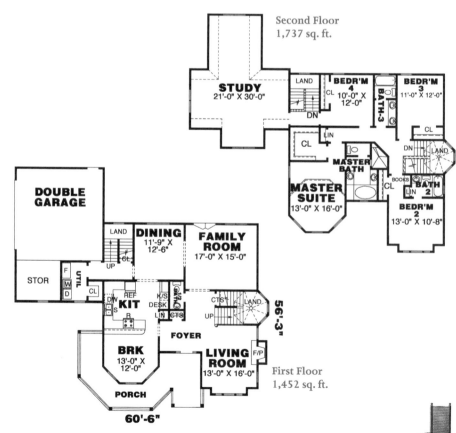

Second Floor
1,737 sq. ft.

STUDY
21'-0" X 30'-0"

LAND

BEDR'M 4
10'-0" X 12'-0"

BEDR'M 3
11'-0" X 12'-0"

BATH-3

CL

LIN

DN

CL

MASTER BATH

BOOKS

DN

LAND

BATH 2

MASTER SUITE
13'-0" X 16'-0"

CL

BEDR'M 2
13'-0" X 10'-8"

DOUBLE GARAGE

STOR

F
W
D

UTIL

CL

LAND

UP

DINING
11'-9" X 12'-6"

FAMILY ROOM
17'-0" X 15'-0"

REF

DW
S

KIT

R

DESK

K/S

LIN

CTS

CTS

LAND

UP

56'-3"

BRK
13'-0" X 12'-0"

FOYER

LIVING ROOM
13'-0" X 16'-0"

F/P

First Floor
1,452 sq. ft.

PORCH

60'-6"

Plan #578-019D-0012

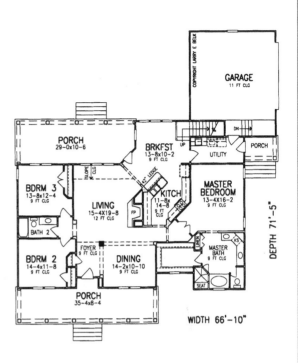

Country Farmhouse Appeal

Features

- 1,993 total square feet of living area
- Charming front and rear porches
- 12' ceiling in living room
- Exquisite master bath with large walk-in closet
- 3 bedrooms, 2 baths, 2-car side entry garage
- Crawl space foundation, drawings also include slab foundation

Plan #578-052D-0011

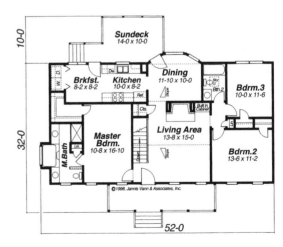

Formal Country Charm

Features

- 1,325 total square feet of living area
- Sloped ceiling and a fireplace in the living area create a cozy feeling
- Formal dining and breakfast areas have an efficiently designed kitchen between them
- Master bedroom has a walk-in closet and luxurious private bath
- 3 bedrooms, 2 baths, 2-car drive under garage
- Basement foundation

To order call toll-free 1-800-DREAM HOME **or visit** www.houseplansandmore.com

Wrap-Around Front Country Porch

Features

- 2,665 total square feet of living area
- 9' ceilings on the first floor
- Spacious kitchen features many cabinets, a center island cooktop and bayed breakfast area adjacent to the laundry room
- Second floor bedrooms boast walk-in closets, dressing areas and share a bath
- Twin patio doors and fireplace grace living room
- 4 bedrooms, 3 baths, 2-car rear entry garage
- Slab foundation, drawings also include crawl space foundation

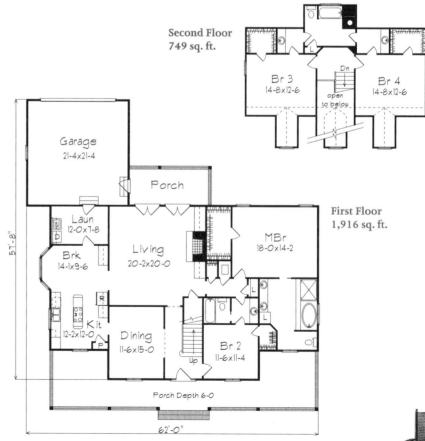

Second Floor
749 sq. ft.

Br 3
14-8x12-6

Br 4
14-8x12-6

Dn
open to below

First Floor
1,916 sq. ft.

Garage
21-4x21-4

Porch

Laun
12-0x7-8

Brk
14-1x9-6

Living
20-2x20-0

MBr
18-0x14-2

Kit
12-2x12-0

Dining
11-6x15-0

Br 2
11-6x11-4

Up

Porch Depth 6-0

51'-8"

62'-0"

Vaulted Rooms Brighten Interior

Features

- 1,290 total square feet of living area
- The kitchen is located conveniently between the dining room and breakfast area
- Master suite has a private luxurious bath with walk-in closet
- Decorative plant shelves through-out this plan add style
- 3 bedrooms, 2 baths, 2-car side entry garage
- Slab, crawl space or walk-out base-ment foundation, please specify when ordering

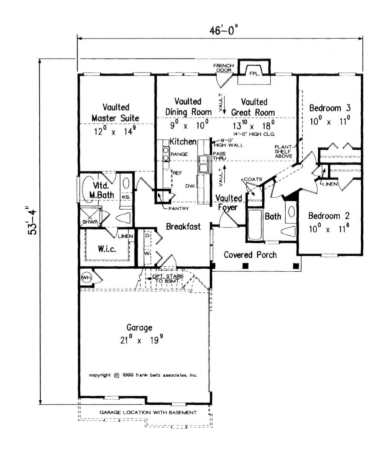

Well-Designed Ranch With Plenty Of Space

Features

- 1,820 total square feet of living area
- Living room has a stunning cathedral ceiling
- Spacious laundry room with easy access to kitchen, garage and the outdoors
- Plenty of closet space throughout
- Covered front porch enhances outdoor living
- 3 bedrooms, 2 baths, 2-car garage
- Basement foundation

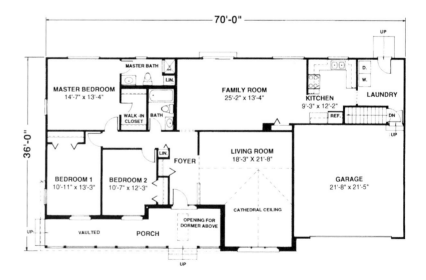

To order call toll-free 1-800-DREAM HOME or visit www.houseplansandmore.com

Delightful Victorian

Features

- 1,985 total square feet of living area
- Cozy family room features a fireplace and double French doors opening onto the porch
- The open kitchen includes a convenient island
- Extraordinary master bedroom has a tray ceiling and a large walk-in closet
- Lovely bayed breakfast area has easy access to the deck
- 3 bedrooms, 2 1/2 baths
- Basement or crawl space foundation, please specify when ordering

Second Floor
976 sq. ft.

TRAY CEILING

MASTER BDRM
16'-4" x 15'-0"

D W

DN

BEDROOM 2
12'-0" x 12'-8"

BEDROOM 3
12'-8" x 12'-0"

WINDOW SEAT

DECK
30'-6" x 11'-7"

BRKFST

PNTRY

KITCHEN
15'-0" x 17'-0"

DINING
14'-8" x 12'-8"

42'-0"

UP

ENTRY
7'-11" x 15'-6"

FAMILY
18'-8" x 16'-0"

COATS

First Floor
1,009 sq. ft.

PORCH
30'-6" x 7'-7"

31'-2"

Authentic Country Cottage

Features

- 2,143 total square feet of living area
- The kitchen handles every task because of its efficiency
- A cozy casual family room has a fireplace for warmth and a convenient log bin accessible from the garage as well
- Dining and living rooms combine, perfect for entertaining
- 4 bedrooms, 3 baths, 2-car garage
- Basement foundation

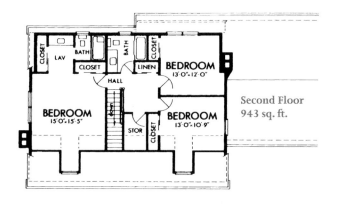

Second Floor
943 sq. ft.

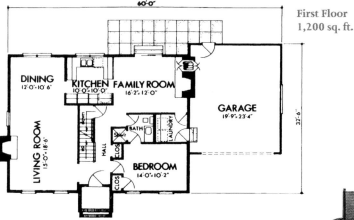

First Floor
1,200 sq. ft.

Plan #578-038D-0007

Country Farmhouse Appeal

Features

- 1,907 total square feet of living area
- Two-story living room is a surprise with skylight and balcony above
- Master bedroom is positioned on the first floor for convenience
- All bedrooms have walk-in closets
- 3 bedrooms, 2 1/2 baths
- Basement, crawl space or slab foundation, please specify when ordering

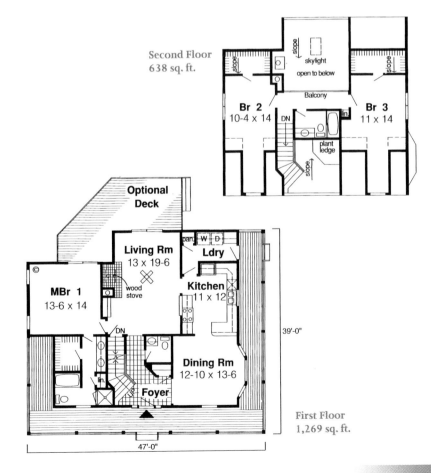

Second Floor
638 sq. ft.

skylight
open to below
Balcony

Br 2
10-4 x 14

Br 3
11 x 14

plant ledge

Optional Deck

Living Rm
13 x 19-6

Ldry

wood stove

Kitchen
11 x 12

MBr 1
13-6 x 14

Dining Rm
12-10 x 13-6

Foyer

39'-0"

47'-0"

First Floor
1,269 sq. ft.

All The Luxuries For Family Living

Features

- 4,100 total square feet of living area

- Family room connects to other casual living areas for convenience

- French doors keep the cozy private den from the rest of the first floor

- A beautiful sitting area extends the master bedroom

- The bonus room on the second floor is included in the square footage

- 4 bedrooms, 3 1/2 baths, 3-car side entry garage

- Crawl space foundation

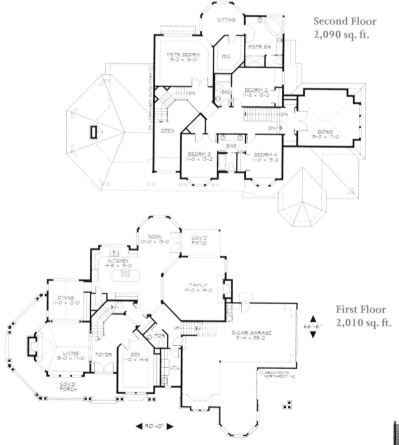

Second Floor
2,090 sq. ft.

First Floor
2,010 sq. ft.

Cozy Covered Front Porch

Features

- 1,749 total square feet of living area
- Tray ceiling in master suite
- A breakfast bar overlooks the vaulted great room
- Additional bedrooms are located away from the master suite for privacy
- Optional bonus room above the garage has an additional 308 square feet of living area
- 3 bedrooms, 2 baths, 2-car garage
- Slab, crawl space or walk-out basement foundation, please specify when ordering

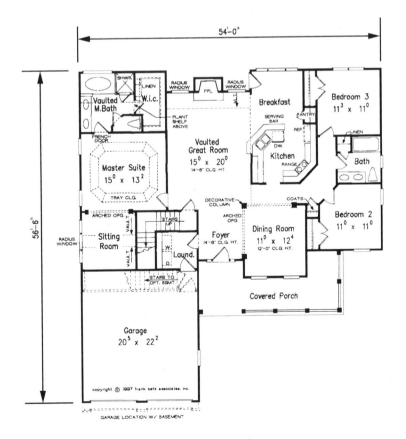

Arches Add Drama To Facade

Features

- 1,982 total square feet of living area
- Large screened porch creates a great casual living area and connects to a covered deck leading into the master suite
- Dramatic formal living room has a sunny bay window and a high ceiling
- Master suite has a private sitting area as well as a pampering luxury-filled bath
- 3 bedrooms, 2 1/2 baths, 3-car side entry garage
- Basement, crawl space or slab foundation, please specify when ordering

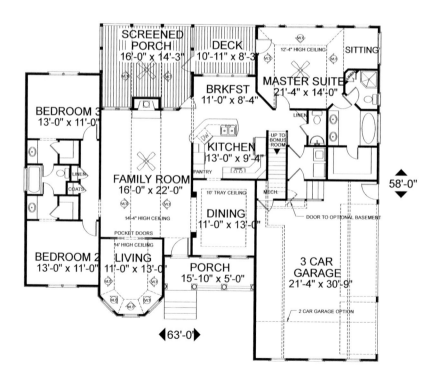

Kitchen With Island Sink

Features

- 2,010 total square feet of living area
- Oversized kitchen is a great gathering place with eat-in island bar, dining area nearby and built-in desk
- First floor master bedroom has privacy
- Unique second floor kid's living area for playroom
- Optional bonus room has an additional 313 square feet of living area
- 3 bedrooms, 2 1/2 baths, 2-car side entry garage
- Basement foundation

First Floor 1,269 sq. ft.

Garage 22 x 24/7

Width: 43'-0"
Depth: 69'-4"

Dining 13 x 11
9' Clg.

Utility

Desk

W D

Kitchen
Bar
12/11 x 11/9

Up
Down

Stoop

Master 13/4 x 16
9' Clg.

Family Room 14/3 x 18
9' Clg.

Foyer

Porch 21 x 8

Second Floor 741 sq. ft.

Optional Bonus 24/7 x 11/4

Kid's Living 10/8 x 11/3
8' Clg.

Attic Storage

Rail

Down

Bedroom #3 13/4 x 11
8' Clg.
Sloped Clg.

Linen

Bedroom #2 14/4 x 15/7
8' Clg.

Classic Farmhouse Design

Features

- 2,464 total square feet of living area
- The dining room is perfect for hosting elegant meals
- Master bedroom is oversized and offers a large shower and a separate dressing area
- The family room features a second fireplace and the kitchen beyond
- 4 bedrooms, 3 baths, 2-car garage
- Basement foundation

Second Floor
1,176 sq. ft.

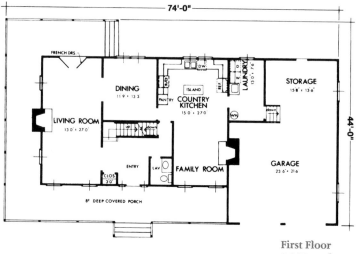

First Floor
1,288 sq. ft.

To order call toll-free **1-800-DREAM HOME** or visit www.houseplansandmore.com

Perfect Compact Ranch

Rear View

Features

- 1,738 total square feet of living area
- A den in the front of the home can easily be converted to a third bedroom
- Kitchen includes an eating nook for family gatherings
- Master bedroom has an unforgettable bath with a super skylight
- Large sunken great room is centralized with a cozy fireplace
- 2 bedrooms, 2 baths, 3-car garage
- Basement, crawl space or slab foundation, please specify when ordering

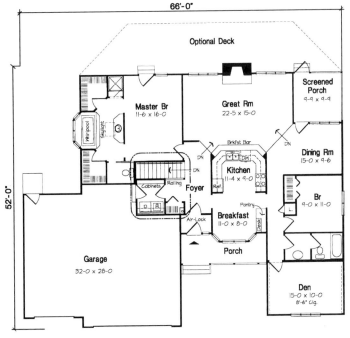

66'-0"

52'-0"

Optional Deck

Master Br
11-6 x 16-0

Great Rm
22-5 x 15-0

Screened Porch
9-9 x 9-9

Whirlpool

Skylight

Brkfst Bar

Dining Rm
15-0 x 9-6

Cabinets

Railing

Foyer

Kitchen
11-4 x 9-0

DN

Ref

Br
9-0 x 11-0

Pantry

Air-Lock

Breakfast
11-0 x 8-0

Desk

Garage
32-0 x 28-0

Porch

Den
15-0 x 10-0
8'-6" Clg.

Furn.

Crawl Space Access

Perfect Home For Escaping To The Outdoors

Features

- 1,200 total square feet of living area
- Enjoy lazy summer evenings on this magnificent porch
- Activity area has a fireplace and ascending stair from the cozy loft
- Kitchen features a built-in pantry
- Master bedroom enjoys a large bath, walk-in closet and cozy loft overlooking the room below
- 2 bedrooms, 2 baths
- Crawl space foundation

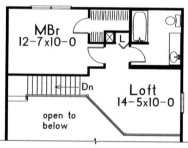

Second Floor
416 sq. ft.

MBr
12-7x10-0

Loft
14-5x10-0

Dn

open to below

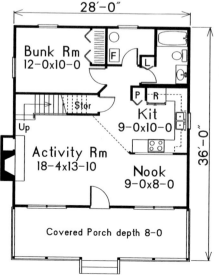

28'-0"

36'-0"

First Floor
784 sq. ft.

Bunk Rm
12-0x10-0

F

L

Stor

Up

Kit
9-0x10-0

P R

Activity Rm
18-4x13-10

Nook
9-0x8-0

Covered Porch depth 8-0

Quaint Country Home Is Ideal

Features

- 1,028 total square feet of living area
- Well-designed bath contains laundry facilities
- L-shaped kitchen has a handy pantry
- Tall windows flank family room fireplace
- Cozy covered porch provides unique angled entry into home
- 3 bedrooms, 1 bath
- Crawl space foundation

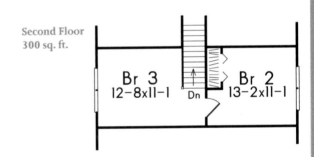

Second Floor
300 sq. ft.

Br 3
12-8x11-1

Dn

Br 2
13-2x11-1

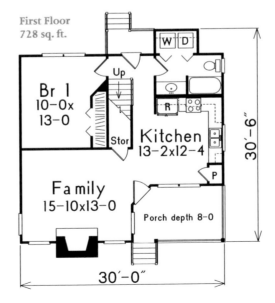

First Floor
728 sq. ft.

Up

W D

Br 1
10-0x
13-0

Stor.

Kitchen
13-2x12-4

Family
15-10x13-0

Porch depth 8-0

P

30'-6"

30'-0"

Modest Ranch Is A Great Layout For Family Living

Features

- 1,557 total square feet of living area
- Vaulted dining room extends off the great room and features an eye-catching plant shelf above
- Double closets adorn the vaulted master bedroom which also features a private bath with tub and shower
- Bedroom #3/den has the option to add a double-door entry creating the feeling of a home office if needed
- 3 bedrooms, 2 baths, 2-car garage
- Crawl space foundation

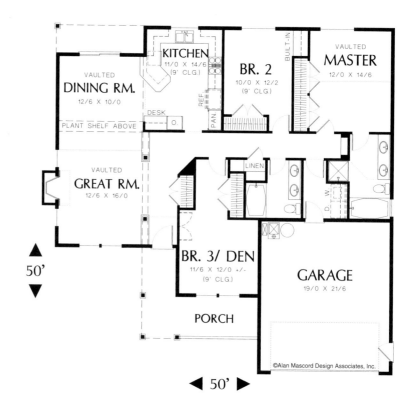

Open Living Centers On Windowed Dining Room

Features

- 2,003 total square feet of living area
- Octagon-shaped dining room boasts a tray ceiling and deck overlook
- L-shaped island kitchen serves the living and dining rooms
- Master bedroom boasts a luxury bath and walk-in closet
- Living room features columns, elegant fireplace and a 10' ceiling
- 3 bedrooms, 2 baths, 2-car garage
- Basement foundation

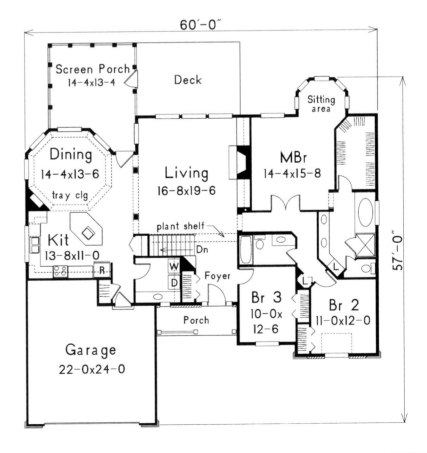

Open And Airy Grand Room

Features

- 2,111 total square feet of living area
- 9' ceilings throughout first floor
- Formal dining room has columns separating it from other areas while allowing it to maintain an open feel
- Master bedroom has privacy from other bedrooms
- Bonus room on the second floor has an additional 345 square feet of living area
- 3 bedrooms, 2 baths, 2-car side entry garage
- Basement foundation

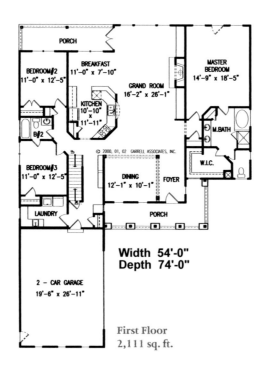

Width 54'-0"
Depth 74'-0"

First Floor
2,111 sq. ft.

Optional
Second Floor

Plan #578-040D-0030

Price Code B

Relax On The Covered Front Porch

Features

- 1,543 total square feet of living area
- Fireplace serves as the focal point of the large family room
- Efficient floor plan keeps hallways at a minimum
- Laundry room connects the kitchen to the garage
- Private first floor master bedroom has a walk-in closet and bath
- 3 bedrooms, 2 1/2 baths, 2-car detached side entry garage
- Slab foundation, drawings also include crawl space foundation

First Floor
1,040 sq. ft.

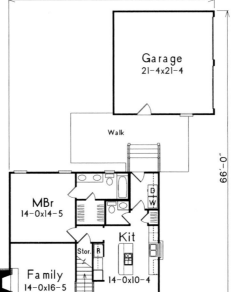

44'-6"

66'-0"

Garage
21-4x21-4

Walk

MBr
14-0x14-5

Kit
14-0x10-4

Stor.

Family
14-0x16-5

Up

Dining
14-0x10-0

Porch depth 8-0

Second Floor
503 sq. ft.

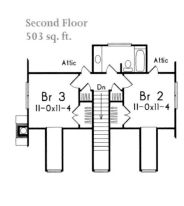

Attic

Attic

Br 3
11-0x11-4

Dn

Br 2
11-0x11-4

To order call toll-free 1-800-DREAM HOME or visit www.houseplansandmore.com

401

Prominent Hall Connects Rooms

Features

- 1,609 total square feet of living area
- The laundry area is adjacent to the kitchen for convenience
- Two storage areas; one can be accessed from the outdoors and the other from the garage
- Eating bar overlooks from kitchen into dining area
- 3 bedrooms, 2 baths, 2-car side entry garage
- Slab foundation

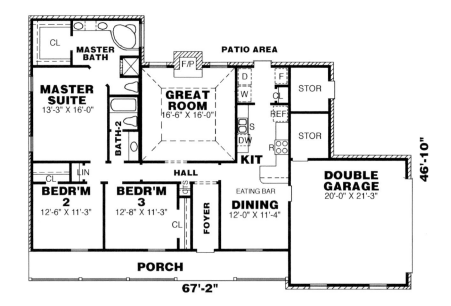

Dramatic Central Staircase

Features

- 3,085 total square feet of living area
- Enter the foyer to find symmetrical formal living and dining rooms both with decorative columns
- Central two-story family room is spectacular with fireplace and beamed ceiling
- Unique see-through area from master bedroom into bath
- Bonus room on the second floor has an additional 315 square feet of living area
- 4 bedrooms, 2 1/2 baths, 3-car tandem garage
- Crawl space foundation

Second Floor
1,460 sq. ft.

First Floor
1,625 sq. ft.

Country Style With This Design

Features

- 2,156 total square feet of living area
- Secluded master bedroom has spa-style bath with corner whirlpool tub, large shower, double sinks and a walk-in closet
- Kitchen overlooks rear patio
- Plenty of windows add an open, airy feel to the great room
- 4 bedrooms, 3 baths, 2-car side entry garage
- Basement, crawl space or slab foundation, please specify when ordering

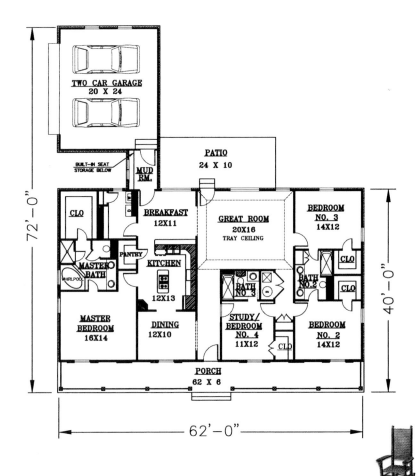

Large Expansive Living Spaces

Features

- 2,064 total square feet of living area
- Second floor has a luxurious master suite, walk-in closet, private bath and a sloped loft
- Angled island extends the kitchen into the dining room with bay window
- Beamed two-story great room is a cozy, rustic retreat
- 3 bedrooms, 2 baths
- Crawl space foundation

Second Floor
774 sq. ft.

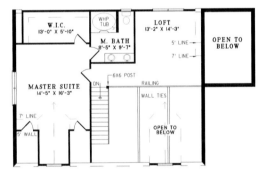

First Floor
1,290 sq. ft.

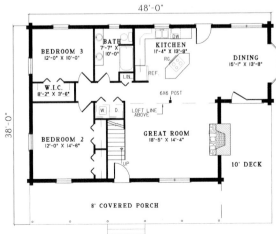

Southern Styling With Covered Porch

Features

- 1,491 total square feet of living area
- Two-story family room has a vaulted ceiling
- Well-organized kitchen has serving bar which overlooks family and dining rooms
- First floor master suite has a tray ceiling, walk-in closet and master bath
- 3 bedrooms, 2 1/2 baths, 2-car drive under garage
- Walk-out basement foundation

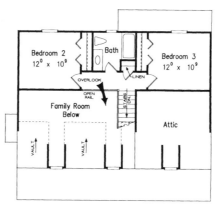

Second Floor
430 sq. ft.

Bedroom 2
12⁰ x 10⁸

Bath

Bedroom 3
12⁰ x 10⁹

OVERLOOK

OPEN RAIL

LINEN

Family Room Below

STAIRS DN

Attic

VAULT   VAULT

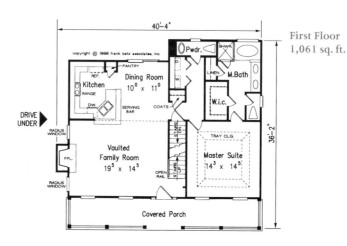

First Floor
1,061 sq. ft.

40'-4"

copyright © 1998 frank betz associates, inc.

Pwdr.   SHWR

PANTRY

REF.

Kitchen

RANGE

DW.

Dining Room
10⁰ x 11⁰

LINEN   M.Bath

W.i.c.

SERVING BAR

COATS

TRAY CLG.

DRIVE UNDER

RADIUS WINDOW

FPL.

Vaulted Family Room
19⁵ x 14⁵

STAIRS DN

STAIRS UP

OPEN RAIL

Master Suite
14³ x 14⁵

36'-2"

RADIUS WINDOW

Covered Porch

Outdoor Living Areas Surround Home

Features

- 2,770 total square feet of living area
- Formal living and dining areas combine for optimal entertaining possibilities including access outdoors and a fireplace
- The cheerful family and breakfast rooms connect for added spaciousness
- A double-door entry into the master bedroom leads to a private covered deck, sitting area and luxurious bath
- 4 bedrooms, 2 1/2 baths, 3-car side entry garage
- Crawl space foundation

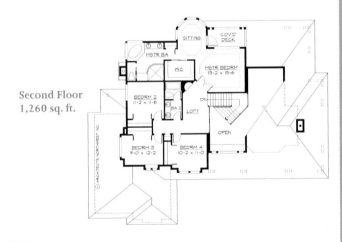

Second Floor
1,260 sq. ft.

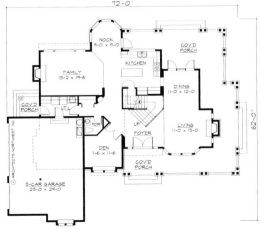

First Floor
1,510 sq. ft.

Country Ranch With Spacious Wrap-Around Porch

Features

- 1,541 total square feet of living area
- Dining area offers access to a screened porch for outdoor dining and entertaining
- Country kitchen features a center island and a breakfast bay for casual meals
- Great room is warmed by a wood-stove
- 3 bedrooms, 2 baths, 2-car garage
- Basement or crawl space foundation, please specify when ordering

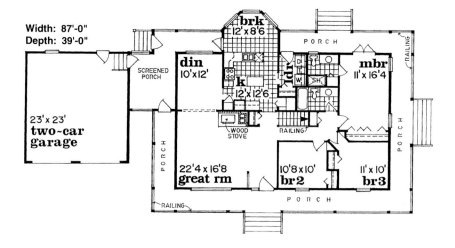

Width: 87'-0"
Depth: 39'-0"

SCREENED PORCH

23' x 23' two-car garage

brk 12' x 8'6

PORCH

din 10'x12'

k 12'x12'6

mbr 11' x 16'4

RAILING

WOOD STOVE

RAILING

22'4 x 16'8 great rm

10'8 x 10' br2

11' x 10' br3

PORCH

RAILING

Double Gables Draw Attention To The Facade

Features

- 4,650 total square feet of living area
- Two-story foyer, living and family rooms create a sense of spacious-ness throughout the first floor
- Double walk-in closets create plenty of storage in the master bath
- The second floor media room is sure to be a gathering place near the bedrooms
- 5 bedrooms, 4 1/2 baths, 3-car rear entry garage
- Crawl space foundation

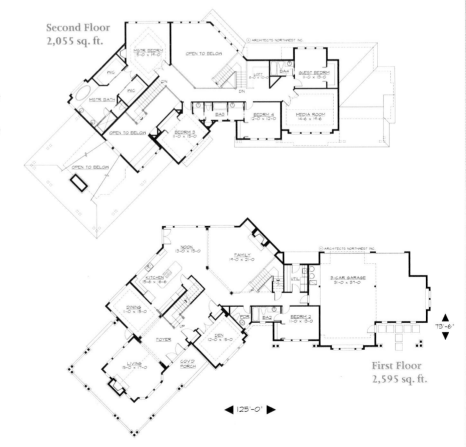

Second Floor
2,055 sq. ft.

First Floor
2,595 sq. ft.

125'-0"

73'-6"

Entertainment Center In Great Room

Features

- 1,791 total square feet of living area
- A whirlpool tub adds luxury to the master bath
- Breakfast nook leads to a covered porch
- Double closets create plenty of storage in the foyer
- 3 bedrooms, 2 baths, 2-car side entry garage
- Basement foundation

Width: 63'-8"
Depth: 51'-0"

Quaint Home Made For Country Living

Features

- 1,578 total square feet of living area
- A fireplace warms the great room and is flanked by windows overlooking the rear deck
- Bedrooms are clustered on one side of the home for privacy from living areas
- Master bedroom has a unique art niche at its entry and a private bath with separate tub and shower
- 3 bedrooms, 2 baths, 2-car side entry garage
- Basement or crawl space foundation, please specify when ordering

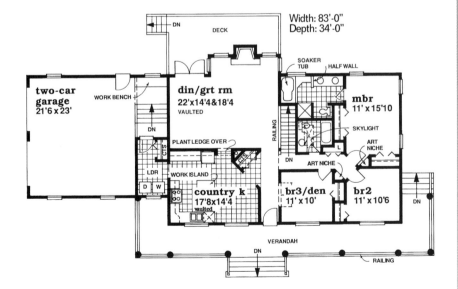

Width: 83'-0"
Depth: 34'-0"

DECK

DN

two-car garage
21'6 x 23'

WORK BENCH

DN

din/grt rm
22'x14'4 & 18'4
VAULTED

PLANT LEDGE OVER

SOAKER TUB

HALF WALL

mbr
11' x 15'10

RAILING

SKYLIGHT

ART NICHE

DN

ART NICHE

LDR

WORK ISLAND

D W

country k
17'8 x 14'4
vaulted

br3/den
11' x 10'

br2
11' x 10'6

DN

VERANDAH

DN

RAILING

Angled Eating Bar Is Great For Family Living

Features

- 1,686 total square feet of living area
- Secondary bedrooms are separate from the master suite maintaining privacy
- Island in kitchen is ideal for food preparation
- Dramatic foyer leads to the great room
- Covered side porch has direct access into the great room
- 3 bedrooms, 2 baths, 2-car side entry garage
- Slab foundation

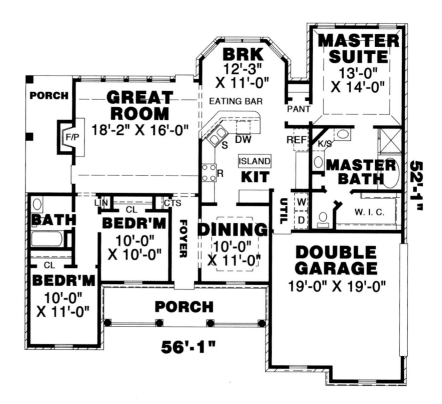

Double Gables Add Warmth To Exterior

Features

- 1,300 total square feet of living area
- Bayed dining room has sliding glass doors that open onto an outdoor patio
- Large bedroom #2 has a built-in desk
- Charming wrap-around front porch
- 3 bedrooms, 2 baths, 2-car garage
- Basement foundation

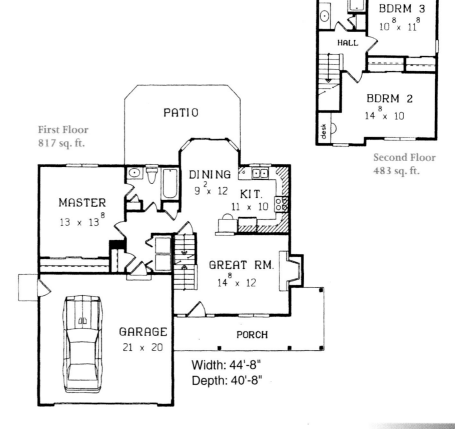

First Floor
817 sq. ft.

PATIO

MASTER
13 x 13⁸

DINING
9²x 12

KIT.
11 x 10

GREAT RM.
14⁸ x 12

GARAGE
21 x 20

PORCH

Width: 44'-8"
Depth: 40'-8"

Second Floor
483 sq. ft.

BDRM 3
10⁸ x 11⁸

HALL

BDRM 2
14⁸ x 10

desk

Traditional Farmhouse Feeling With This Home

Features

- 2,582 total square feet of living area
- Both the family and living rooms are warmed by hearths
- The master bedroom on the second floor has a bayed sitting room and a private bath with whirlpool tub
- Old-fashioned window seat in second floor landing is a charming touch
- 4 bedrooms, 3 baths, 2-car side entry garage
- Basement or crawl space foundation, please specify when ordering

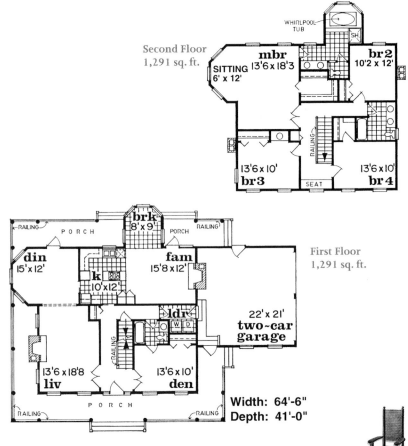

Second Floor
1,291 sq. ft.

WHIRLPOOL TUB

mbr 13'6 x 18'3

SITTING 6' x 12'

br 2 10'2 x 12'

13'6 x 10'
br 3

SEAT

13'6 x 10'
br 4

RAILING

First Floor
1,291 sq. ft.

RAILING   PORCH   brk 8' x 9'   PORCH   RAILING

din 15' x 12'

fam 15'8 x 12'

k 10' x 12'

ldr
W D

22' x 21'
two-car garage

RAILING

13'6 x 18'8
liv

13'6 x 10'
den

PORCH

RAILING   RAILING

Width: 64'-6"
Depth: 41'-0"

Country Home With Plenty Of Style

Features

- 1,829 total square feet of living area
- Entry foyer with coat closet opens to a large family room with fireplace
- Two second floor bedrooms share a full bath
- Optional bedroom #4 on the second floor has an additional 145 square feet of living area
- Cozy porch provides a convenient side entrance into the home
- 3 bedrooms, 2 1/2 baths, 2-car side entry garage
- Partial basement/crawl space foundation

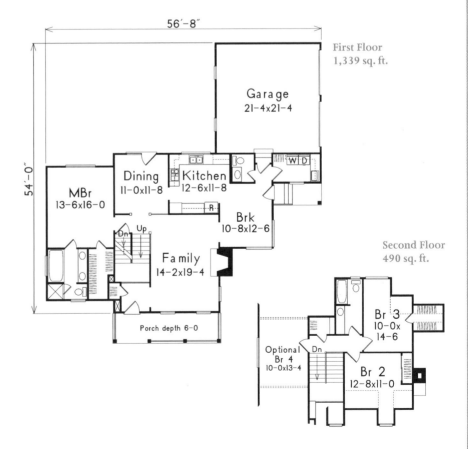

First Floor
1,339 sq. ft.

Second Floor
490 sq. ft.

Ranch With Traditional Feel

Features

- 1,985 total square feet of living area
- 9' ceilings throughout home
- Master suite has direct access into the sunroom
- Sunny breakfast room features a bay window
- Bonus room on the second floor has an additional 191 square feet of living area
- 3 bedrooms, 3 baths, 2-car side entry garage
- Slab foundation

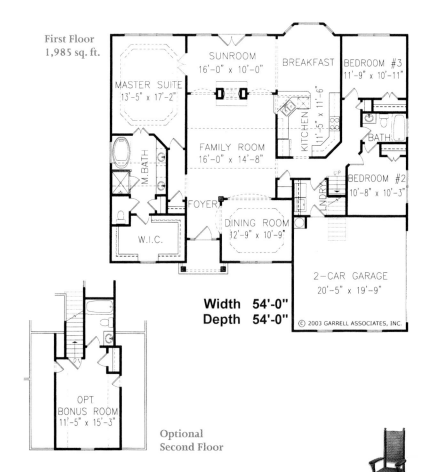

First Floor
1,985 sq. ft.

SUNROOM
16'-0" x 10'-0"

BREAKFAST

BEDROOM #3
11'-9" x 10'-11"

MASTER SUITE
13'-5" x 17'-2"

KITCHEN
11'-5" x 11'-6"

BATH

FAMILY ROOM
16'-0" x 14'-8"

BATH

M. BATH

BEDROOM #2
10'-8" x 10'-3"

FOYER

LNDRY

UP

W.I.C.

DINING ROOM
12'-9" x 10'-9"

2-CAR GARAGE
20'-5" x 19'-9"

Width 54'-0"
Depth 54'-0"

© 2003 GARRELL ASSOCIATES, INC.

OPT.
BONUS ROOM
11'-5" x 15'-3"

Optional
Second Floor

Master Bedroom Provides Retreat

Features

- 1,687 total square feet of living area
- Family room with built-in cabinet and fireplace is the focal point of this home
- U-shaped kitchen has a bar that opens to the family room
- Back porch opens to the dining room and leads to the garage via a walkway
- Convenient laundry room is located near the center of activity
- 4 bedrooms, 2 1/2 baths, 2-car detached garage
- Basement foundation

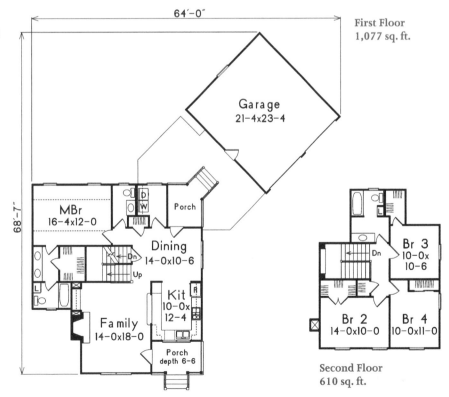

First Floor
1,077 sq. ft.

Garage
21-4x23-4

MBr
16-4x12-0

Porch

Dining
14-0x10-6

Kit
10-0x
12-4

Family
14-0x18-0

Porch
depth 6-6

Br 3
10-0x
10-6

Br 2
14-0x10-0

Br 4
10-0x11-0

Second Floor
610 sq. ft.

Compact And Convenient Farmhouse

Features

- 1,958 total square feet of living area
- Spacious kitchen and breakfast area is open to the rear deck
- A charming rail separates the family room and breakfast area keeping an open feel
- Dormers add interest and spaciousness in bedroom #2
- Bonus room on the second floor is included in the square footage
- 3 bedrooms, 2 1/2 baths, 2-car side entry garage
- Basement foundation, drawings also include slab and crawl space foundations

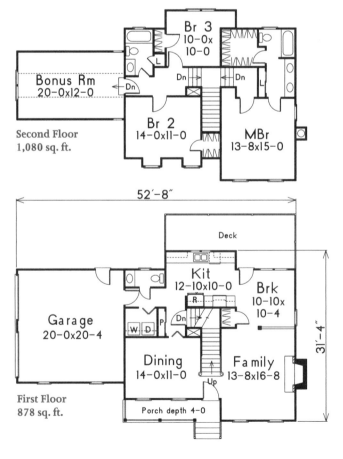

A Great Country House

Features

- 1,669 total square feet of living area
- Windows add exciting visual elements to the exterior as well as plenty of natural light to the interior
- Two-story great room has a raised hearth
- Second floor loft/study would easily make a terrific home office
- 3 bedrooms, 2 baths
- Crawl space foundation

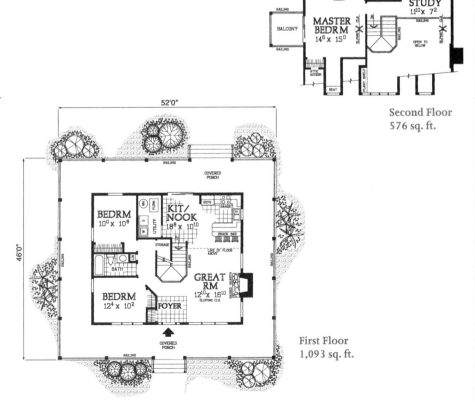

Second Floor
576 sq. ft.

First Floor
1,093 sq. ft.

Charming Home Arranged For Open Living

Features

- 1,609 total square feet of living area
- Kitchen captures full use of space with pantry, ample cabinets and workspace
- Master bedroom is well secluded with a walk-in closet and private bath
- Large utility room includes a sink and extra storage
- Attractive bay window in the dining area provides light
- 3 bedrooms, 2 1/2 baths, 2-car garage
- Slab foundation

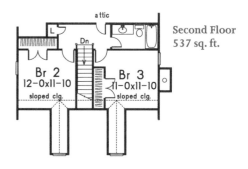

Second Floor
537 sq. ft.

attic

Br 2
12-0x11-10
sloped clg.

Br 3
11-0x11-10
sloped clg.

Dn

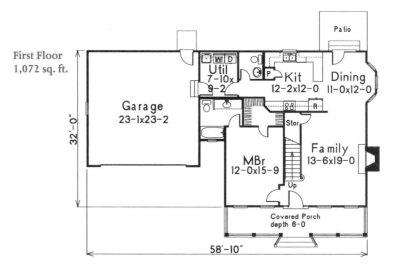

First Floor
1,072 sq. ft.

Patio

Util
7-10x
9-2

Kit
12-2x12-0

Dining
11-0x12-0

Garage
23-1x23-2

32'-0"

MBr
12-0x15-9

Stor

Family
13-6x19-0

Up

Covered Porch
depth 6-0

58'-10"

To order call toll-free 1-800-DREAM HOME or visit www.houseplansandmore.com

Stately Home Features Porch With Balcony Above

Features

- 2,216 total square feet of living area
- Luxury master bedroom suite features full-windowed bathtub bay, double walk-in closets and access to the front balcony
- Spacious kitchen has enough space for dining
- Second floor laundry facility is centrally located
- 4 bedrooms, 2 1/2 baths, 2-car drive under garage
- Basement foundation

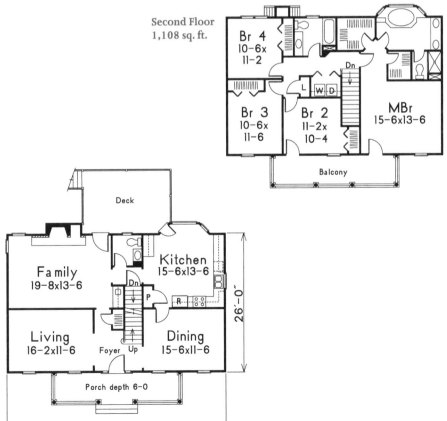

Second Floor
1,108 sq. ft.

Br 4
10-6x
11-2

Br 3
10-6x
11-6

Br 2
11-2x
10-4

MBr
15-6x13-6

Balcony

Deck

Family
19-8x13-6

Kitchen
15-6x13-6

First Floor
1,108 sq. ft.

Living
16-2x11-6

Dining
15-6x11-6

Foyer   Up

26'-0"

Porch depth 6-0

42'-0"

Corner Windows Grace Library

Features

- 1,824 total square feet of living area
- Living room features a 10' ceiling, fireplace and media center
- Dining room includes a bay window and convenient kitchen access
- Master bedroom features a large walk-in closet and luxurious bath with a double-door entry
- Modified U-shaped kitchen features pantry and bar
- 3 bedrooms, 2 baths, 2-car detached garage
- Slab foundation

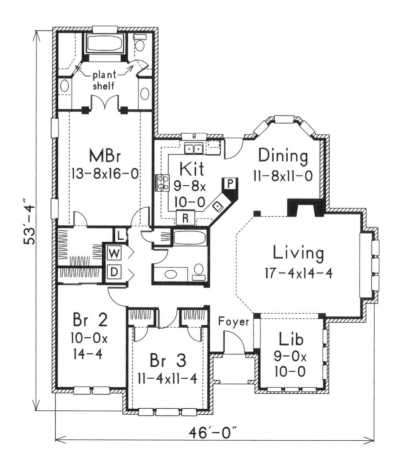

Formal Living And Dining Rooms

Features

- 1,890 total square feet of living area
- Inviting covered porch adds a unique touch with partial stone pillars
- Vaulted ceilings in the living, dining and family rooms
- Kitchen is open to the family room and nook
- Large walk-in pantry in the kitchen
- Arch accented master bath has a spa tub, double sinks and walk-in closet
- 3 bedrooms, 2 baths, 2-car garage
- Crawl space foundation

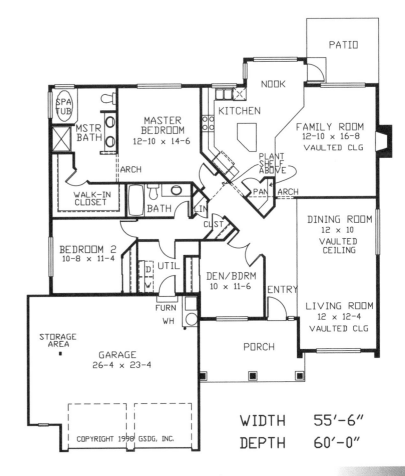

WIDTH   55'-6"
DEPTH   60'-0"

Private Bedroom Area

Features

- 1,550 total square feet of living area
- Wrap-around front porch is an ideal gathering place
- Handy snack bar is positioned so the kitchen flows into the family room
- Master bedroom has many amenities
- 3 bedrooms, 2 baths, 2-car detached side entry garage
- Slab or crawl space foundation, please specify when ordering

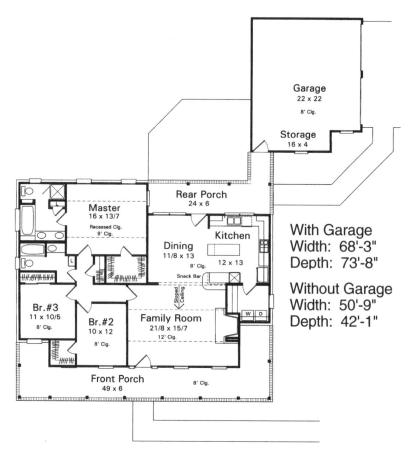

With Garage
Width: 68'-3"
Depth: 73'-8"

Without Garage
Width: 50'-9"
Depth: 42'-1"

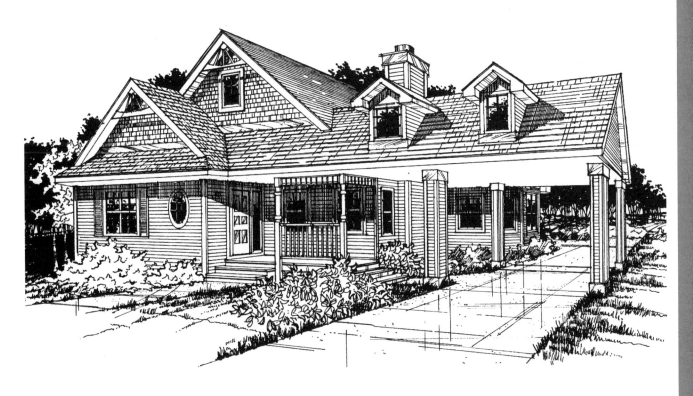

Fits Well On A Narrow Lot

Features

- 1,631 total square feet of living area
- Vaulted living room creates a spacious feeling upon entering the home
- Master bedroom has private bath with plant shelf accents
- Bedroom #3 can easily convert to a den or home office
- 3 bedrooms, 2 baths, 2-car side entry garage, 1-car carport
- Basement foundation

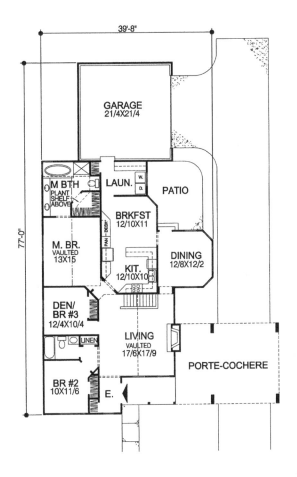

39'-8"

77'-0"

GARAGE
21/4X21/4

M BTH
PLANT SHELF ABOVE

LAUN.

PATIO

BRKFST
12/10X11

M. BR.
VAULTED
13X15

KIT.
12/10X10

DINING
12/8X12/2

DEN/
BR #3
12/4X10/4

LINEN

LIVING
VAULTED
17/6X17/9

PORTE-COCHERE

BR #2
10X11/6

E.

Lattice Is An Uncommon Touch

Features

- 2,080 total square feet of living area
- Gallery hall creates a grand entrance into the great room
- Computer nook located in the breakfast room is a functional living area near the center of activity
- A window seat in one of the secondary bedrooms adds enjoyment
- Built-in entertainment center and bookshelves make relaxing a breeze in the great room
- 3 bedrooms, 2 baths, 2-car side entry garage
- Basement, crawl space or slab foundation, please specify when ordering

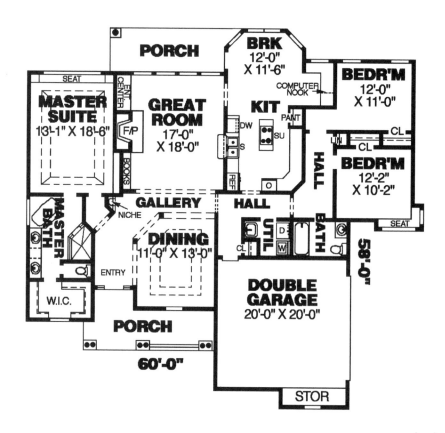

Decorative Roof Lines Add Character

Features

- 2,367 total square feet of living area
- The spacious kitchen offers an abundance of counterspace including an extra-large center island
- A butler's pantry is located outside the formal dining room to assist with entertaining
- The airy living room features a cathedral ceiling and grand fireplace
- All bedrooms are located on the second floor for privacy
- 4 bedrooms, 2 1/2 baths, 3-car garage
- Basement foundation

Second Floor
1,188 sq. ft.

First Floor
1,179 sq. ft.

Outdoor Exposure Front And Back

Features

- 2,685 total square feet of living area
- 9' ceilings throughout the first floor
- Vaulted master bedroom, isolated for privacy, boasts a magnificent bath with garden tub, separate shower and two closets
- Laundry area near bedrooms for the ultimate in convenience
- Screened porch and morning room are both located off the well-planned kitchen
- 4 bedrooms, 2 1/2 baths, 3-car garage
- Basement foundation

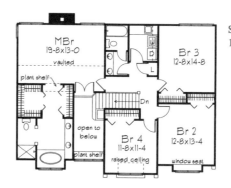

Second Floor
1,325 sq. ft.

MBr
19-8x13-0
vaulted

Br 3
12-8x14-8

Br 4
11-8x11-4
raised_ceiling

Br 2
12-8x13-4
window seat

open to below

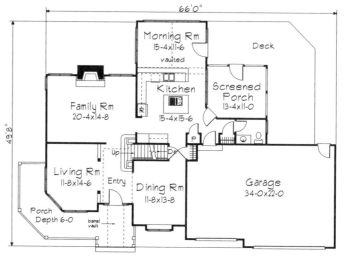

66'0"

49'8"

Morning Rm
15-4x11-6
vaulted

Deck

Family Rm
20-4x14-8

Kitchen
15-4x15-6

Screened Porch
13-4x11-0

Living Rm
11-8x14-6

Entry

Dining Rm
11-8x13-8

Garage
34-0x22-0

Porch Depth 6-0

First Floor
1,360 sq. ft.

Inviting Covered Porch Entry

Features

- 2,034 total square feet of living area
- Oversized tub in master bath adds luxury
- Rustic touches are present in the great room which features a beamed ceiling and a large brick fireplace
- Center island in kitchen features extra seating
- 3 bedrooms, 2 1/2 baths, 2-car garage
- Basement foundation

Charming Covered Porch

Features

- 1,963 total square feet of living area
- Spacious breakfast nook is a great gathering place
- Master bedroom has its own wing with a private bath and lots of closet space
- Large laundry room with closet and sink
- 3 bedrooms, 2 baths, 2-car side entry garage
- Slab or crawl space foundation, please specify when ordering

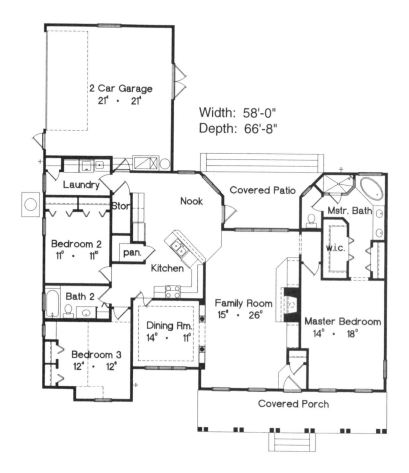

Width: 58'-0"
Depth: 66'-8"

Charming Victorian With Turret

Features

- 2,364 total square feet of living area
- Master bedroom features a turret and private balcony
- Family room enjoys a fireplace and dual French doors that access the porch and sundeck
- First floor has 9' ceilings
- Laundry room is located on the second floor
- 4 bedrooms, 2 1/2 baths, 2-car drive under garage
- Basement foundation

Second Floor
1,209 sq. ft.

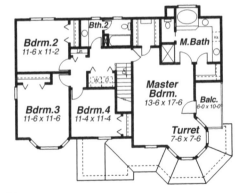

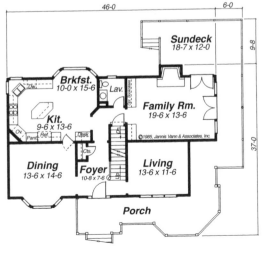

First Floor
1,155 sq. ft.

Covered Porch Adds Charm

Features

- 2,069 total square feet of living area
- 9' ceilings throughout this home
- Kitchen has many amenities including a snack bar
- Large front and rear porches offer outdoor living spaces
- 3 bedrooms, 2 1/2 baths, 2-car garage
- Slab or crawl space foundation, please specify when ordering

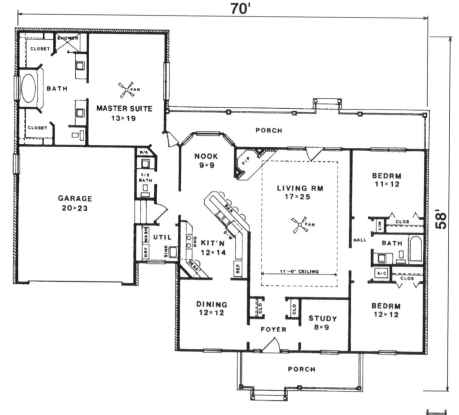

Casual Country Home With Unique Loft

Features

- 1,673 total square feet of living area
- Great room flows into the break-fast nook with outdoor access and beyond to an efficient kitchen
- Master bedroom on the second floor has access to loft/study, private balcony and bath
- Covered porch surrounds the entire home for outdoor living area
- 3 bedrooms, 2 baths
- Crawl space foundation

Second Floor
580 sq. ft.

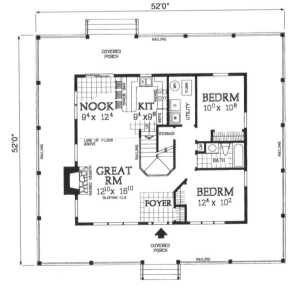

First Floor
1,093 sq. ft.

Large Ranch With Well-Organized Living Area

Features

- 2,083 total square feet of living area
- A handy server counter located between the kitchen and formal dining room is ideal for entertaining
- Decorative columns grace the entrance into the great room
- A large island in the kitchen aids in food preparation
- 3 bedrooms, 2 1/2 baths, 2-car garage
- Basement foundation

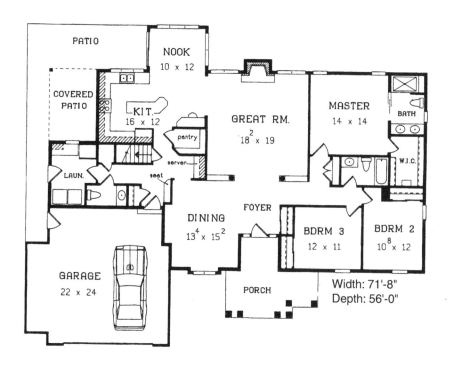

Width: 71'-8"
Depth: 56'-0"

Triple Dormers Add Curb Appeal

Features

- 3,383 total square feet of living area

- Large vaulted activity center on the second floor has a built-in entertainment center perfect for a computer or media center

- First floor includes a secluded home office off the master suite that has direct access to the out-doors

- A large fireplace divides the dining room from the great room while maintaining a feeling of openness

- 4 bedrooms, 3 1/2 baths, 2-car side entry garage

- Slab or crawl space foundation, please specify when ordering

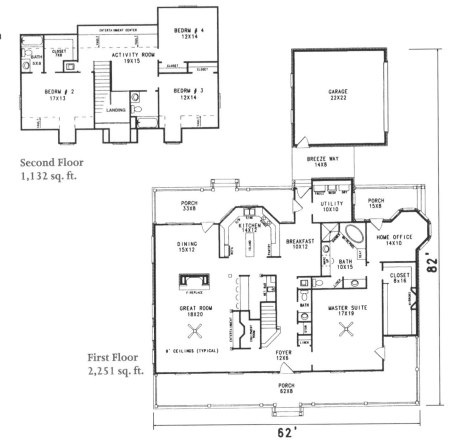

Second Floor
1,132 sq. ft.

First Floor
2,251 sq. ft.

© 2003, Garrell Associates, Inc.

Interesting Arched Front Porch Detail

Features

- 1,761 total square feet of living area
- 9' ceilings throughout this home
- Vaulted grand room has a beautiful fireplace surrounded by book-shelves
- Secondary bedrooms are separated from the master bedroom for privacy
- Kitchen includes counter for extra dining space
- 3 bedrooms, 2 baths, 2-car garage
- Slab foundation

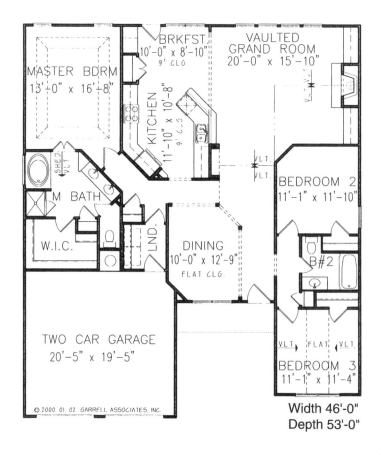

Width 46'-0"
Depth 53'-0"

To order call toll-free 1-800-DREAM HOME or visit www.houseplansandmore.com

Pillars And Dormers Add Charm

Features

- 2,293 total square feet of living area
- Formal dining area flows into large family room making great use of space
- Cozy nook off kitchen makes an ideal breakfast area
- Covered patio attaches to master bedroom and family room
- Optional second floor has an additional 509 square feet of living area
- Framing - only concrete block available
- 4 bedrooms, 2 baths, 2-car side entry garage
- Slab foundation

Optional
Second Floor

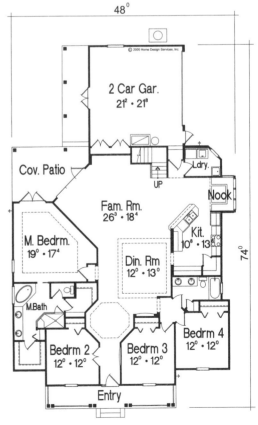

First Floor
2,293 sq. ft.

Two-Story Home With Uncommon Charm

Features

- 1,695 total square feet of living area
- Facade features a cozy wrap-around porch, projected living room window and repeating front gables
- Balcony overlooks to the entry below
- Kitchen has a full-view corner window with adjacent eating space that opens to the screened porch
- Vaulted master bedroom enjoys double closets and a private bath
- 3 bedrooms, 2 1/2 baths, 2-car garage
- Basement foundation

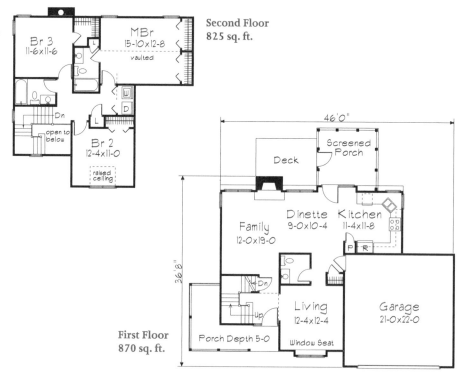

Br 3
11-6x11-6

MBr
15-10x12-8
vaulted

Second Floor
825 sq. ft.

Dn

open to
below

Br 2
12-4x11-0

raised
ceiling

46'0"

Deck

Screened
Porch

Family
12-0x19-0

Dinette
9-0x10-4

Kitchen
11-4x11-8

P   R

36'8"

Dn

Up

Living
12-4x12-4

Garage
21-0x22-0

First Floor
870 sq. ft.

Porch Depth 5-0

Window Seat

Splendid Ranch Full Of Amenities

Features

- 2,730 total square feet of living area
- See-through fireplace is a focal point shared by the master bedroom and master bath
- Great room has a window wall flooding the entire room with sunlight
- Arched soffits add a stunning element to the interior
- 3 bedrooms, 2 1/2 baths, 3-car side entry garage
- Basement foundation

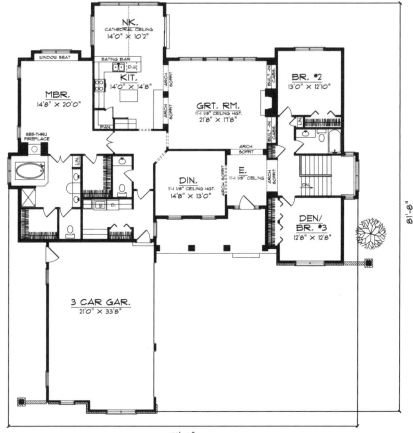

Lovely Arched Touches On The Covered Porch

Features

- 1,594 total square feet of living area
- Corner fireplace in the great room creates a cozy feel
- Spacious kitchen combines with the dining room creating a terrific gathering place
- A handy family and guest entrance is a casual and convenient way to enter the home
- 3 bedrooms, 2 baths, 2-car garage
- Slab or crawl space foundation, please specify when ordering

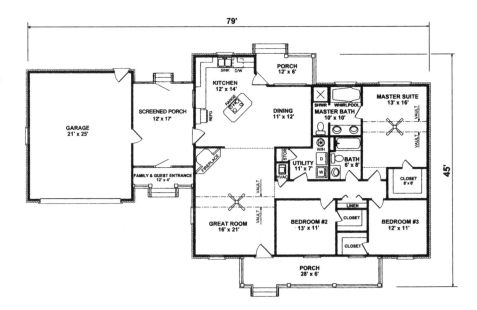

439

Central Gathering Room

Features

- 3,272 total square feet of living area
- Living room with fireplace accesses rear patio and wrap-around front porch
- Large formal dining room
- Master bedroom has a walk-in closet and deluxe bath
- Future area on the second floor has an additional 452 square feet of living area
- 4 bedrooms, 3 full baths, 2 half baths, 2-car side entry garage
- Basement, crawl space or slab foundation, please specify when ordering

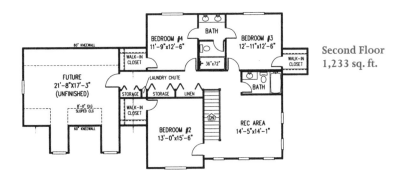

Second Floor
1,233 sq. ft.

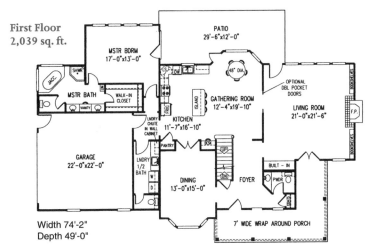

First Floor
2,039 sq. ft.

Width 74'-2"
Depth 49'-0"

Plan #578-068D-0007

Price Code B

Colossal Great Room

Features

- 1,599 total square feet of living area
- Efficiently designed kitchen includes a large pantry and easy access to the laundry room
- Bedroom #3 has a charming window seat
- Master bedroom has a full bath and large walk-in closet
- 4 bedrooms, 2 baths, 2-car garage
- Basement foundation, drawings also include crawl space and slab foundations

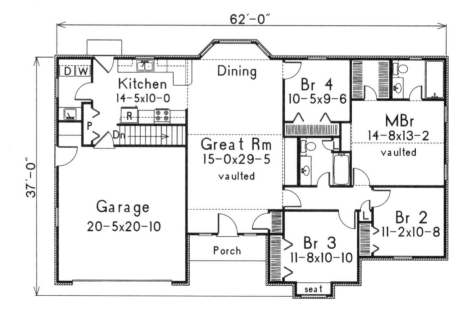

Trim Layout Separates Living Area

Features

- 2,361 total square feet of living area
- Octagon-shaped front porch is the focal point of this facade
- Large living room with a vaulted ceiling couples the front porch with the rear patio for open entertaining
- Family room with fireplace and kitchen with ample breakfast bar are situated in a secluded corner
- Master bedroom boasts a vaulted ceiling and an oversized bay window
- 4 bedrooms, 2 1/2 baths, 2-car garage
- Basement foundation

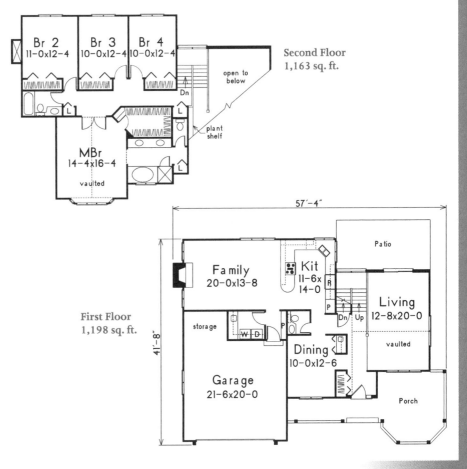

Second Floor
1,163 sq. ft.

Br 2
11-0x12-4

Br 3
10-0x12-4

Br 4
10-0x12-4

open to below

plant shelf

MBr
14-4x16-4
vaulted

First Floor
1,198 sq. ft.

57'-4"

41'-8"

Family
20-0x13-8

Kit
11-6x 14-0

Patio

Living
12-8x20-0
vaulted

storage

Dining
10-0x12-6

Garage
21-6x20-0

Porch

Cozy Mountain Farmhouse

Features

- 2,326 total square feet of living area
- A glorious sunroom with skylights brightens the home and creates a relaxing atmosphere
- The centrally located kitchen serves the formal and informal dining areas with ease
- The secondary bedrooms share a private bath with double-bowl vanity
- The bonus room above the garage has an additional 358 square feet of living area
- 3 bedrooms, 2 1/2 baths, 2-car side entry garage
- Basement, walk-out basement or slab foundation, please specify when ordering

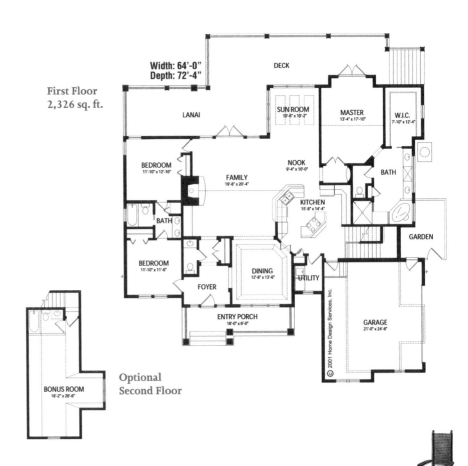

First Floor
2,326 sq. ft.

Width: 64'-0"
Depth: 72'-4"

Optional
Second Floor

To order call toll-free 1-800-DREAM HOME or visit www.houseplansandmore.com

Comfortable One-Story Country Home

Features

- 1,367 total square feet of living area
- Neat front porch shelters the entrance
- Dining room has a full wall of windows and convenient storage area
- Breakfast area leads to the rear terrace through sliding doors
- Large living room with high ceiling, skylight and fireplace
- 3 bedrooms, 2 baths, 2-car garage
- Basement foundation, drawings also include slab foundation

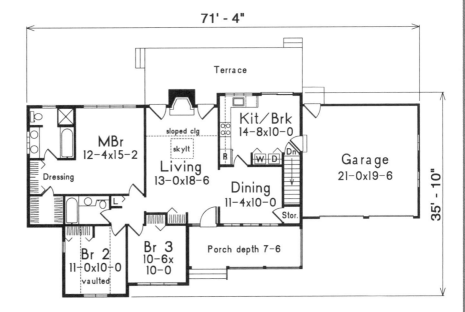

Appealing Master Suite

Features

- 1,896 total square feet of living area
- Living room has lots of windows, a media center and a fireplace
- Centrally located kitchen with breakfast nook
- Extra storage in garage
- Covered porch in front and rear of home
- Optional balcony on second floor
- 4 bedrooms, 2 1/2 baths, 2-car garage
- Basement, crawl space or slab foundation, please specify when ordering

Second Floor
661 sq. ft.

First Floor
1,235 sq. ft.

Raised Plantation Styling

Features

- 2,287 total square feet of living area
- Two-story foyer has balcony
- Great room includes a fireplace and decorative fixed glass between dining room
- Large kitchen and breakfast room with great view to rear
- Second floor has two bedrooms, balcony and large playroom
- 3 bedrooms, 2 1/2 baths, 2-car side entry garage
- Slab or crawl space foundation, please specify when ordering

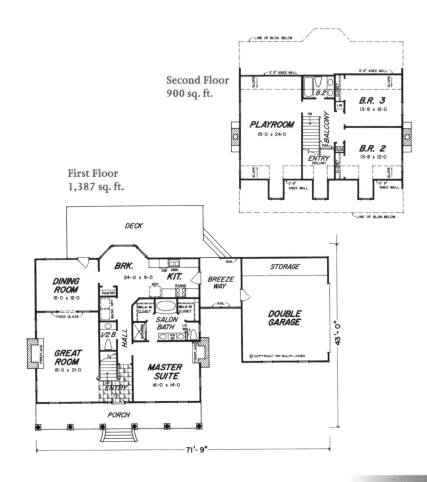

Second Floor
900 sq. ft.

First Floor
1,387 sq. ft.

Charming Country Comfort

Features

- 2,988 total square feet of living area
- Bedrooms #2 and #3 share a common bath
- Energy efficient home with 2" x 6" exterior walls
- Rear porch has direct access to the master bedroom, living and dining rooms
- Spacious utility room located off garage entrance features a convenient bath with shower
- Large L-shaped kitchen has plenty of workspace
- Oversized master bedroom is complete with a walk-in closet and master bath
- 3 bedrooms, 3 1/2 baths, 2-car side entry garage
- Partial basement/crawl space foundation

A Home For Family Of Living

Features

- 2,940 total square feet of living area
- Two sets of twin dormers add outdoor charm while lighting the indoors
- Massive central foyer leads into the sunken living room below and has access to the second floor attic
- Private master bedroom is complete with a luxurious corner tub and large walk-in closet
- A novel bridge provides view of living room below and access to second floor attic
- 4 bedrooms, 3 baths, 2-car side entry garage
- Basement foundation

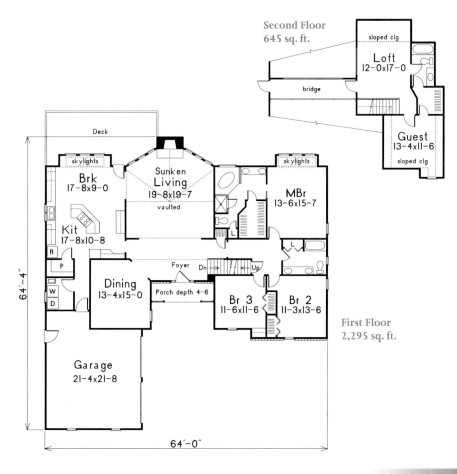

Second Floor
645 sq. ft.

sloped clg

Loft
12-0x17-0

bridge

Guest
13-4x11-6

sloped clg

Deck

skylights

Brk
17-8x9-0

Sunken
Living
19-8x19-7
vaulted

skylights

MBr
13-6x15-7

Kit
17-8x10-8

Foyer

Dn

Up

Dining
13-4x15-0

Porch depth 4-6

Br 3
11-6x11-6

Br 2
11-3x13-6

First Floor
2,295 sq. ft.

Garage
21-4x21-8

64'-4"

64'-0"

Superb Home Accented With Victorian Details

Features

- 2,420 total square feet of living area
- Master bedroom is filled with extras such as a unique master bath and lots of storage
- Extending off great room is a bright sunroom with access to an optional deck
- Compact kitchen with nook creates a useful breakfast area
- 4 bedrooms, 2 1/2 baths, 2-car garage
- Basement foundation

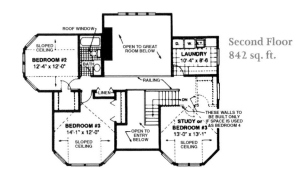

Second Floor
842 sq. ft.

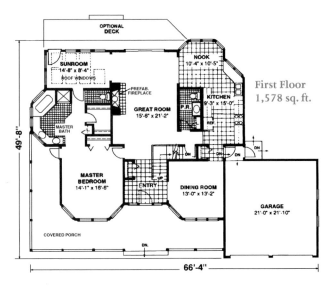

First Floor
1,578 sq. ft.

Sprawling Family Farmhouse

Features

- 2,972 total square feet of living area
- Extra storage available off the second floor bedroom
- Angled staircase in entry adds interest
- Charming screened porch is accessible from the breakfast room
- Bonus room above the garage has an additional 396 square feet of living area
- 4 bedrooms, 3 1/2 baths, 3-car side entry garage
- Basement foundation

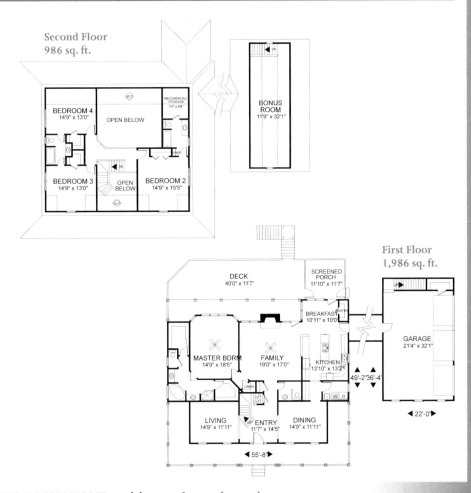

Second Floor
986 sq. ft.

BEDROOM 4
14'9" x 13'0"

OPEN BELOW

MECHANICAL STORAGE
7'5" x 8'8"

BONUS ROOM
11'9" x 32'1"

BEDROOM 3
14'9" x 13'0"

OPEN BELOW

BEDROOM 2
14'9" x 15'5"

First Floor
1,986 sq. ft.

DECK
40'0" x 11'7"

SCREENED PORCH
11'10" x 11'7"

BREAKFAST
10'11" x 10'0"

GARAGE
21'4" x 32'1"

MASTER BDRM
14'9" x 18'5"

FAMILY
19'0" x 17'0"

KITCHEN
13'10" x 13'2"

49'-2"36'-4"

LIVING
14'9" x 11'11"

ENTRY
11'7" x 14'5"

DINING
14'9" x 11'11"

22'-0"

55'-8"

Country Classic With Modern Floor Plan

Features

- 1,921 total square feet of living area
- Energy efficient home with 2" x 6" exterior walls
- Sunken family room includes a built-in entertainment center and coffered ceiling
- Sunken formal living room features a coffered ceiling
- Master bedroom dressing area has double sinks, spa tub, shower and French door to private deck
- Large front porch adds to home's appeal
- 3 bedrooms, 2 1/2 baths, 2-car garage
- Basement foundation

Second Floor
863 sq. ft.

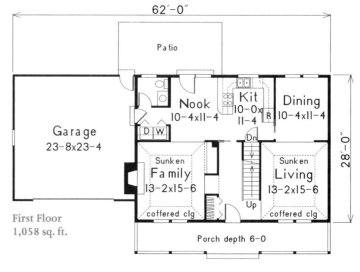

First Floor
1,058 sq. ft.

To order call toll-free 1-800-DREAM HOME or visit www.houseplansandmore.com

Grand Victorian Home

Features

- 2,590 total square feet of living area
- Energy efficient home with 2" x 6" exterior walls
- Utility room is located on the second floor for convenience
- Master bedroom has private bath with double vanity, oversized shower and freestanding tub in bay window
- Bonus room above the garage has an additional 459 square feet of living area
- 3 bedrooms, 2 1/2 baths, 2-car garage
- Basement foundation

Second Floor
1,238 sq. ft.

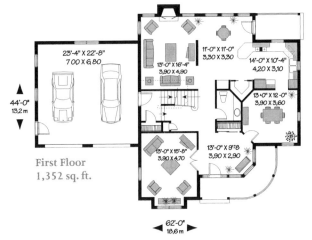

First Floor
1,352 sq. ft.

Wonderful Views From The Rear Of This Home

Features

- 2,911 total square feet of living area
- Wrap-around porch is adorned with double columns
- Optional living area and bedroom above two-car garage has 512 square feet of living area
- Beautiful master bath with corner tub, separate shower and large walk-in closet
- Large sundeck offers a great area to relax
- 3 bedrooms, 2 1/2 baths, 2-car side entry garage
- Partial basement/crawl space foundation

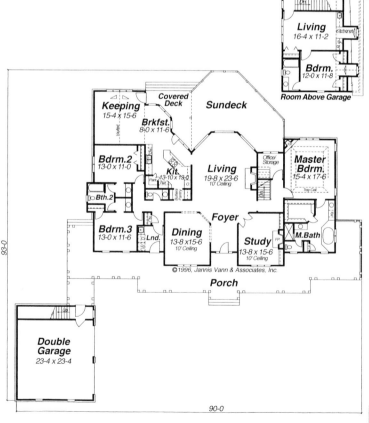

Living 16-4 x 11-2

Bdrm. 12-0 x 11-8

Room Above Garage

Keeping 15-4 x 15-6

Covered Deck

Sundeck

Brkfst. 8-0 x 11-6

Bdrm.2 13-0 x 11-0

Kit. 13-10 x 13-0

Living 19-8 x 23-6 10' Ceiling

Office/ Storage

Master Bdrm. 15-4 x 17-6

Bth.2

Bdrm.3 13-0 x 11-6

Lnd.

Dining 13-8 x15-6 10' Ceiling

Foyer

Study 13-8 x 15-6 10' Ceiling

M.Bath

©1996, Jannis Vann & Associates, Inc.

93-0

Porch

Double Garage 23-4 x 23-4

90-0

Rear View

Plan #578-073D-0037

A Grand Beamed Entry With Arched Window

Features

- 1,665 total square feet of living area
- Central loft on second floor is a nice retreat
- Oversized dining room has access to outdoor grilling porch
- A deck wraps around the home for an additional outdoor living area
- 3 bedrooms, 2 baths
- Crawl space foundation

Second Floor
663 sq. ft.

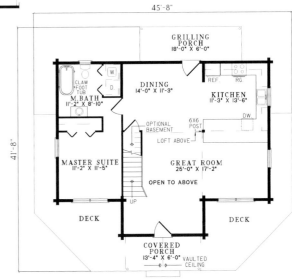

First Floor
1,002 sq. ft.

Covered Rear Porch

Features

- 1,253 total square feet of living area
- Sloped ceiling and fireplace in family room add drama
- U-shaped kitchen is efficiently designed
- Large walk-in closets are found in all the bedrooms
- 3 bedrooms, 2 baths, 2-car garage
- Crawl space or slab foundation, please specify when ordering

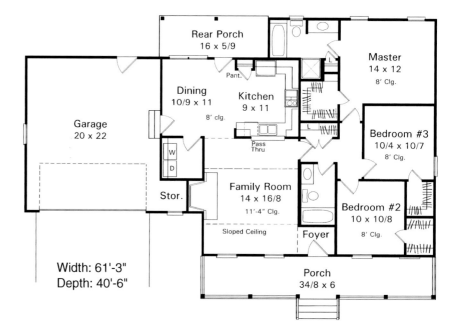

Rear Porch
16 x 5/9

Master
14 x 12
8' Clg.

Dining
10/9 x 11
8' clg.

Kitchen
9 x 11

Pant.

Bedroom #3
10/4 x 10/7
8' Clg.

Garage
20 x 22

Pass Thru

W
D

Stor.

Family Room
14 x 16/8
11'-4" Clg.

Bedroom #2
10 x 10/8
8' Clg.

Foyer

Sloped Ceiling

Width: 61'-3"
Depth: 40'-6"

Porch
34/8 x 6

Charming Screened-In Gazebo Porch

Features

- 1,442 total square feet of living area
- Energy efficient home with 2" x 6" exterior walls
- Kitchen accesses bayed area and porch which provide a cozy atmosphere
- Open living area makes relaxing a breeze
- 3 bedrooms, 2 baths
- Basement foundation

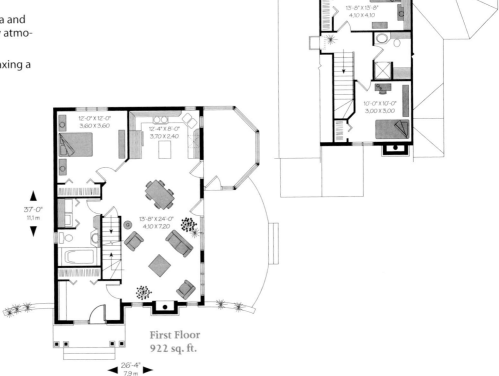

Second Floor
520 sq. ft.

13'-8" X 13'-8"
4,10 X 4,10

10'-0" X 10'-0"
3,00 X 3,00

12'-0" X 12'-0"
3,60 X 3,60

12'-4" X 8'-0"
3,70 X 2,40

37'-0"
11,1 m

13'-8" X 24'-0"
4,10 X 7,20

First Floor
922 sq. ft.

26'-4"
7,9 m

Plenty Of Built-Ins

Features

- 3,012 total square feet of living area
- Master bedroom has a sitting area with an entertainment center/library
- Utility room has a sink and includes lots of storage and counterspace
- Future space above garage has an additional 336 square feet of living area
- 4 bedrooms, 3 1/2 baths, 2-car side entry garage
- Crawl space foundation, drawings also include slab and basement foundations

Width: 62'-0"
Depth: 86'-0"

First Floor
2,202 sq. ft.

Second Floor
810 sq. ft.

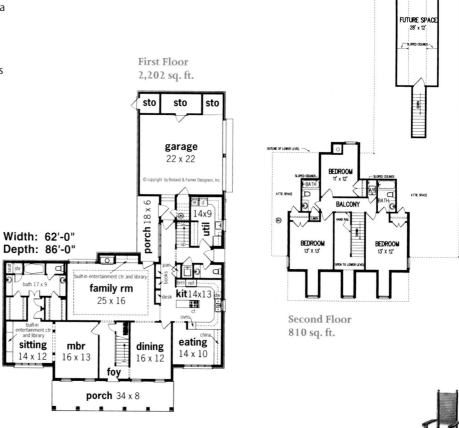

To order call toll-free **1-800-DREAM HOME** or visit www.houseplansandmore.com

Two-Story Has A Country Feel

Features

- 3,422 total square feet of living area
- Oversized kitchen island includes space for the stove as well as a desk and bookshelves underneath
- Corner whirlpool tub is the focal point in the master bath
- A corner fireplace is enjoyed by both the hearth room and the breakfast room nearby
- Bonus room on the second floor has an additional 228 square feet of living area
- 4 bedrooms, 3 1/2 baths, 3-car side entry garage
- Basement foundation

Second Floor
1,055 sq. ft.

First Floor
2,367 sq. ft.

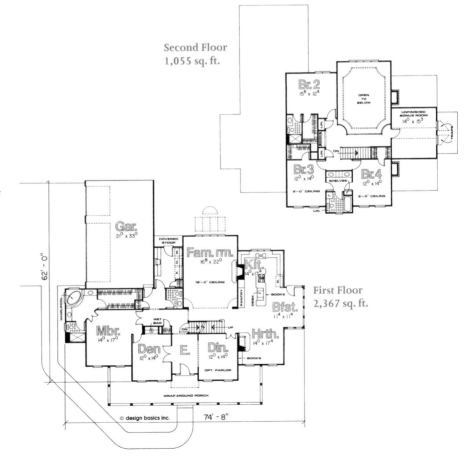

Built-In Computer Desk

Features

- 1,525 total square feet of living area
- Corner fireplace is highlighted in the great room
- Unique glass block window over the whirlpool tub in the master bath brightens the interior
- Open bar overlooks both the kitchen and great room
- Breakfast room leads to an outdoor grilling and covered porch
- 3 bedrooms, 2 baths, 2-car garage
- Basement, walk-out basement, crawl space or slab foundation, please specify when ordering

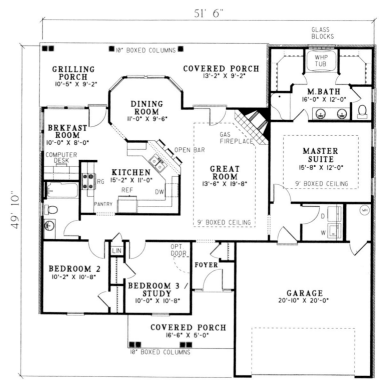

Rear View

Plan #578-039D-0022

Office Or Fourth Bedroom

Features

- 2,158 total square feet of living area
- Private master suite has a walk-in closet and bath
- Sloped ceiling in family room adds drama
- Secondary bedrooms include 9' ceilings and walk-in closets
- Covered porch adds a charming touch
- 4 bedrooms, 3 baths, 2-car side entry garage
- Crawl space or slab foundation, please specify when ordering

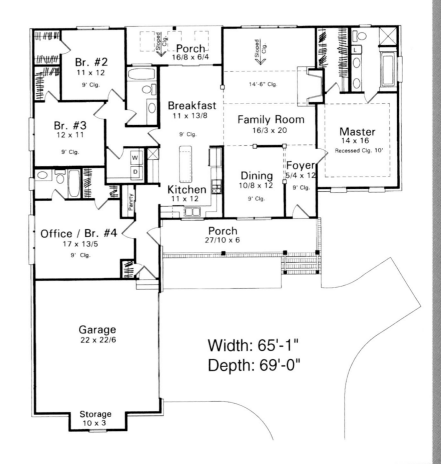

Width: 65'-1"
Depth: 69'-0"

Breezeway Joins Living Space With Garage

Features

- 1,874 total square feet of living area
- 9' ceilings throughout the first floor
- Two-story foyer opens into the large family room with fireplace
- First floor master bedroom includes a private bath with tub and shower
- 4 bedrooms, 2 1/2 baths, 2-car garage
- Basement foundation, drawings also include slab foundation

Second Floor
633 sq. ft.

Br 2
11-0x10-7

Br 3
11-4x11-0

Br 4
11-4x11-0

Dn

open to foyer

plant shelf

73'-4"

38'-6"

Garage
21-4x23-4

First Floor
1,241 sq. ft.

Dining
13-4x10-0

Kitchen
13-4x10-0

Family
13-4x18-2

MBr
13-4x15-0

Foyer

plant shelf

Porch
41-4x8-0

A Cozy Home With Rustic Touches

Features

- 2,272 total square feet of living area
- 10' ceilings throughout the first floor and 9' ceilings on the second floor
- Lots of storage area on the second floor
- First floor master bedroom has a lovely sitting area with an arched entry
- Second floor bedrooms share a Jack and Jill bath
- 3 bedrooms, 2 1/2 baths, 2-car rear entry garage
- Slab foundation

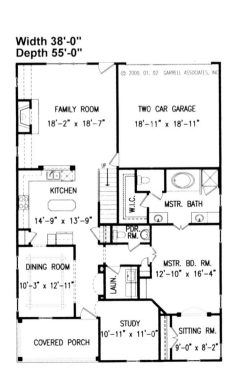

Width 38'-0"
Depth 55'-0"

© 2000, 01, 02 GARRELL ASSOCIATES, INC

FAMILY ROOM
18'-2" x 18'-7"

TWO CAR GARAGE
18'-11" x 18'-11"

KITCHEN
14'-9" x 13'-9"

UP

W.I.C.

MSTR. BATH

PDR. RM.

DINING ROOM
10'-3" x 12'-11"

LAUN.

MSTR. BD. RM.
12'-10" x 16'-4"

STUDY
10'-11" x 11'-0"

SITTING RM.
9'-0" x 8'-2"

COVERED PORCH

First Floor
1,587 sq. ft.

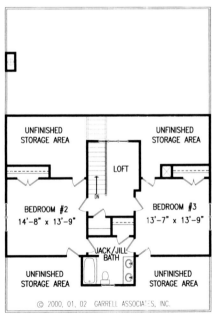

UNFINISHED STORAGE AREA

UNFINISHED STORAGE AREA

LOFT

DN

BEDROOM #2
14'-8" x 13'-9"

BEDROOM #3
13'-7" x 13'-9"

JACK/JILL BATH

UNFINISHED STORAGE AREA

UNFINISHED STORAGE AREA

© 2000, 01, 02 GARRELL ASSOCIATES, INC.

Second Floor
685 sq. ft.

Traditional Classic, Modern Features Abound

Features

- 3,035 total square feet of living area
- Front facade includes large porch
- Private master bedroom with win-dowed sitting area, walk-in closet, sloped ceiling and skylight
- Formal living and dining rooms adjoin the family room through at-tractive French doors
- Energy efficient home with 2" x 6" exterior walls
- 4 bedrooms, 3 1/2 baths, 2-car detached side entry garage
- Crawl space foundation, drawings also include slab and basement foundations

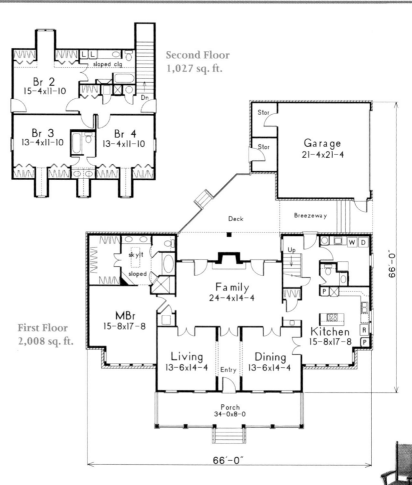

Double French Doors Grace Living Room

Features

- 2,333 total square feet of living area
- 9' ceilings on the first floor
- Master bedroom features a large walk-in closet and an inviting double-door entry into a spacious bath
- Convenient laundry room is located near the kitchen
- 4 bedrooms, 3 baths, 2-car side entry garage
- Slab foundation, drawings also include crawl space and partial crawl space/basement foundations

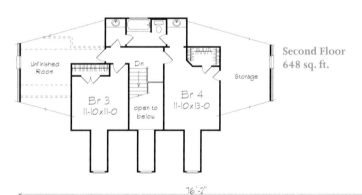

Second Floor
648 sq. ft.

Br 3
11-10x11-0

Br 4
11-10x13-0

Unfinished Room

Storage

Dn

open to below

76'-2"

44'-5"

First Floor
1,685 sq. ft.

Patio

Covered Porch

Garage
21-8x23-4

MBr
15-0x13-6

Living
19-4x17-4

Brk
10-8x10-0

Kit
10-8x
12-0

Br 2
11-10x11-7

Dining
11-10x13-3

Porch
33-0x6-0

Up

Small Ranch For A Perfect Country Haven

Features

- 1,761 total square feet of living area
- Exterior window dressing, roof dormers and planter boxes provide visual warmth and charm
- Great room boasts a vaulted ceiling, fireplace and opens to a pass-through kitchen
- The vaulted master bedroom includes a luxury bath and walk-in closet
- Home features eight separate closets with an abundance of storage
- 4 bedrooms, 2 baths, 2-car side entry garage
- Basement foundation

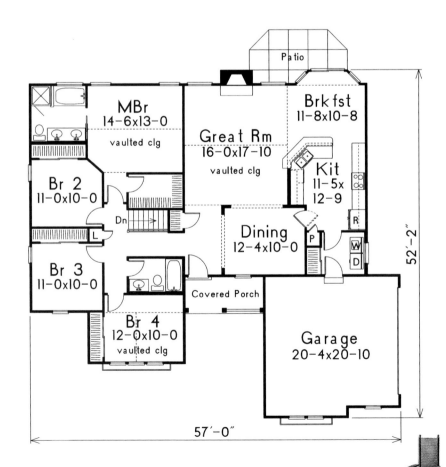

Victorian Home Has A Custom Feel

Features

- 3,746 total square feet of living area
- Upon entering a large foyer guests are greeted by a beautiful central two-story rotunda with circular staircase
- An oval tray ceiling in the formal dining room creates a Victorian feel
- Two-story family room is sunny and bright with windows on two floors
- Bonus room on the second floor has an additional 314 square feet of living area
- 4 bedrooms, 3 1/2 baths, 3-car garage
- Crawl space foundation

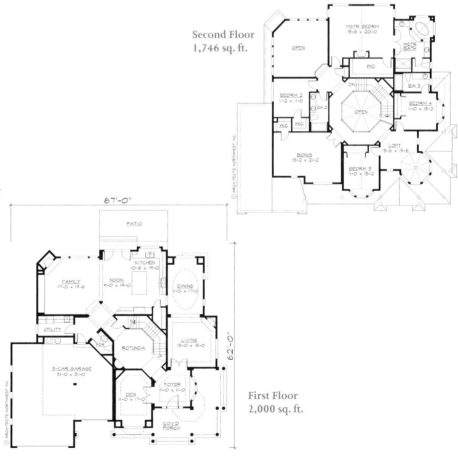

Second Floor
1,746 sq. ft.

First Floor
2,000 sq. ft.

Roomy Two-Story Has Covered Porch

Features

- 1,600 total square feet of living area
- Energy efficient home with 2" x 6" exterior walls
- First floor master bedroom is accessible from two points of entry
- Master bath dressing area includes separate vanities and a mirrored makeup counter
- Second floor bedrooms have generous storage space and share a full bath
- 3 bedrooms, 2 baths, 2-car side entry garage
- Crawl space foundation, drawings also include slab foundation

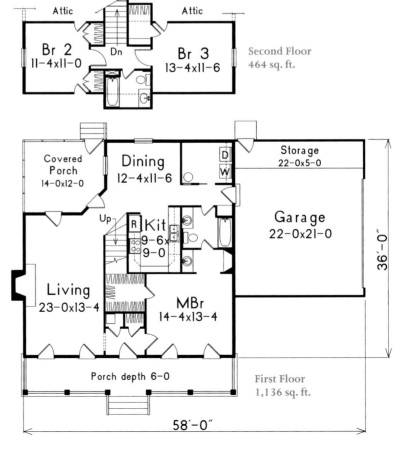

Attic

Br 2
11-4x11-0

Dn

Attic

Br 3
13-4x11-6

Second Floor
464 sq. ft.

Covered Porch
14-0x12-0

Dining
12-4x11-6

D
W

Storage
22-0x5-0

Up

R Kit
9-6x
9-0

Garage
22-0x21-0

Living
23-0x13-4

MBr
14-4x13-4

36'-0"

Porch depth 6-0

First Floor
1,136 sq. ft.

58'-0"

Victorian Accents Create A Custom Feel

Features

- 2,750 total square feet of living area

- Spacious dining room is connected to the kitchen for ease and also has access onto the wrap-around porch

- A double-door entry leads into the master bedroom enhanced with a spacious walk-in closet and a private bath with whirlpool tub

- Secluded den is an ideal place for a home office

- 4 bedrooms, 2 1/2 baths, 2-car side entry garage

- Basement or crawl space foundation, please specify when ordering

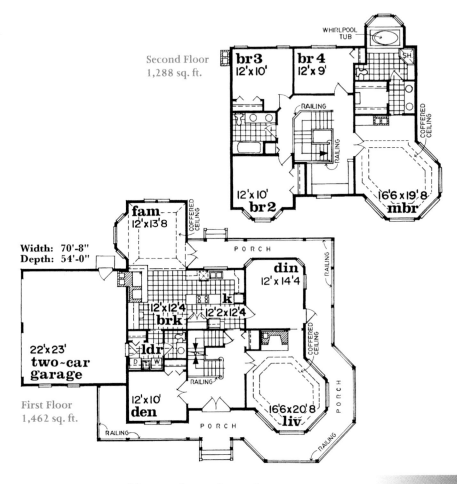

Second Floor
1,288 sq. ft.

Width: 70'-8"
Depth: 54'-0"

First Floor
1,462 sq. ft.

Plan #578-022D-0028

Price Code D

Master Bath Features Curved Glass Block Wall

Features

- 2,223 total square feet of living area
- Vaulted master bedroom opens to a private courtyard
- The master bath features a curved glass block wall around the tub and shower
- Vaulted family room combines with the breakfast room and kitchen to create a large casual living area
- Second floor includes secondary bedrooms and a possible loft/office
- 3 bedrooms, 2 1/2 baths, 2-car garage
- Basement foundation

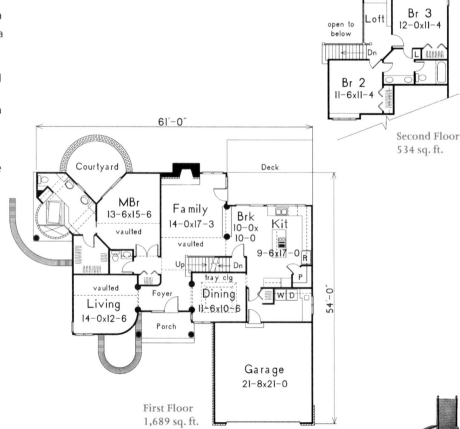

Second Floor
534 sq. ft.

First Floor
1,689 sq. ft.

Columns And Dormers Grace Stylish Exterior

Features

- 3,216 total square feet of living area
- All bedrooms include private full baths
- Hearth room and combination kitchen/breakfast area create a large informal gathering area
- Oversized family room boasts a fireplace, wet bar and bay window
- Master bedroom has two walk-in closets and a luxurious bath
- 4 bedrooms, 4 1/2 baths, 3-car side entry garage
- Basement foundation

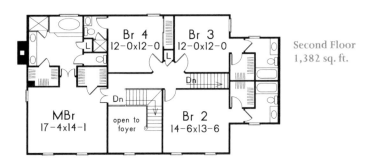

Second Floor
1,382 sq. ft.

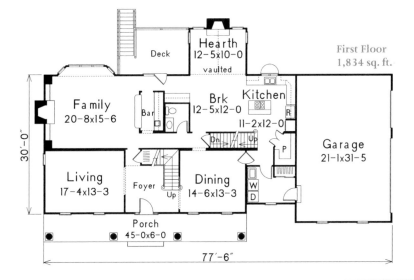

First Floor
1,834 sq. ft.

Covered Porch Adds Charm

Features

- 1,595 total square feet of living area
- The front secondary bedroom could easily convert to a library or home office especially with its convenient double-door entry
- An expansive deck is enjoyed by the open great room and bayed dining area
- A walk-in closet organizes the master bedroom
- 3 bedrooms, 2 baths, 2-car garage
- Walk-out basement foundation

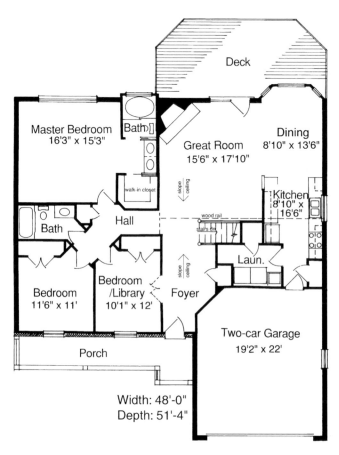

Deck

Master Bedroom
16'3" x 15'3"

Bath

Great Room
15'6" x 17'10"

Dining
8'10" x 13'6"

walk-in closet

Kitchen
8'10" x 16'6"

Bath

Hall

wood rail

stairs dn

Laun.

Bedroom
11'6" x 11'

Bedroom
/Library
10'1" x 12'

Foyer

Two-car Garage
19'2" x 22'

Porch

Width: 48'-0"
Depth: 51'-4"

To order call toll-free 1-800-DREAM HOME **or visit** www.houseplansandmore.com

Plan #578-052D-0002

Raised Ranch Style

Features

- 1,208 total square feet of living area
- Master bath is graced with an over-sized tub, plant shelf and double vanity
- A U-shaped kitchen promotes organization while easily accessing the dining area
- Hall bath includes a laundry closet for convenience
- 3 bedrooms, 2 baths, 2-car drive under garage
- Basement foundation

Sundeck
10-0 x 10-0

10-0

M.Bath

Bedroom 2

Kitchen
8-0 x 10-0

Dw.

Bath 2

W.D.

Dining
10-4 x 10-0

Ref.

OPT PLANT SHELF
OPEN TO BDRM

Master
Bedroom
11-6 x 14-6

Cts.

Down

Family Room
18-4 x 13-0

29-0

Bedroom 3
11-0 x 10-0

Entry

© 1998, Jannis Vann & Associates, Inc.

48-0

2-4

Craftsman Country Cottage

Features

- 1,649 total square feet of living area
- Energy efficient home with 2" x 6" exterior walls
- Ideal design for a narrow lot
- Country kitchen includes an island and eating bar
- Master bedroom has 12' vaulted ceiling and a charming arched window
- 4 bedrooms, 2 1/2 baths, 2-car side entry garage
- Basement or crawl space foundation, please specify when ordering

Width: 30'-0"
Depth: 52'-0"

Second Floor
791 sq. ft.

First Floor
858 sq. ft.

Special Planning In This Compact Home

Features

- 977 total square feet of living area
- Comfortable living room features a vaulted ceiling, fireplace, plant shelf and coat closet
- Both bedrooms are located on the second floor and share a bath with double-bowl vanity and linen closet
- Sliding glass doors in the dining room provide access to the deck
- 2 bedrooms, 1 1/2 baths, 1-car garage
- Basement foundation

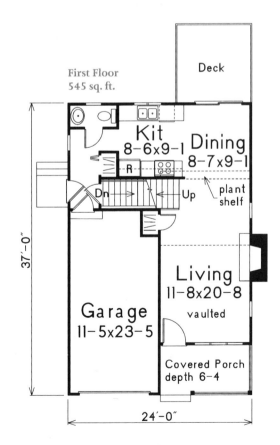

First Floor
545 sq. ft.

Deck

Kit
8-6x9-1

Dining
8-7x9-1

plant
shelf

Dn

Up

37'-0"

Living
11-8x20-8
vaulted

Garage
11-5x23-5

Covered Porch
depth 6-4

24'-0"

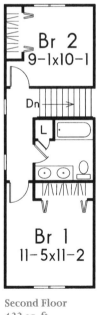

Br 2
9-1x10-1

Dn

L

Br 1
11-5x11-2

Second Floor
432 sq. ft.

Our Blueprint Packages Include. . .

Quality plans for building your future, with extras that provide unsurpassed value, ensure good construction and long-term enjoyment.

A quality home - one that looks good, functions well, and provides years of enjoyment - is a product of many things - design, materials, craftsmanship.

But it's also the result of outstanding blueprints - the actual plans and specifications that tell the builder exactly how to build your home.

And with our BLUEPRINT PACKAGES you get the absolute best. A complete set of blueprints is available for every design in this book. These "working drawings," are highly detailed, resulting in two key benefits:

‑ Better understanding by the contractor of how to build your home and...

‑ More accurate construction estimates.

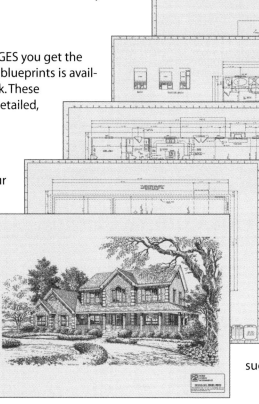

Cover Sheet

Included with many of the plans, the cover sheet is the artist's rendering of the exterior of the home. It will give you an idea of how your home will look when completed and landscaped.

Interior Elevations

Interior elevations provide views of special interior elements such as fireplaces, kitchen cabinets, built-in units and other features of the home.

Foundation Plan

The foundation plan shows the layout of the basement, crawl space, slab or pier foundation. All necessary notations and dimensions are included. See plan page for the foundation types included. If the home plan you choose does not have your desired foundation type, our Customer Service Representatives can advise you on how to customize your foundation to suit your specific needs or site conditions.

Details

Details show how to construct certain components of your home, such as the roof system, stairs, deck, etc.

Sections

Sections show detail views of the home or portions of the home as if it were sliced from the roof to the foundation. This sheet shows important areas such as load-bearing walls, stairs, joists, trusses and other structural elements, which are critical for proper construction.

Floor Plans

The floor plans show the placement of walls, doors, closets, plumbing fixtures, electrical outlets, columns, and beams for each level of the home.

Exterior Elevations

Exterior elevations illustrate the front, rear and both sides of the house, with all details of exterior materials and the required dimensions.

Home Plans Index

What Kind Of Plan Package Do You Need?

Once you find the home plan you've been looking for, here are some suggestions on how to make your Dream Home a reality. To get started, order the type of plans that fit your particular situation.

Your Choices:

The 1-set package - We offer a 1-set plan package so you can study your home in detail. This one set is considered a study set and is marked "not for construction." It is a copyright violation to reproduce blueprints.

The Minimum 5-set package - If you're ready to start the construction process, this 5-set package is the minimum number of blueprint sets you will need. It will require keeping close track of each set so they can be used by multiple subcontractors and tradespeople.

The Standard 8-set package - For best results in terms of cost, schedule and quality of construction, we recommend you order eight (or more) sets of blueprints. Besides one set for yourself, additional sets of blueprints will be required by your mortgage lender, local building department, general contractor and all subcontractors working on foundation, electrical, plumbing, heating/air conditioning, carpentry work, etc.

Reproducible Masters - If you wish to make some minor design changes, you'll want to order reproducible masters. These drawings contain the same information as the blueprints but are printed on erasable and reproducible paper which clearly indicates your right to copy or reproduce. This will allow your builder or a local design professional to make the necessary drawing changes without the major expense of redrawing the plans. This package also allows you to print copies of the modified plans as needed. The right of building only one structure from these plans is licensed exclusively to the buyer. You may not use this design to build a second or multiple dwelling(s) without purchasing another blueprint. Each violation of the Copyright Law is punishable in a fine.

Mirror Reverse Sets - Plans can be printed in mirror reverse. These plans are useful when the house would fit your site better if all the rooms were on the opposite side than shown. They are simply a mirror image of the original drawings causing the lettering and dimensions to read backwards. Therefore, when ordering mirror reverse drawings, you must purchase at least one set of right-reading plans. Some of our plans are offerred mirror reverse right-reading. This means the plan, lettering and dimensions are flipped but read correctly. See the Home Plans Index on pages 477-478 for availability.

Other Great Products...

The Legal Kit - Avoid many legal pitfalls and build your home with confidence using the forms and contract featured in

this kit. Included are request for proposal documents, various fixed price and cost plus contracts, instructions on how and when to use each form, warranty statements and more. Save time and money before you break ground on your new home or start a remodeling project. All forms are reproducible. The kit is ideal for homebuilders and contractors. **Cost: $35⁰⁰**

Detail Plan Packages - Framing, Electrical & Plumbing Packages - Three separate packages offer homebuilders details for con-

structing various foundations; numerous floor, wall and roof framing techniques; simple to complex residential wiring; sump and water softener hookups; plumbing connection methods; installation of septic systems, and more. Each package includes three-dimensional illustrations and a glossary of terms. Purchase one or all three. **Cost: $20⁰⁰ each or all three for $40⁰⁰** Note: These drawings do not pertain to a specific home plan.

Other Helpful Building Aids...

Your Blueprint Package will contain the necessary construction information to build your home. We also offer the following products and services to save you time and money in the building process.

Express Delivery - Most orders are processed within 24 hours of receipt. Please allow 7-10 business days for delivery. If you need to place a rush order, please call us by 11:00 a.m. Monday-Friday CST and ask for express service (allow 1-2 business days).

Technical Assistance - If you have questions, call our technical support line at 1-314-770-2228 between 8:00 a.m. and 5:00 p.m. Monday-Friday CST. Whether it involves design modifications or field assistance, our designers are extremely familiar with all of our designs and will be happy to help you. We want your home to be everything you expect it to be.

Material List - Material lists are available for many of our plans. Each list gives you the quantity, dimensions and description of the building materials necessary to construct your home. You'll get faster and more accurate bids from your contractor and material suppliers, and you'll save money by paying for only the materials you need. Refer to the Home Plan Index on pages 477-478 for availability. **Cost: $125⁰⁰** Note: Material Lists are not refundable.

How To Order

For fastest service, Call Toll-Free 1-800-DREAM HOME (1-800-373-2646) day or night

FOUR Easy Ways To Order

1. CALL toll-free 1-800-373-2646 for credit card orders. MasterCard, Visa, Discover and American Express are accepted.

2. FAX your order to 1-314-770-2226.

3. MAIL the Order Form to: **HDA, Inc.**
   944 Anglum Rd.
   St. Louis, MO 63042

4. ONLINE visit www.houseplansandmore.com

Order Form

Please send me -

PLAN NUMBER 578- _____

PRICE CODE _____ (see Plan Index)

Specify Foundation Type *(see plan page for availability)* $ _____
- ☐ Slab ☐ Crawl space ☐ Pier
- ☐ Basement ☐ Walk-out basement

☐ Reproducible Masters $ _____
☐ Eight-Set Plan Package $ _____
☐ Five-Set Plan Package $ _____
☐ One-Set Study Package *(no mirror reverse)* $ _____
Additional Plan Sets*
- ☐____(Qty.) at $45.00 each $ _____

Mirror Reverse*
- ☐Right-reading $150 one-time charge
  (see index on pages 477-478 for availability) $ _____
- ☐Print in Mirror Reverse *(where right-reading is not available)*
  _____ (Qty.) at $15.00 each $ _____

☐ Material List* $125 *(see pages 477-478 for avail.)* $ _____
☐ Legal Kit *(see page 479)* $ _____
Detail Plan Packages: *(see page 479)*
- ☐Framing ☐Electrical ☐Plumbing $ _____

SUBTOTAL $ _____
Sales Tax - MO residents add 6% $ _____
☐ Shipping / Handling (see chart at right) $ _____
TOTAL *(US funds only - sorry no CODs)* $ _____

I hereby authorize HDA, Inc. to charge this purchase to my credit card account (check one):

☐ MasterCard ☐ VISA ☐ DISCOVER ☐ American Express Cards

Credit Card number _____

Expiration date _____

Signature _____

Name _____
(Please print or type)

Street Address _____
*(Please **do not** use PO Box)*

City _____

State _____

Zip _____

Daytime phone number (_____) - _____

E-mail address _____

I'm a ☐ Builder/Contractor ☐ Homeowner ☐ Renter
I ☐ have ☐ have not selected my general contractor

480 *Thank you for your order!*

Important Information To Know Before You Order

- **Exchange Policies -** Since blueprints are printed in response to your order, we cannot honor requests for refunds. However, if for some reason you find that the plan you have purchased does not meet your requirements, you may exchange that plan for another plan in our collection within 90 days of purchase. At the time of the exchange, you will be charged a processing fee of 25% of your original plan package price, plus the difference in price between the plan packages (if applicable) and the cost to ship the new plans to you.

  Please note: Reproducible drawings can only be exchanged if the package is unopened.

- **Building Codes & Requirements -** At the time the construction drawings were prepared, every effort was made to ensure that these plans and specifications meet nationally recognized codes. Our plans conform to most national building codes. Because building codes vary from area to area, some drawing modifications and/or the assistance of a professional designer or architect may be necessary to comply with your local codes or to accommodate specific building site conditions. We advise you to consult with your local building official for information regarding codes governing your area.

Questions? Call Our Customer Service Number 314-770-2228

Blueprint Price Schedule — **BEST VALUE**

Price Code	1-Set	SAVE $110 5-Sets	SAVE $200 8-Sets	Reproducible Masters
AAA	$225	$295	$340	$440
AA	$325	$395	$440	$540
A	$385	$455	$500	$600
B	$445	$515	$560	$660
C	$500	$570	$615	$715
D	$560	$630	$675	$775
E	$620	$690	$735	$835
F	$675	$745	$790	$890
G	$765	$835	$880	$980
H	$890	$960	$1005	$1105

**Plan prices are subject to change without notice.
Please note that plans and material lists are not refundable.**

- **Additional Sets* -** Additional sets of the plan ordered are available for $45.00 each. Five-set, eight-set, and reproducible packages offer considerable savings.

- **Mirror Reverse Plans* -** Available for an additional $15.00 per set, these plans are simply a mirror image of the original drawings causing the dimensions and lettering to read backwards. Therefore, when ordering mirror reverse plans, you must purchase at least one set of right reading plans. Some of our plans are offered mirror reverse right-reading. This means the plan, lettering and dimensions are flipped but read correctly. To purchase a mirror reverse right-reading set, the cost is an additional $150. See the Home Plans Index on pages 477-478 for availability.

- **One-Set Study Package -** We offer a one-set plan package so you can study your home in detail. This one set is considered a study set and is marked "not for construction." It is a copyright violation to reproduce blueprints.

Available only within 90 days after purchase of plan package or reproducible masters of same plan.

Shipping & Handling Charges

U.S. SHIPPING - AK & HI express only	1-4 Sets	5-7 Sets	8 Sets or Reproducibles
Regular *(allow 7-10 business days)*	$15.00	$17.50	$25.00
Priority *(allow 3-5 business days)*	$25.00	$30.00	$35.00
Express* *(allow 1-2 business days)*	$35.00	$40.00	$45.00
CANADA SHIPPING (to/from) - Plans with suffix 032D & 062D			
Standard *(allow 8-12 business days)*	$25.00	$30.00	$35.00
Express* *(allow 3-5 business days)*	$40.00	$40.00	$45.00

Overseas Shipping/International - Call, fax, or e-mail (plans@hdainc.com) for shipping costs.
* For express delivery please call us by 11:00 a.m. Monday-Friday C